ACCIDENTAL FEMINISTS

JANE CARO

MELBOURNE UNIVERSITY PRESS

MELBOURNE UNIVERSITY PRESS
An imprint of Melbourne University Publishing Limited
Level 1, 715 Swanston Street, Carlton, Victoria 3053, Australia
mup-contact@unimelb.edu.au
www.mup.com.au

First published 2019

Text design and typesetting by Megan Ellis
Cover design by Design by Committee
Cover image by Josh Durham/Bigstockphoto
Printed in Australia by McPherson's Printing Group

NATIONAL LIBRARY OF AUSTRALIA
A catalogue record for this book is available from the National Library of Australia

9780522872835 (paperback)
9780522872842 (ebook)

To Ralph

May we continue to grow old together

CONTENTS

INTRODUCTION

The generation born after World War II are usually referred to as the baby boomers. The boomers, both male and female, have had a huge impact on the world. They were bound to, I suppose, considering when they were born and their sheer numbers. However, it is boomer women who, in my opinion, have really made the greatest and most lasting difference. They have changed everything but they didn't grow up expecting to be revolutionary. They are the accidental feminists.

They are the first generation of women in the history of the world who have mostly earned their own money for most of their lives. That, in itself, is revolutionary.

They are also my generation. I am a tail-end boomer, born in 1957. I grew up when they grew up and have lived through the world the boomers were raised in, absorbed the messages we were sent about our futures, and experienced the way all those seemingly immutable assumptions were blown out of the water. It's been a hell of a ride, and it's not over yet. Nevertheless, I somehow feel as if the revolution that has occurred in the lives of women remains relatively unacknowledged. It's as if each step forward is regarded in isolation and many people still seem to live with the expectation that any day now, women will go back into their box and live the way they always used to. I don't think that is going to happen, and this book is my attempt to explain why.

It is also an attempt to tell the life story of my generation of women. As I was raised in Australia, it focuses on the experiences of women from that country—but I do not think those experiences are radically different from those of women over fifty-five in other parts of the Western world. We all lived through and benefited from the technology that changed our opportunities and the way we were able to contribute. The two particular technologies that enabled us to live such different lives are reliable contraception and the tampon. We also lived through and benefited from what is called the second wave of feminism in the 1970s, when I was still an impressionable teenager. (The first wave of feminism was the fight for the vote.) We are currently living through what will probably end up being called the third wave, and it is accelerating the change in women's lives at a speed that makes my head spin.

I have been an active participant in the changes in women's lives, as a rebellious teenager, a university student, a career woman, a wife, a mother, a grandmother and—always—a feminist. I have also been a grateful beneficiary. Like many of my peers, I have lived a much more interesting, varied and exciting life than almost any woman from the generations who came before me. But this book is neither a memoir nor a biography, although where my own life and experiences have seemed relevant I have not hesitated to draw on them. Rather, it is the story of a generation who grabbed their unexpected opportunities and ran with them.

But this book is also the story of two fates, because not all the women of my generation have benefited in the same way. Far too many of my boomer sisters now find themselves staring down the barrel of a poverty-stricken old age. Indeed, it was my horror at discovering a few years ago that so many of my contemporaries had been left high and dry that motivated the writing of the article that led to this book.

I began by asking myself why so many women of my generation were doing well and, conversely, why so many were doing badly. I am not sure I have found the definitive answer, but what I have found is that society has not kept pace with women. Indeed, I argue in these pages that many sectors of society have done their damnedest to hold back women every step of the way. Many remain hostile to women's economic independence and set up all sorts of barriers to women having the same chances as men, even while they deny that any such difficulties exist. I hope that I have been able to expose just how high, wide, thick and deep these supposedly non-existent barriers remain. These obstacles—some are the legacy of the world we grew up in, some are brand-new hurdles set up specifically to slow us down, some are conscious and some are unconscious—accumulate and so make women vulnerable throughout their lives, but particularly as they age.

As I explored the story of my generation, I did not restrict myself to research, reports and discussions of a formal, academic or theoretical kind, although of course you'll find plenty of those referred to in these pages. I wanted to hear first-hand from the women themselves. To that end, I sent a questionnaire to a range of women from my generation, some who were living in precarious circumstances. Some of the women generously responded to those questionnaires, and their thoughts, experiences and ideas enrich this book. As I promised them, I have disguised their identities, giving them false names and, in some cases, dividing the experiences of a single respondent among a series of fictitious names. I have done this out of respect for them and their privacy, but the words I quote are verbatim. I want to thank all of the women who trusted me with their answers, both for the time they took and for the honesty of their responses. The book would not be the same without them.

I also want to point out that in this book when I refer to 'women' I am referring to everyone who identifies as a woman. I am not discriminating on the basis of race, social class, education, creed, sexual orientation, gender at birth, age or anything else—not consciously, anyway. If you present yourself to the world as a woman, as far as I am concerned you are one. Women are not a job lot. We are as varied as all other groups of human beings. What we share is the burden of assumptions that are made about what a woman should be like, what she should do, say, wear, think and express. To be a woman, no matter your background, is to have to fight for your territory in a way that most men never have to. We even have to fight a seemingly endless and repetitive battle to retain control over our own bodies. Women of colour, of course, women who live with a disability, poor women, migrant women, trans women and non-heterosexual women must navigate all the usual prejudices and barriers against their gender and then some. Many women must fight multiple levels of bias and discrimination including ageism. I have tried to pay due respect within these pages to the different degrees of difficulty women face while also wanting to emphasise the universally limiting effect of sexism. This has not been easy, but I have done my best. Like every author, I hope that all my readers, including male ones, can identify with the stories of struggle and triumph I tell. After all, every human being, regardless of age, gender, race, religion, or accident of birth, wants to be treated fairly, and that's all this generation of women have been fighting for—even if, as the title of this book implies, they have sometimes engaged in that fight without quite meaning to.

When I point out how revolutionary this generation of women are and how big a deal it is to be the first generation in history who have mostly earned their own money, people invariably respond with surprise, and even this reaction is an example of how little notice we take of women's lives. How often are women who fight for their own rights told that they should put their efforts on hold as long as there remain others who are worse off? Women are always being asked to put others' needs ahead of their own, which is a brilliant way to make sure their own needs never get met. What happens to women is still seen as peripheral, of minor importance—even trivial. Serious matters focus on men, apparently. In fact, I now believe that feminism is really a centuries-long fight by one half of the human race to be taken seriously by the other half.

I hope that when you have finished reading about the women who have changed everything, you will take them and what they have achieved very seriously.

1

DAUGHTERS OF FEMINISM

Her name was Kerrie (we were all called Kerrie, Debbie, Jane, Lynne or Sue in those days). It was 1972 and we were fifteen and reaching the end of what was then called Fourth Form. They call it Year 10 now.

We were both students at a bog-standard, co-ed public high school in the boondocks of Sydney's Northern Beaches. It wasn't a posh school, and in those days it enrolled the children of the entire local community. My father was a company director. Maybe Kerrie's dad was too, or perhaps he was a tradie or operated a small business. Back then, we didn't know what our friends' dads did and we didn't care. Our mums generally didn't do paid work, unless you were the unlucky offspring of the ostracised and whispered-about 'deserted wife'. The term 'single mother' was not used because it was dads who took off, not mums. Mums couldn't, no matter how miserable or mistreated they might be. They had little choice: not only did they rarely earn any money, but the social stigma attached to a woman who left her family (black eyes and bruises notwithstanding) was terrifying.

Kerrie was in tears. We were about to do our School Certificate, which was a much more significant exam then—when most students left school at 15 and it was their highest educational qualification—than it is now, but that wasn't the problem. Kerrie was a bright girl. She'd worked her way up from the bottom classes in First Form (Year 7) to the top English class. She knew she was going to ace the exam. Kerrie was distraught because her father had just informed her that no matter how well she did in the School Certificate, she would not be going on to Fifth and Sixth Form. He could not afford to have both his kids out of the workforce for another few years, and as she was 'just a girl' she was the one who would have to leave and get herself a job. The injustice of this hit my friend hard. She knew she was a better student than her brother and that she enjoyed school while he hated it. She had ambitions to go to university; he'd rather poke his eyes out with a fork. But he was a boy and she was a girl, and that was that.

I was outraged on her behalf. My mother was a feminist, a member of the Women's Electoral Lobby, and hardly a day went by without her fulminating about the injustices visited upon women because of their gender. But I was the child of a well-to-do family. No tough decisions had to be made about whether we could afford to let me stay on at school or go to university. I comforted Kerrie as best I could and urged her to fight her MCP (male chauvinist pig, as they were called in 1972) of a father. All to no avail, of course. Kerrie left at the end of that year and disappeared into the ranks of the shop assistants, filing clerks, receptionists and apprentice hairdressers that swallowed more than half of the girls I'd shared classes with.

Looking back on it, for both the girls and the boys who stayed on for their last two years of secondary education, entering the senior school was a class marker. Our fathers tended to have white-collar jobs and wanted us to have them too, even if we were girls and only expected to work for a few years until we had kids.

When Amanda, a student at a Catholic high school in the 1970s, thought about her future—something she did very rarely—she says that she 'hoped to find a spunk to link up with, and didn't think too much about what happened after'. A 'spunk', as I recall with great fondness, is what teenage girls called attractive teenage boys back then. Debbie imagined 'living a comfortable life'. She says, 'I dreamed of owning an apartment near the ocean somewhere. I imagined that my hard work would pay off.' Theresa did well at school and expected to go to university. She says, 'I expected (hoped) I would marry and have a family one day. I don't think I really ever thought beyond that.' Susan's adoptive father was abusive and frightening, so she barricaded herself into her room and lost herself in sci-fi and horror novels. She also became obsessed with her horse. Nevertheless, she describes herself as a teenage girl who lived 'just one day to the next. Most of it is simply a grey fog.'

The Australia of the 1960s and 1970s, the era when I grew up and when most of the women now over fifty did as well, was a different world from today. I suspect that, apart from the labour-saving devices and shorter skirts, men and women from the 1860s and 1870s would not have found much that surprised them a century on. The traditional family was still just that for most people. Us kids called our friends' parents Mr and Mrs, and never used their first names in the way children routinely do now. We were all terrified of fathers as a species and avoided having anything whatsoever to do with them. This was the era of 'spare the rod and spoil the child', and fathers were often the disciplinarians. My friends would casually talk about 'getting a belting' from their dad, a punishment that sometimes involved their dad's actual belt. Susan's adoptive father invented horrific punishments for his two daughters, including being forced to walk around the house naked or in their underwear. When as a small child Susan confided in her teachers about her home life, she was taken out of primary school, her family moved house and everyone was told she 'was a liar who would make things up'. In those days, no-one in authority ever followed up and families were often allowed to just disappear.

Fortunately, for most of the rest of us, avoiding fathers was not difficult as they were rarely home, even on weekends. My own rather unconventional father (I was certainly not afraid of him, and he never hit us) worked all week and then played cricket for most of the weekend. My mother resented this mightily and—as women's lib began to make headlines—her discontent was increasingly verbalised. But, and I can't emphasise this strongly enough, she was very unusual.

When the current generation look back at the world of my childhood and adolescence, the world I shared with the cohort who are the focus of this book, they see the rising tides of revolutionary social movements—the anti-war demonstrations, the fight against apartheid, the rise of black power, social justice movements of all kinds, the youth-quake in general, and, of course, the rise of women's liberation. These are the things that stand out, particularly in hindsight. They were also the focus of our nightly TV news—in flickering black and white until 1975. However, they hardly affected most of us at the time. We did what people do as the great tides of history break around them: we jogged along with our lives just as we had always done.

Most of my girlfriends were not ambitious. They did not expect to have careers. I know this because I argued with them about it as we did the drawback on our Marlboro ciggies, hiding from our teachers round the back of the senior studies block. My girlfriends knew what their future looked like. It looked like their mothers' had, back in the 1940s and 1950s. They would work for a few years, have some fun, meet a guy (a spunk), marry, save for a deposit on a house or a block of land, and then they'd have kids. Even the girls who wanted to go to uni were all hoping to get teacher scholarships. It was the only job we could think of that worked around having children. Leanne considered being a teacher but decided that 'because it was a typical job that women did, I didn't want to do it'. I had a similar thought and did a straight arts degree at uni. But Leanne and I were the exceptions. Most of the girls I went to school with were not feminists. Indeed, the 'women's libbers' we saw on the news irritated them. Their demands and arguments made my friends uncomfortable, perhaps because they drew attention to things they did not want to think about. Many of my schoolfriends' mothers fed their daughters' dislike. They saw the slogans, the demos and the demands of feminists as a criticism of their lives as homemakers. They reacted defensively and often actively discouraged their daughters from having any ideas above their allotted female station.

This attitude persists. Only a couple of years ago, I remember a female school principal (she was well into her forties) telling me with tears in her eyes that when she told her mother she had been elected president of the area's Primary Principals' Association, her mother rolled her eyes and asked her what made her think she could manage a job like that. The lack of confidence our mothers often had in their own ability to navigate the world is the poisoned chalice they bequeathed to their daughters.

It is hardly surprising that the women of the 1950s and 1960s had this profound distrust of their own abilities. Women were routinely infantilised and patronised. Briefly allowed a modicum of agency and value when their labour was required during World War II, efforts were redoubled in the immediate postwar decades to remind women of their inferiority and their 'natural place' in the home. Indeed, as civil rights for other groups in the community gathered momentum, particularly in the US, women's rights, if they were included at all, were literally included as a joke. On 8 February 1964 (what a seminal year it was) an elderly congressman, Howard Smith, who favoured segregation, added an amendment to President Johnson's 1964 Civil Rights Act. He proposed adding the word 'sex' after race, colour, religion and national origin.

According to author Gillian Thomas, Congressman Smith 'played his amendment for laughs', cracking sexist jokes that are hair-raising in retrospect but were quite unexceptional at the time, and his suggestion was greeted with obliging guffaws by the male-dominated

Congress. Some of the twelve (out of 435) women members rose to try and combat the laughter and make some serious arguments in support of the amendment that would make discrimination against women illegal. Thomas quotes Democratic congresswoman Martha Griffiths as saying to the House: 'I presume that if there had been any necessity to point out that women were a second-class sex the laughter would have proved it.' Despite the laughter, both the amendment (an attempt, according to Thomas, by segregationists to derail the Civil Rights Act) and the bill were passed.

Australia was certainly not immune to this routine disrespect towards women and their work, their rights and their achievements. In 2003, the ABC ran series two of *A Big Country Revisited*. The program compared the Australia portrayed in the original documentary series (1968–91) with the Australia of the twenty-first century. I remembered *A Big Country* well from my youth and enjoyed its resurrection. The episode that etched itself into my consciousness was called 'Grey Hair Doesn't Mean You're a Fuddy Duddy', and looked at the Country Women's Association then and now.

What struck me was the extraordinary tone taken by the male narrator of the original program from the 1960s. He spoke of these women with the same patronising derision that the US Congress had indulged in a few years earlier. No matter how hard these women worked or how much money they raised, the narrator saw them as a joke. They were spoken of as if they were children who were aping the grown-ups (aka men). What they did might be cute, but it was also futile—an attitude that goes right back to Samuel Johnson (1709–84) and his much-quoted response to attending a Quaker meeting: 'Sir, a woman's preaching is like a dog's walking on his hind legs. It is not done well; but you are surprised to find it done at all.' This attitude of condescending astonishment towards any achievement by a woman had survived virtually unchanged for over 300 years, well into the 1960s.

For the women of my generation (and no doubt for every previous generation throughout history), this derision mattered.

The almost universal scorn and ridicule towards women very effectively undermined their confidence and self-worth. Susan's adoptive father routinely referred to his cowed and submissive wife as 'my little turd'. You can perhaps imagine the effect that had on his growing daughters. Social researcher Hugh Mackay in his book *What Makes Us Tick?* lists the ten desires that need to be met before you can live a satisfying life. He says he lists them in no particular order except for the first one, which is the most important. He calls it 'the desire to be taken seriously'. When I first read Mackay's book it was as if a light had been turned on. I saw clearly that feminism is the struggle by half the human race to be taken seriously by the other half. 'Indelible in the hippocampus is the laughter' said Christine Blasey Ford as she testified about her alleged abuse at the hands of Supreme Court nominee Brett Kavanaugh at his confirmation hearing. A phrase that resonated with women all over the world. When I was young, when the women of my generation were in their formative years, we were not taken seriously either. Nor, just as damagingly, were our mothers, or our grandmothers. Indeed, when I asked a number of women of my generation to answer some questions about their youth, aspirations, relationships and lives, not one of them said she wanted to be like her mother. Bev was unequivocal: 'Trying not to be like my mother has driven me in untold ways throughout my life.' Veronica agreed: 'Anyone but her' was her heartfelt response.

Feminism has had a considerable impact in the decades since my generation were quietly rejecting the lives their mothers lived, but the damage that had been done to the women who came before us was hard to shake off. As I half-joke on occasion, 2000 years of people being disappointed when you were born is not overcome in a few decades—and, make no mistake, when I was born, the birth of a boy was still cause for more celebration than the birth of a girl.

The major effect I can remember feminism having on my peers in the Frenchs Forest and Belrose of the 1970s was in terms of sexual liberation. We were all on the pill by the time we were sixteen, and most of us were having sex. My teenage years were also awash with illegal drugs, particularly marijuana and, for the really daring, LSD. Oddly, I was radical politically, especially about the position of women, but I was very square about drugs. Most of my friends were the exact opposite.

I am not arguing, however, that second-wave feminism had no effect other than sexual liberation on the women I knew. It revolutionised my mother's life, giving her the courage to do a mature-age matriculation course at tech (as TAFE was then called) and go on to take advantage of Gough Whitlam's education reforms. When the new Australian Labor Party (ALP) government abolished university tuition fees in 1974, a wave of mature-age women like my mother grasped their second chance with both, highly motivated hands. They could finally get the university education that their fathers (poor Kerrie) had denied them. Peta missed out on a free university education, but nevertheless went to Wollongong University and studied social science. She says graduating in 1994 boosted her confidence to such an extent that for the first time in her life she felt 'I can do anything, or at least try'. Many other women who had been trained from birth to think poorly of themselves and their capacity had the same epiphany as they found, to their astonishment, that they had gained high marks on the university essays they'd handed in, despite their sense of inadequacy. Their confidence and self-esteem blossomed thanks to their unexpected success.

Women's liberation had a huge effect on our teachers, too. We still had to put up with humiliating policing of our uniforms—particularly skirt lengths—but we knew enough to protest and we also knew many of our teachers fully supported our objections. That was liberating. Whether we were up for competing with blokes in the workplace or not, schoolgirls in the late 1960s and early 1970s were no longer as compliant and well behaved as those who had gone before us. This was shocking and unsettling, particularly to older generations.

Even so, the consequences for girls who rebelled when I was a teenager could be very daunting. I remember friends of mine being threatened by teachers, parents and religious leaders with the possibility they would be charged (yes, charged) with being 'in moral danger' and sent to what was ominously referred to as 'The Girls' Home'. Decades later, when I read some of the revelations about Jimmy Savile's predatory paedophilia, particularly at a school for what was referred to as 'emotionally disturbed girls' (aka mouthy and defiant girls), my blood ran cold. In Ireland, of course, they ran the risk of being sent to the infamous Magdalene Laundries. And, no doubt, some of my peers were whisked off to Homes for Unmarried Mothers to await the birth of illegitimate babies that they were then not permitted to keep. The treatment of Indigenous girls was even more terrifying and horrific. In every case, it was the girls who were seen as bad and deserving of punishment, never those who preyed upon them—a routine cruelty that was accepted almost without comment in my youth, except, to their credit, by feminists. And, worse, the stigma attached to 'wayward' (or 'emotionally disturbed') girls made them sitting ducks for predators in ways that are only just coming to light now. Many of the women I interviewed hinted at abuse when they were young. Susan became pregnant at sixteen and was coerced into giving up her baby. As an adopted child herself, she says her situation was presented to her 'as if it ran in the family'.

As always, vulnerability increased the lower the rung of the social ladder you occupied—but none of us were immune. Going to university might have been a marker of social class at Forest High in the 1970s, but sexism was having the same effects in posher schools and suburbs too. One of the most famous Sydney private girls' schools (then and now) was Abbotsleigh in Wahroonga. Through the sister of a boyfriend, I had become friendly with a group of girls from that famous school, run, at the time, by the legendary Betty Archdale. While the private-school girls I knew tended to be called Sally, Fiona,

Pippi and Deirdre rather than Kerrie, Karen or Lynne, they were no more unconventional than we were. They may have expected to marry a professional man rather than a tradie, but otherwise their life plans were much the same: a job (dental nurse, interior decorator, sales assistant in a posh shop), marriage and then children. No matter your social class, a man was still the only financial plan most girls could imagine. After all, it was the only model we had actually seen. The feminists might have talked a good game, but in the early 1970s that was largely what rhetoric about women's rights seemed to be: argument and polemic.

The wave of discontent and rebellion that gave rise to second-wave feminism when I was young took everyone by surprise. No-one anticipated the changes in women's lives that were to come. My favourite illustration of how blind the world was to the coming revolution is the famous *Up* series of films by Michael Apted. Beginning in 1964 (there's that year again), the series continues today. A now-elderly Apted has been visiting the same fourteen Britons every seven years, starting when they were seven-year-olds. They are now sixty-one. The first episode was made for the British TV series *World in Action.*

The concept behind the series was the famous Jesuit motto 'Give me a child until he is seven and I will show you the man'. The producers thought they were creating an exposé on the effects of social class—which they certainly did—but the series also turned out to be an essay on the revolution in the lives of women that has occurred in the last half-century. It is a revolution that in 1964 was unimaginable—so unimaginable that the fourteen seven-year-olds chosen by the producers for the original episode included ten boys but only four girls. Yes, four girls: one from an upper-class background, and three working-class friends. It is impossible that such a project today would be similarly cast. Indeed, even if it was tried, the outcry would be deafening. In 1964, nobody so much as noticed.

So why did the producers choose only four girls? Well, no-one thought girls' lives would be very interesting, not even the girls themselves. They, like my friends a few short years later, assumed girls would just grow up, work for a bit, marry and have kids. Their lives would be shaped by their husbands' lives, as women's had been for millennia.

For many of the women who are over fifty in the early twenty-first century, this is another of the assumptions that formed them. Even if you had a feminist mother like mine, you still absorbed the messages about our limited future through the pores of your skin. As Australia's former sex discrimination commissioner Liz Broderick brilliantly put it, sexism is like asbestos in the walls: you just breathe it in. We were baby-making machines, always had been, always would be, and we were supposed to be satisfied with that. The women who were beginning to assert their full and separate humanity were often caricatured as harpies, termagants and shrews. They were held up to us as awful warnings, not as women to admire or emulate. Undaunted, feminists—like all good revolutionaries before them—took on the language that was used to belittle and marginalise them and owned it. One of the first feminist publishing houses was called Virago, and an early feminist newspaper flexed its defiant muscles under the banner of *Spare Rib*.

Feminism and its supporters—the unladylike, shrill 'women's libbers'—persisted, despite the mockery, scorn and ridicule. And thanks to them, the lives of women and girls have changed beyond recognition since 1964. Yet it is important to point out just what attitudes to women were like during my generation's childhood and adolescence. They set the context for the rest of this book, because we heard the contradictory messages and absorbed them. On the one hand we saw the limited lives most women then lived. We saw the disrespect in which women—no matter who they were or what they did—were held. But we were also encouraged to get a decent education, and, as we reached our adolescence, many of the women in our lives began to rebel and directly challenge the shackles that bound them and the attitudes that held them down. As we grew up, we found that we were expected to be in paid work while still doing the lion's share of the unpaid work at home. We married, but—thanks to those paid jobs—if we were unhappy with our husbands we could leave them, and many of us did. Intellectually, we knew we had a right to lives just as rich and varied as those of our brothers. Emotionally, we still struggled against our own and others' unconscious assumptions. We fought guilt, disapproval and the sense that whatever we did was somehow wrong. Karen concentrated on being a parent and is pleased in one way that she did, but she still beats herself up: 'I failed totally at finding out what I was good at and having a career. I had the potential and I failed.'

Women who are over fifty grew up in one world and now must exist in quite another. They are the generation that has experienced the greatest change in women's lives in recorded history. Yet such is our lingering inability to take women's lives seriously that society barely acknowledges that there has been such a fundamental shift. It is almost as if the world has spent the past fifty-odd years waiting for women to get back into their kitchens and for everything to return to normal. Indeed, one could arguably see much of Donald Trump's triumph over Hillary Clinton in the 2016 US presidential election as being symptomatic of precisely that. However, the furious response by so many women to Trump's presidency is also a clear indication that most of those who used to be considered 'the second sex' have changed and will not put themselves second anymore.

Indeed, the likelihood that women (in the West, anyway) will ever return to the small lives they were sentenced to in previous generations is growing increasingly unlikely for all sorts of reasons, not least economic. As I have said, women over fifty today are the first women ever to have almost universally earned their own money for most of their lives. Yet it is almost as if what happens to women remains largely invisible. Nevertheless, these momentous changes have brought both great benefits and great challenges.

Sadly, not all women over fifty have benefited equally from women's invasion of the workplace or our triumph in education (women and girls now enrol in universities in greater numbers than men and boys, and also win most of the academic prizes) or our expanded choices. Some women have found themselves increasingly left behind. They grew up in a world that taught them to expect that they would be looked after by somebody else, but now live in a world that expects them to look after themselves. Because so many older women have not benefited from the change in women's lives, feminism remains an incomplete project. As long as women make up the poorest of the poor—and the fastest-growing group among the homeless is women over fifty-five—there remains work to be done.

Interestingly, we can pinpoint exactly when this work began. It started, as always, with a new technology.

The contraceptive pill was first prescribed to women in 1960. 'The pill' (as it quickly became known) was controversial. Its inventors intended it to give married women control over how many children they would have and how they would space their pregnancies. Doctors were very well aware of the negative effect constant childbearing had on the health of women. However, they never imagined it being used by single women to enjoy their sexuality because they could now safely and effectively avoid the usual consequences. This anxiety was probably behind the refusal of many religious organisations, notably the Catholic Church, to embrace safe contraception with the same enthusiasm as most of their followers. In fact, if control of female sexuality is your aim, then their concerns were well founded. Once the pill was made available, all sorts of women started taking it—from the onset of menstruation until the end of menopause, and everywhere in between.

In combination with other equally effective and reliable forms of contraception, the pill enabled women to escape the chains of their biology and make choices about their own lives in much the same way as men could. Not to put too fine a point on it, the pill liberated them. My generation of women could get educated, they could work, they could earn, travel, fall in and out of love, and still decide when and if they would have children. With greater control over reproduction came greater control of every part of their lives. This was the change that became known, in popular culture, as 'having it all'. ('Having it all', by the way, just means having meaningful paid work and a family—something men had just assumed was their birthright since time immemorial.) For women, the idea that they might live lives as full as those of men was (and still is, in some quarters) seen as selfish. Disapproved of or not, the improvements in contraception, combined with much better prenatal and antenatal care, obstetrics and medical science in general (most children who are born now live beyond infancy), meant my generation of women could choose to have children around their paid work. It wasn't easy, but it was doable.

While I am eulogising the pill, I feel the need to give a little nod to the tampon, which also freed women from the potential embarrassment that accompanied menstruation. Indeed, whenever people nominate the world's most important inventions (the internal combustion engine, the world wide web, battery storage), I always suggest the pill and the tampon. I simply can't imagine what my life would have been like without them. Actually, I can imagine, and vividly. It would have been like that of all the generations of women who lived before me. The very idea makes me shudder.

I believe that women's liberation—or second-wave feminism, as it is now known—was born from the pill, not the other way around. Safe, effective, affordable contraception allowed half the human race to imagine and create a different future for themselves. That is certainly how it worked for me.

Unlike Kerrie, I did go on to do my HSC and then went to university. When I graduated in 1977, despite my decidedly lack-lustre Bachelor of Arts, I got an entry-level job in marketing for a multinational company. This was still unusual enough that I felt rather proud of myself. Even though I majored in English literature, the degree was the reason that I could be considered for such a career opportunity. In 1977, 10 per cent of Australians went to university. These days, 30 per cent do. It was simply less common in those days, particularly for girls, to have a degree.

As part of my induction into this graduate position in marketing, I went to a week-long residential training course. At the farewell drinks, I remember the course leader confiding that he'd been running the training for a decade or more but this was the first year when the female trainees were equal in number to the male trainees. My peers and I, it seemed, were on the frontier of something, and that is never a comfortable place to be.

There was a lot of resentment expressed towards us, particularly from women in more conventionally female work roles. When I was offered the (incredibly lowly and poorly paid) graduate trainee position of marketing officer, I was warned there was one person who had vociferously objected to me getting the job. It was the only other woman in the team—the secretary/typist. I was told that she was very hostile about working for a woman and that it was my responsibility to win her over. As I hung up the phone after accepting the position, my new boss's parting words were ringing in my ears. 'And remember, she is much more important to us than you are.'

If I'd been nervous before, I was now rigid with terror. Fear being a great motivator, I did win over the only other woman in the team, and it is no small thing to learn to be polite and helpful to all your colleagues, no matter their position in the hierarchy. However, it stung to see the two other (male) marketing officers just drop their typing onto her desk as they breezed by, while I cringed and genuflected, always making my request politely and tentatively, prefacing it with 'If you have time', 'Is there anything I can help you with?' or 'It's not urgent'. To the team secretary, working for any man, even one so wet behind the ears he couldn't yet grow facial hair, was preferable to working for a woman. Men had status. They were natural leaders. Women had no status, and woe betide us if we put on any airs and graces (aka behaved like the men did).

There were a handful of senior women in the company, but most of them were single and in slightly off-centre jobs (personnel, as it was called then, or market research) rather than on the career ladder. None of them had children, either. When I first started in the paid workforce, it was career or children for women—never both. Career women were not admired. Rather, they were pitied, seen as peculiar, lonely, unable to get a man.

However, there were plenty of 'working mothers' (as they were beginning to be called) in the company. Many of them worked on the same floor as I did. They were not considered part of any 'team'. They were the women who sat at small desks in the centre of the open-plan office (all the male managers had offices with their names embossed on the door and windows overlooking the harbour) and crunched numbers on adding machines from dawn to dusk, creating long ribbons of paper that flowed over their desks and onto the floor. This was before computers.

The lives of these working mothers did not look like much fun. They rushed in at 8.30, crunched numbers until 12.30, and dashed out to the shops during their half-hour lunch to buy the groceries they needed to make that night's dinner. They came back to their desks and crunched numbers again until 4.30, then rushed home on public transport, lugging those bags of groceries, before picking up kids, supervising homework, cooking a meal, cleaning it up, doing some laundry, collapsing into bed, waking to the alarm and starting all over again—for a pittance. Everyone knew why they worked: they needed the money. If they'd had a decent husband who could provide for them properly, they wouldn't have had to work. We felt sorry for them. I am not sure they felt sorry for themselves. I was very fond of some of those women. They were motherly towards me and had a strong sense of camaraderie and a ribald, subversive sense of humour that was most often at the expense of the men in their lives, including the oblivious blokes staring at their harbour view behind the closed doors of their offices.

Those women were all a lot older than I was, and I have no idea what happened to any of them. They had realistic expectations for their lives and expected to work—both for money and at home—every second God sent. They'd been trained for it all their lives. I was different. I wanted the kind of life my father had had, not the one I saw my mother struggling to get away from. I thought I was peculiar in this desire, but, as things have turned out, it seems such secret ambitions burning in young female breasts were not so uncommon.

2

HAGS, CRONES, WITCHES AND MOTHERS-IN-LAW

There was a moment in my fifties when I realised that I was being called almost every name in the title of this chapter, although only one was literally true: I had officially become someone's mother-in-law. Thoughtful (?) respondents on Twitter suddenly delighted in reminding me of my hagdom (a common notification included at least some of the following sentiments: that I was a bitter, dried-up old hag). I don't know that anyone, as yet, has ascribed to me any of the supernatural powers of witchcraft, but I live in hope.

I think I attract such responses because I am an older woman who refuses to remain silent. What is it conservative US pundits keep asking Hillary Clinton to do? It generally involves going away, shutting up and walking in the woods. Apparently that is the only dignified option for such an accomplished woman in defeat. Conservative Australians seem to wish the same fate for ex-PM Julia Gillard. Women of a certain age are called names like these in an attempt to shame them into silence. We are superfluous to requirements, meant to accept our invisibility without complaint. If we don't, we are … well, see chapter title above.

About a decade ago, my husband and I took our two almost-grown daughters on a trip to Europe. The younger was sixteen and the older was nineteen. What was interesting (to me, anyway) was how this drove home just how invisible I had become. Young men were attracted to us like flies. I say 'us', but really they were attracted to our daughters. If they began talking to us in a cafe or at a museum or (appropriately enough) an ancient monument, the young men would engage my husband with a few polite remarks before they attempted to gain the attention of the girls. However, when it came to me, it was as if there was a woman-shaped vacant space wherever I was standing.

The experience of being rendered invisible is a peculiar one. It happened again recently on another overseas trip (appearing on the telly in Australia keeps me from being quite so invisible in my own country). This time, it was just my husband and me travelling, so young people routinely ignored us both. However, when we went on a day tour, usually with people around our own age, I again found that while everyone engaged my husband in conversation ('Where are you from? What do you do?'), I was rarely asked a question. At one lunch, every time I opened my mouth to offer a comment relevant to the political discussion we were having, one of the men at the table interrupted and spoke over the top of me. It wasn't done maliciously—it was as if he literally could not hear my voice. The other men had stopped speaking, so clearly it was now his turn. I checked with my husband after the lunch was over, wondering whether I was being hypersensitive, but he confirmed that what I had experienced was also what he had seen. I have become quite accustomed, when travelling, to never having a question directed my way. It doesn't upset me or annoy me—in fact, it is almost amusing in its predictability. But it is impossible not to notice.

Nonetheless, becoming irrelevant and invisible as we age comes as a shock to many women, even though we get an inkling very early of what it might be like. The first time I felt I had disappeared, I was thirty-one and walking past a building site. My experience of building sites until that point was the typical one for young women of my generation: I was catcalled, whistled at and loudly appraised. This time, however, my journey past the workmen was greeted by an eerie silence—tumbleweeds-blowing-down-main-street level silence. Why? Well, I was walking past the building site while pushing a stroller. My baby daughter had rendered me invisible, at least to the men perched on the scaffolding. They literally could no longer see me or, if they could make out a passing human, I was now a decidedly non-sexual one.

This sense of disappearing—particularly in public—may be one of the reasons why so many women fear ageing. We've been trained since birth to believe that our looks are the most important thing about us. Girls are routinely complimented on their appearance rather than their capabilities, so it's no wonder invisibility hits us so hard.

Girls were relentlessly groomed to be passive recipients of the male gaze when I was young, but for anyone who thinks those days are long gone, it seems old habits die hard. Arguably, the pressure to be gorgeous has intensified in this era of Instagram and Snapchat and the obsession with so-called celebrity lives is relentlessly documented in all their excruciating triviality on social media. And this grooming starts painfully young.

As I wrote this chapter, a scandal erupted around children's shoe manufacturer Clarks. They were under attack from outraged parents—mostly mothers—for marketing a black school shoe for little girls called 'Dolly Babe' that featured lavish hearts on a pink background on the insole. The equivalent Clarks black school shoe for boys, on the other hand (or should that be foot), was called 'Leader' and featured football details (sigh!). The job of the female, from childhood, it seems, is still primarily to be cute, pretty and lovable. Agency and action, just as it was for the producers who chose the kids featured in *Seven Up!* in 1964, remain the province of boys.

That scandals like the kerfuffle around the school shoes still erupt so regularly makes you wonder whether marketers just refuse to notice how much the world has changed or are cynically manipulating our responses for the free publicity. Knowing the marketing business as intimately as I do, I think it is much more likely to be the former than the latter. Contrary to popular opinion, most marketers are not that clever.

Silly old Clarks shoes are just the latest in a seemingly endless list of clothing, toys, films, books, you-name-it that have been criticised for grooming girls for a lifetime of accepting their place as the second sex, as the passive object of the male gaze. Another scandal that went viral at the same time, thanks to a furious blog post from a female surfer, concerned photographs on the homepage of the website of the surfing retailer and clothing designer Billabong. It was once again the contrast between the portrayals of women and men that triggered the outrage. As the blogger pointed out, the woman in the advertising photograph was portrayed as a passive and highly sexualised object of desire. She lay with her back arched and her head thrown back while reclining (uncomfortably) on the sand—the better to display the Billabong bikini she wore. Her unnatural but sexually provocative pose revealed that her purpose was the gratification of others. The man in the shot next to hers was portrayed completely differently, and perhaps it was the two photographs' close juxtaposition that made the contrast so stark. He was depicted as a highly skilled, powerful athlete busy taming a wave. His purpose was to experience self-gratification. Some people like to claim that this stuff is trivial and not worth getting upset about, but surfer Karen Knowlton, the blogger whose critical post not only went viral but caused Billabong to change its homepage, articulated why representations like this matter: 'We soak this sh*t up, these images that tell us who we are and what we are for, what our bodies are good for.' As a result, she explains, women who surf have to silence their own doubts about whether they belong in the surf and whether they have the same right as male surfers to compete for waves. Knowlton says she struggles against the feeling that she shouldn't take up male space and isn't even entitled to be in the surf at all.

In other words, female surfers are meant to disappear and not claim any right to the waves that we all (even the female surfers themselves, apparently) see as natural male territory. We can be admired for our appearance (until we reach a certain age, anyway) but we may not take up any real-world, contested space. And it starts young. According to writer Madonna King, the top ten boys' and girls' schools in Queensland (as defined by matriculation results) make abundantly clear this difference in the space the male gender may occupy compared to the female gender. The elite boys' schools occupy fifteen times more physical area than the comparable schools for girls, and receive ten times more in bequests and donations.

This debate about the right of women to take up space in the world is a very important one, and it is not just actual physical space that women are forced to hand over. It can include psychological and emotional space, time, attention and even the space inside their own bodies. Susan, the adoptee who as a pregnant sixteen-year-old was coerced into giving up her baby, makes a tragic point about how this assumption of the right of men to claim all kinds of space can affect vulnerable young girls: 'My adoptive mother spoke to me quietly and said that if I could possibly have the baby on my (abusive) adoptive father's birthday, that would be a nice thing for him. Now I was further diminished as a human. Even the birth of a date-rape baby belonged to a man.'

Despite it being a very lopsided bargain, beauty and male approval are things girls are taught to aspire to from the moment they are born, and that message is continually reinforced throughout our lives. Yet physical beauty has no actual moral value. It not only did not launch a thousand ships (the men made their own choices—Helen of Troy could not help how she looked; she was not an admiral, gave no orders and had no power of command) but cannot change the world. Being beautiful is largely an accident of genes. You can make what is called 'the best of yourself', certainly, but unless you are rich enough (and insecure enough) to go to extreme surgical lengths, we all have our natural physical limitations. Behind the universal fetishisation of female beauty is a prettily disguised message about passivity and submission (cross your legs, Susan, and don't have that baby until a man tells you it's the right day).

There's another message, too. When women are praised for their physical beauty they have not earned this admiration—they have merely lucked into it. Women are meant to yearn to be looked at and admired but aspire to nothing more. To claim attention in any other way is to be seen as pushy, demanding, shrill, selfish and unfeminine—haggish, even. We are asking for too much space. Many older women fall silent even as they disappear for fear of being judged in this way. Yet if we want to attract any attention at all, as our looks fade, what else can we do but make a noise and express ourselves? Is it any wonder, therefore, that so many of us concentrate every ounce of our energy and funds on clinging to our youthful appearance as best we can? A woman who has 'let herself go' is an object of both pity and blame. That is why 'old hag', 'old bag', 'old battleaxe' are common insults about older women. They are not just comments about chronological age: they are also judgements about our failure to maintain our looks. To age and get ugly is seen as a moral failing rather than as a misfortune or, better yet, an irrelevance. To get fat (something that also often accompanies ageing) means you are treated in much the same way. Close your eyes and look at the images you see in your head when you hear the words 'crone', 'hag', 'witch' and 'mother-in-law'. Are any of them pretty?

Women who are famous and admired—with a few honourable exceptions—are often required to be beautiful. Their appearance is obsessively and harshly policed. Any kilo gained is tut-tutted. Any fashion faux pas is cruelly mocked and ridiculed. TV personality and journalist Lisa Wilkinson dedicated her 2013 Andrew Olle Media Lecture to discussing the obsession viewers, commentators, media executives, producers and all the rest of us have with the hair, clothes and weight of female TV personalities and celebrities. The expectation that the famous woman will do her duty as eye candy is so inexorable that female celebrities are routinely humiliated for any deviation from the standard of gorgeousness expected.

British TV presenter and professor of classics at Cambridge University Mary Beard routinely attracts a storm of sexist abuse about her unconventional appearance whenever she appears on screen. It is as if many people (most of them men) find it fundamentally offensive when a woman earns her place in the spotlight because of her knowledge, personality and experience rather than because of her appearance. Indeed, when the British TV series *Civilisations* aired in the US in 2018, Beard, who was one of the three hosts, complained that she had been virtually edited out of her episodes in the US version. Beard is sixty-three years old and describes herself as a 'slightly creaky old lady with long grey hair'. Mind you, one of her co-hosts is Simon Schama, who is seventy-three and, while charming, no oil painting. His appearances in the show remained.

Although Beard's appearance (and appearances) seem to earn the ire of men, such is the complexity of our relationship with our own physical presence (trying to view yourself from the outside as well as the inside does your head in) that it is often other women who feed this obsession with the fashion failures of their famous sisters. When Wilkinson was co-host of Channel 9's breakfast TV show, *Today*, the other host, Karl Stefanovic, emphasised the difference between the way men's appearance on TV is viewed compared to women's by wearing the same suit every day on the show for a year. Despite (or perhaps because of) the relentless scrutiny of Wilkinson, no-one even noticed.

Ageing, of course, is the inevitable way that most of us will fall from the ranks of the 'beautiful'—if we ever earned a spot in the first place. Cruel clickbait along the lines of 'You won't believe what this 70s star looks like now' is ubiquitous on the internet.

But it is not simply that the majority of women in films, television and even books are defined by their beauty and desirability. Paradoxically, girls are trained from an early age to accept a far higher level of invisibility than boys ever have to put up with. When my daughters were young I returned to paid work as a copywriter in the advertising industry, working on the Kellogg's account, among others. The girls were watching TV one afternoon after school when the elder turned to me after yet another commercial for breakfast cereal and said, wearily, 'Don't they think girls eat cereal, Mum?' Her observation shocked me, and I began to take more notice. The number of little girls in ads—unless the product featured was for a toy, clothing or snack that was directly designed for them—was minuscule in comparison to the number of boys. If the product, like breakfast cereal, was aimed generically at children, it almost invariably featured only boys.

Thanks to my daughter's question, I went back to work and did what I could to change that. It wasn't easy. The conventional wisdom was (and still is) that while girls will happily identify with boys, boys will not do the same with girls. I also remember that I tried to correct the overwhelming preponderance of male voice-overs in both radio and TV commercials, regardless of whether the ad was aimed at women. (The majority of ads are, by the way—women still do most of the shopping.) Every time I suggested a female voice-over, I'd have to fight for it. Blokes never tired of telling me that women didn't identify with female voices and preferred male voice-overs. They even had the research to prove it. Well, no wonder. Women, just like men, had been trained from an early age to watch and listen to men, and so this was considered 'just the way things are'. I didn't believe the research and I didn't believe what the blokes were telling me. I fought back and—sometimes—I won. Other women in the industry must have waged a similar fight, because it is gratifying how often we hear female voices now. (I wonder whatever happened to all that authoritative 'research'?) I believe strongly that the usual explanation about girls being happy to identify with boys, rather than vice versa, is a rationalisation of a deeper and more sexist motive. I believe we actively resist allowing boys to identify with female protagonists. We remain terrified that allowing boys to imaginatively identify with girls will 'feminise' them. Contrary to the claims made by some conservative pundits, it is not social engineering to make representations more equal, or to make products aimed at kids more gender neutral (and inclusive). It is simply reversing the social engineering that has policed rigid gender roles for centuries.

The relative invisibility of women in media is, of course, not new. In fact, gender ratios have not changed much in film and TV since 1946, when ratios actually improved slightly because fewer war films were being made. Since that year, the percentage of women in crowd scenes, just to give one example, has been stuck fast at 17 per cent. This is despite the fact that women make up 51 per cent of the population. In other words, even when it comes to extras, there are more roles for men than women.

Just as I was not the only female copywriter of my generation pushing back against the overwhelming sexism in my industry, nor was I the only parent of daughters who noticed their lack of representation. Ten years ago, Academy Award–winning actor Geena Davis established the Institute on Gender in Media in response to what she had observed about her own industry after having her children. Davis had fraternal twins—a boy and a girl—and began to notice how many portrayals of boys were available for her son to identify with and how few were available for her daughter. Shocked by what she saw, she created the institute and pioneered the largest-ever research project into gender depictions in the media. What she uncovered was that the general ratio of male to female representations was 3:1. Her work has begun to bear fruit, and gender representations have improved. But don't get too excited: 2016 was the best year for the representation of women in film so far, but even so, the percentage of women protagonists only climbed to 29 per cent.

When the women of my generation were growing up, we hardly saw our own gender represented at all. When we did, they were most often the love interest of the hero. I remember as a child becoming infuriated when the heroine inevitably fell and twisted her ankle as she and the hero tried to flee the bad guys. The hero then scooped her up, proving his worth by escaping while carrying a swooning female in his manly arms. I didn't fall over every time I ran anywhere, nor did any of the women and girls I knew. Even as a child, it drove me nuts to watch how blatantly women's supposed weakness was used to emphasise men's supposed strength.

The point I am making is that women have been ruthlessly and consistently groomed to accept their invisibility. A study that looked at almost 6000 children's books published between the first year of the twentieth century and the first year of the twenty-first (that's a solid 100 years of data) found that 'males are the central characters in 57 per cent of children's books each year, with just 31 per cent having female central characters'. According to the same study, even when the children's book features an animal as the central character, it is male 23 per cent of the time and female a mere 7.5 per cent. Thank goodness for Jemima Puddle-Duck!

I remember as a young girl searching in vain for female heroes, whether they were fictional characters in books or real-life women. They were very hard to find, although I loved Jane Eyre (*Jane Eyre* by Charlotte Brontë), Mary Lennox (*The Secret Garden* by Frances Hodgson Burnett) and Jo March (*Little Women* by Louisa May Alcott). But when it came to real-life women to admire, they were as rare as hen's teeth. Perhaps it is no coincidence that I grew up to write young adult novels about Elizabeth Tudor. When I was a girl, she felt like a beacon of hope in a stiflingly male universe. Elizabeth I not only ruled a kingdom, she was universally acknowledged to have done it well. She was the closest woman I could find who was recognised as a genius (we almost never use that description when speaking of women). Even better, she ruled her kingdom entirely alone, refusing to ever marry or have children. I devoured everything I could lay my hands on about Elizabeth I. I still do. Knowing she existed felt as necessary to me when I was a girl as breathing. She was a talisman against the commonly held view that women were incapable of doing anything that mattered except have children. She was also—and this is vital—not beautiful.

For women of my generation (and, regrettably, I suspect this is still true today), it is only for a brief time that our youth gave us a spurious kind of power. Between the ages of fifteen and twenty-five, most women are at their most beautiful and—for a while—can allow themselves to believe that they will always be the adored focus of the male gaze. This is often the time when women of my generation fell in love and got married. We were seduced by the promise of 'happily ever after' (another form of grooming perpetrated on women when they were occasionally permitted to be the hero of the story). Many of my generation aspired to nothing much beyond the romantic dream of a frilly white entry to the land of never-ending love. Most of the girls I knew even promised to 'obey' their husband in their vows and happily, excitedly even, changed their last name. I did neither but still found myself occasionally addressed as 'Mrs Ralph Dunning' (!)—something I experienced as another act of obliteration. My separate identity along with my name had literally disappeared upon my marriage. Almost worse, addressing me in that fashion was then explained to me as an example of good manners!

Despite these constant reminders throughout our lives of women's irrelevance and secondary status, the invisibility that comes with ageing remains shocking. Yet there is a paradox at the centre of our attitudes to older women: we routinely ignore them, yet we also seem to fear them.

The human female is a remarkable creature. Almost alone among life on this planet (I believe this may also apply to some species of whale), the human female can and does live many decades past her fertility. There are many theories as to why this may be so; most involve the length of time and complexity of raising human young. Grandmothers, so the theory goes, are very important for the survival of their daughters' offspring and so cannot also be burdened with new babies of their own. Studies of hunter-gatherer societies have shown that children with a living grandmother (particularly a maternal grandmother) were both taller and heavier than those without, and were more likely to survive to adulthood.

Whatever the reason, the years we live past the menopause can be both the most liberating of our lives and also the most bewildering. It was only relatively recently that older women stopped being routinely sneered at by comedians and comic films and TV shows. The universally despised and derided figure of the 'mother-in-law' was once the only role model Western women had to look forward to as they aged. 'Take my mother-in-law … please' was the standard icebreaker of the (not-very-talented) comedian. The mother-in-law figure of my youth was a gorgon, a dragon and a grotesque. She was ugly, loud, interfering, fat, badly dressed and—yet—powerful. Her son-in-law lived in fear of her, perhaps because she was the one person who could challenge his dominance over his wife. She also acted as an awful warning of what his wife might become as she aged and gained confidence in her own powers and was correspondingly less convinced about his.

Older women in fairytales are also both despised and yet terrifying. They are the witches and the crones, the hideous hags who curse the plucky hero. They entice children into gingerbread houses so they can fatten them up to eat them. They are the wicked stepmothers homicidally jealous of the heroine's youth and beauty. At the very least they live in lonely cottages deep in dark woods, unprotected against attacks by wolves, cast out from the safety and community of the world that matters. In history, older women were often horribly vulnerable, particularly if they acted as midwives or healers. The fear of witches was pathological in Europe until the industrial revolution. Indeed, it may be no coincidence that James I, the king who succeeded to the throne after the death of Elizabeth I, was an enthusiastic witch-hunter and that many, often older, women suffered horribly during his reign. I do not think you have to be expert in human psychology to draw a fairly straight line between the fear of witches and the fear of women released from the burden of child-bearing and rearing (oh, and the fear of a powerful and revered Virgin Queen, perhaps). Nor is witch-hunting entirely a thing of the past. Vulnerability to accusations of witchcraft remains a terrifying reality for women (and, recently, young girls) in places such as Papua New Guinea, and the punishments meted out to them can include torture and murder.

Given such a dark history and the relentlessly negative portrayal of older women, is it any wonder that so many women are terrified of the passing of time? The fear lasts to this day and, like all fears, is very handy economically as far as capitalism is concerned. Transparency Market Research recently announced that the market for anti-ageing products and services will be worth an estimated US$191.7 billion globally by 2019.

Yet for many of the women of my generation it is not all bad news and expensive (but useless) skincare. Thanks to the revolution in women's lives, there is an unexpected bonus to getting older, particularly if you are financially secure and independent. As women age they are gradually freed from the onerous responsibilities of bearing and raising children, or the potential of doing so. If they have money, they also find they have time to—at last—start doing the things they want to do. Being in paid employment for most of their lives has given women a freedom and a power that no other previous generation has had in such numbers. Even better, the lucky ones are set to inherit what has been called one of the largest generational shifts of wealth ever. This is because women generally live longer than their brothers and their husbands. *Investment News* in the US has estimated that '(US)$22 trillion in assets will shift to women by 2020', and business is noticing. Perhaps it is no coincidence that the old trope of the dreaded 'mother-in-law' appears to have completely disappeared in the last few years. Sure, the resurgence of feminism that has occurred thanks to social media has had its effect, but controlling the majority of wealth generates respect like nothing else.

Perhaps the loathing of the older woman was only possible when the power of older women was safely constrained and limited by their lack of economic independence and control. It is a lot riskier to bully and deride those you want to sell shit to. Mind you, while that may mean it pays to be nice to women's faces—even wrinkly ones—it does not mean you have to like them. Perhaps this niggling fear of the growing power of older women was one of the problems that Hillary Clinton faced in her failed attempt to be America's first female president. We can't stop older women gaining economic power, perhaps, but we'll be damned if we'll vote them into political power as well.

But none of the above are the worst things that can happen to women of my generation.

We may remain ambivalent about the fate of women over fifty who are fortunate in their circumstances, but most of us are oblivious to the fate of those who have not been so blessed. This generation seems to be heading in two very different directions. For some, they will be the beneficiaries of both their own earnings and the transfer of wealth that comes from inheritance. For others, who have missed out—or lost out—on both, the future looks very bleak. Susan, whose life was blighted by extreme difficulties from the start, has been homeless for three years and has spent the past five months living out of her car. Amanda, who hoped to marry a spunk, has, after a series of failed relationships, finally found a man she loves, but she worries about money daily and spent eighteen months homeless a few years ago. Debbie, who dreamed of a comfortable life, is now on the Newstart Allowance and unable to afford rent. She lives with her children in order to survive. Their stories are far too common. Many of the women I grew up with are living insecure lives full of dread.

Of course, it is likely that penury and insecurity have always been the more common fate for women as they aged, and that it is the older women who are now enjoying both power and money that are the recent phenomenon. Given the weight of silence around women's history in general and that of older women in particular, it is hard to know for sure. Widows throughout history have found themselves thrown on the mercy of their sons—made dependent on those who were once utterly dependent on them—because of the tradition of women being unable to inherit or control their own money. (This may be the origin of the growing phenomenon of economic elder abuse, particularly by sons towards ageing and widowed mothers.) Women who outlived their husbands were less common in the past due to the dangers of childbirth—there is a reason there are so many stepmothers in fairytales. Those who did, however, and did not have living children either willing or able to take them on, were a burden to their community. For centuries in Britain, for example, they became the responsibility of their parish, then after the introduction of the notorious Poor Laws in 1834, they were expected to rely on the slender mercies of the workhouse. But more about that later.

Today, while marketers may be rubbing their hands in glee over the increasing cohort of rich old women, legislators are eyeing with alarm the growing number of poor old women. These are the women without the financial resources to see them through their old age. In the past, perhaps, they were forced to accept their fate more or less silently, thanks to their invisibility. Today, however, another technological revolution has meant that this generation of older women are able to refuse to go quietly. While they have not benefited from their wages in the way that some of their more fortunate sisters have, most of these women have still been in paid work for most of their lives. They are educated, they have access to the internet and, to their eternal credit, they are refusing to be cowed. They are speaking up about their fate—and you can call them nasty names, or sneer and roll your eyes at them behind their backs (or to their faces), but they are not deterred. They are insisting that we take them and their needs seriously. Women over fifty, whether rich or poor, are embracing their hagdom for what it is: hard-won wisdom. It is not the crone or the old bag that is in danger of extinction: it is the 'sweet little old lady'. And not before time, either.

3

DUTIFUL DAUGHTERS, WIVES, MOTHERS AND GRANDMOTHERS

Before the main feature at my neighbourhood cinema (yes, my generation is also helping to keep movie-houses alive) they run one of those slide shows promoting local businesses. The promotional slide that never fails to make me catch my breath is for a business called Dutiful Daughters. It is a provider of home-care services. My stifled gasp is in response to the organisation's business name. The whole idea of dutiful daughters seems at once so old-fashioned and such a nasty, covert little slap to all the actual daughters in the audience. After all, if we really were doing our duty, why would there need to be such an agency?

I sometimes think this is the core conflict that women face as they try to navigate their way through life. We are constantly tugged in two directions. These days we are expected to earn our own money and be financially independent, keeping a weather eye on our superannuation balance. Yet the old assumptions about women and their 'natural' functions remain tenacious. We are still the gender expected to drop everything whenever a member of our family requires care. These two things are not compatible, and they are a contradictory pressure simply not felt by men. After all, there is no home-care agency called Dutiful Sons.

For some, there is nothing that can be done about this. In their view, to be the owner of two X chromosomes condemns you to a life subservient to the needs of others. In 2016, in a speech to the National Press Club, one of our most conservative former prime ministers, John Howard, summed up the traditional attitude perfectly: 'I'm not sure that you will ever have a fifty-fifty thing because it's a fact of society that the caring role, whatever people may say about it and whatever the causes are … women play a significantly greater part of filling the caring role in our communities, which inevitably will place some limits on their capacity.' The belief that this is simply a fact of life, something immutable and unchangeable, part of woman's God-given nature, is one of the reasons why so many women still feel guilty about ever putting their own needs and desires first. Margaret remembers how hard it was to carve out any time for herself when her husband got a job that took him overseas for weeks and sometimes months at a time: 'I tried organising myself an evening class (a fitness class, a first aid class) with him getting home to take over the child-care duties, but he made me late so many times—because of difficulties getting out of the office—I gave up.' With a husband whose work meant he never had time for his family, Margaret felt she had no options: 'So, no, I didn't have a career … And now I am at an age when many of my peers are starting to retire and I haven't found a job/career to retire from yet! I feel like I'm very quickly running out of time. How did I get to be fifty-five and in this position?'

Women of my generation did not anticipate this dilemma. When we were brought up, as I have explained, it was assumed that our caring responsibilities would take precedence over anything else. We were simply expected to be dutiful—especially once we had children. As the romantic poet Lord Byron famously put it, 'Man's love is of man's life a thing apart / 'Tis woman's whole existence'. Our primary duty was, according to blokes, to love them and their offspring. That's why the toys we were given were dolls. They were a way to practise for a future of taking care of others. However, although no-one could have picked it at the time, there was a hint of change in the air, even in the sort of dolls we were being given.

Until 1959, when Mattel developed the Barbie doll, dolls were manufactured in the image of little girls or babies. They were our pretend children and I remember dutifully tucking my collection of dolls into their baby cradle at night, conscientiously kissing them all 'Night-night' and mimicking my mother's actions when she said goodnight to me. But Barbie was a revolution. Barbie was very clearly formed in the image of an adult woman, and she became our avatar. Even though many feminists see Barbie as a stereotypical, eating-disorder-promoting anathema, I see her as a giant leap for womankind. At last, little girls were able to imagine their lives as independent women and not primarily as apprentice mothers. Okay, Barbie was moulded into the plastic version of eye candy, but ... baby steps, baby steps. (Mind you, with those feet, that is all Barbie could ever take.) Interestingly, another period in history when dolls (for aristocratic little girls, anyway) were fashioned to look like adult women rather than children was during another revolutionary time: the Reformation. When the rules get loosened, women have always been quick to try and grab a bit more space for themselves. The depressing side of that observation, however, is how quickly they get pushed back to the margins.

When my friends and I played with our Barbie dolls we were able to imagine a future that included work, fun, parties, boyfriends, adventure and travel. Barbie even had her own campervan, as I recall. I never remember us playing games called 'Barbie has a baby', 'Barbie cleans the house' or 'Barbie takes care of her ageing parents'. Despite what we saw our mothers doing, such scenarios did not enter our minds. Barbie's glamour forced us to imagine a future life that might include some fun rather than just duty.

Despite the subtle subversion of Barbie, as we grew and began to enter romantic relationships we found we had duties that our boyfriends did not. The first was to sexually police the relationship. It was up to us how far what was then called 'petting' went, and if it went too far, we were the ones who were to blame. It was our job—as dutiful girlfriends—to be sexually alluring and up for a fair amount of sexual play (otherwise, we were 'frigid'). Yet we were also supposed to intuitively know exactly when and how to draw the line and call a halt. Our boyfriends complained (I seem to remember a fair bit of whining about a condition called 'blue balls'), but I think most of them were grateful. Teenage boys were no more ready for full-on sex than teenage girls, I think, but it was part of the masculine disguise they were forced to wear that they could not be the one to say no. That was our duty. We were protecting ourselves, no doubt, but we were also protecting them and taking responsibility for them—the beginning of a lifetime of doing so.

The girls who either did 'go all the way' or were rumoured to have done so were comprehensively vilified. They were called 'sluts', 'slags' and even 'the town bike' (because everyone has had a ride). This condemnation of sexually active girls was not restricted to other immature young people, either. Jenny became pregnant and was sent away to have her baby. She went to hospital for a check-up. 'The doctor used a speculum on me so roughly, as if deliberately trying to cause violent, painful penetration. It hurt so much I jumped and turned to face him in horror. The look on his face was as if to say "You deserve that and worse, you slut." His eyes were filled with anger and judgement. I should suffer for being so sinful. It looked like hatred … I was fifteen.'

I remember with pity and shame the girls in my own high school and neighbourhood who were characterised as sluts. It wasn't just the boys (or male doctors) who pilloried and punished them: even (relatively) good girls like me turned our backs. The boys who had participated in the degradation of these very vulnerable young women—often in packs—were admired and valorised. She was disgusting; they were virile. We see this tradition continuing now with the loathsome male-bonding behaviour among sporting teams that is sometimes referred to as 'spit-roasting' (use your imagination). Worse, we still excuse it as boys just being boys. Frankly, if that is true, boys should not be allowed out! A recent example in Northern Ireland dealt with four footballers, three of whom were accused of raping a young woman at a party. Despite eight harrowing days in the witness box by the victim, and texts from the accused boasting about 'spit-roasting', the men were acquitted. The case caused a scandal in Ireland and led to a hashtag campaign on social media, #Ibelieveher, and a debate about what consent actually means. Is it the same as being so frozen with fear you cannot say no? There have been many similar scandals in Australia and all over the world. One of the most famous in this country was that involving an Australian sporting team and a nineteen-year-old New Zealand girl who had either consensually participated in 'group sex' or been gang-raped, depending on who you believe. The events of that infamous evening were the subject of a *Four Corners* episode in 2009. We are often told that such scandals risk 'ruining a young man's life', yet, given how many famous sportsmen have been accused of this stuff and have gone on to have fine careers and seemingly unblemished reputations, it is the women's lives that are forever damaged.

The double standard about girls and sex has stood firm in the face of the pill, Barbie and feminism. Given the chances of any woman winning a rape case (in Victoria, for example, of the 3500 rapes reported to police between 2009 and 2010 only 3 per cent resulted in a conviction), it still does. The girls who 'put out' have failed in their duty as moral guardians. Mind you, for those of us who escaped such a fate or managed to bury it deep in our past, and who married and became respectable, our duties did not cease.

When the women of my generation married, it may still have been considered our duty to promise to obey and take our husband's name as our mothers had, but some things had changed. By the 1970s most of us (even the good girls) were not virgins when we wed and thanks to the pill had probably slept with boys who were not the groom waiting for us at the altar,.

The shotgun weddings that were so much a part of our mothers' experiences were beginning to be a relic of the past. Now, they are virtually unheard of. According to a 2014 study by researchers at Cornell, Duke, Brown and Louisiana State universities and the US Census Bureau and National Center for Health Statistics, in the 1960s, two-thirds of couples who got pregnant outside of marriage had a rushed wedding. By the 1980s (when I got married), this had dropped to about a quarter. My husband (a devout atheist, like his wife) is godfather to a close friend's daughter. Her christening was celebrated at the wedding ceremony and so, as godfather, he was a part of the wedding party. The bride had been adamant she did not want to walk down any kind of 'aisle' (she had a secular wedding) with a pregnant belly, so she waited until her child was almost one before tying the knot.

Between the 1970s and 2000s, shotgun weddings fell from 27 per cent of women with a premarital pregnancy to 7 per cent. This is just another of the silent revolutions women of my vintage have lived through. As the deserted wife disappeared, the de facto partner took her place. In 1976 my boyfriend (now husband) and I moved in together, an arrangement that was then called 'living in sin'. After nine years of sinful cohabitation, we decided we wanted to have children and so, in 1984, we got married. It was a secular wedding in my parents' garden, conducted by a celebrant. As I have already said, I did not promise to 'obey' my husband and did not change my name. Both decisions were relatively unusual at the time but not unheard of, and they are certainly no longer particularly shocking. Nevertheless, when we did have our children, it was me who gave up my career in advertising and stayed home to care for them. This was partly because I was—as is usual for women—the lower-paid, but it was also because I felt the pressure telling me it was my duty as a woman and a mother. I had absorbed the overwhelming message that surrounded my generation of women: if you were going to 'choose' to have children, it was your job to look after them. As a nun midwife said to a friend of mine as she groaned with pain in labour, 'You've made your bed, now you lie in it.' My memory of being a young mother is one of being surrounded by pursed lips, disapproving looks and exasperated, not-my-problem shrugs. Fathers, I remember noticing at the time, got off scot-free.

Mind you, I say I 'gave up' my paid employment, but I was actually made redundant when I was four months pregnant. My 'brilliant career' really did go bung. I ended up having five years out of the workforce, despite doing a little freelance work and retraining for another career. I never started that different career because, like Margaret's partner, my husband was promoted to a job that took him away from home one week out of two and I became a single parent for twenty-six weeks a year. My caring duties absolutely interfered with my ability to maintain an income. Unfortunately, notwithstanding the passage of nearly three decades since I was at home caring for small children, such duties still have a devastating effect on women and their ability to earn a living. The workplace, despite more or less constant pressure for the last few decades, still refuses to recognise that the core worker is no longer a man with a stay-at-home wife who can remove all his caring responsibilities from him.

This refusal by the workplace to adapt to the fundamental changes that have occurred in families has created a horrible crunch for the young parents of this generation, particularly mothers. I was five years out of the workforce, but such a long period caring for children has become increasingly unusual. In 1991, the year my younger daughter was born and the year my husband was promoted, the proportion of mothers who were employed was 55 per cent. It was 56 per cent in 1996—by which time I had been back in the paid workforce for two years, working part time in an ad agency, and it seems I was typical of my generation. The percentage grew to 59 per cent in 2001, 63 per cent in 2006 and 65 per cent in 2011.

I was also typical because I went back to work part time. Thirty-six per cent of working mothers work on a part-time basis compared to 25 per cent who are employed full time. This is great in terms of combining working with caring responsibilities, but it has a lifelong impact on our income and, of course, the amount of superannuation we are able to accumulate—but more about that later. Suffice to say one of the most common estimates is that women earn about $1 million less over their lifetime directly as a result of the cost of caring. Mind you, we've been trained from an early age to accept less reward for our labour. Dr Terry Fitzsimmons from the University of Queensland's Business School surveyed 10,000 male and female students in Brisbane and found boys got an average of $13 a week in pocket money while their sisters got an average of $9.60.

Even when women return to work, as most of them do quite quickly these days, the cost of child care hits them hard. Having a child in day care if you work full time in one of Australia's largest cities can cost as much as $33,000 per annum after tax. If you have two children in full-time care, for many women the cost is more than their take-home pay. Author Polly Dunning (full disclosure: she is also my elder daughter) estimated that returning to full-time work as a schoolteacher after having two children would cost her family $2000 a year more than her income. Rather than her being paid to work, her family would actually be paying for the privilege! It's all very well to advise women to stay in the job market no matter what to safeguard their lifetime earnings and superannuation, but if the short-term cost of going back to work is defaulting on the mortgage, as Dunning says, 'choice is an illusion'.

It sometimes feels as if government policies are designed to be a disincentive for women returning to work. Maybe that is because so many of our elected leaders remain the male members of my generation. They are the men who as boys received all the same messages as their female contemporaries about what was 'natural' for women. Yet it seems to me that while the women I grew up with have changed beyond recognition, whether accidentally or on purpose, most of my male peers have doggedly turned their faces away from the revolution their sisters and wives have experienced. In far too many cases, they have actively refused to change. The messages they received as boys are the messages they still believe are true. I suspect many of them are still waiting for women to give up on the folly of equality and for everything to go back to the way it 'should' be (I am looking at you, John Howard). Perhaps that is why so much of our public policy feels almost as if it has been designed to make women do their so-called duty, regardless of the long-term price we pay. As I have said before, the duty of caring for children and other members of our family who are in need and the duty to look after ourselves financially are contradictory and impossible for most women to fulfil. Yet we get blamed, either way.

Nevertheless, contradictory push-pull forces or not, as the stats quoted above show, women have changed and most mothers do return to work—at least part time. I doubt they return to preserve their living standard in their old age. I suspect it is much more about continuing to pay the mortgage, which now requires two salaries in almost all of our major cities. However, the rising cost of child care (Australia has one of the most expensive child-care systems in the world) and the stagnation in real wages have created a crunch for families and that is where one generation is looking for help from another. Increasingly, our children are turning to us to help out with the child care so they can try to at least keep pace with the rising cost of living. It has fallen to us, many of whom had thought we were finally free of our child-rearing responsibilities, to step into the breach.

Some grandparents—even, perhaps, most of them— are happy to help out with the child care, but there is a vast difference between helping your kids on an ad hoc basis as a favour and becoming the unpaid nanny. In fact, grandparents are now the most popular form of child care, outstripping all other kinds. In 2008, 660,000 children, or around one-fifth of Australians aged between nought and twelve, were being minded regularly by their grandparents.

Grandparents looking after their grandchildren so their children—particularly daughters—can return to work means those grandparents, particularly grandmothers (female grandparents provided 44 per cent of the child care for couple families and 34 per cent for one-parent ones; male grandparents provided just 11.6 per cent and 9 per cent respectively), may have to give up their own chances of gaining employment. If, as is true for far too many women, their financial situation is already precarious, being an unpaid baby-minder can make everything worse. I doubt Centrelink accepts babysitting your grandchildren as a legitimate excuse for missing a job interview. Yet the guilt that accompanies refusing to help a desperate, exhausted daughter struggling (as you once did) with the demands of small children, work and—too frequently—an oblivious husband is often too much for us to contemplate. Many of us sigh, button our lip and, once again, do our duty.

For some of my generation, given how much longer our own parents are living, we can find ourselves wedged between our very young and energetic children or grandchildren and our ageing but just as demanding parents. After caring for her immigrant parents-in-law who lived with her family when her children were small (talk about the sandwich generation), Lesley then became a full-time carer for her own mother as she aged. Since her mother's death, Lesley has been unable to find work and is now on unemployment benefits: 'Being on Newstart is extremely difficult. I am unable to afford rent etc. on my own and live with my children in order to survive.' The cost of caring to the women who do the lion's share of it can be staggeringly high.

And let us be completely up-front about this: the majority of the caring burden for both ends of the age spectrum falls on women.

There are many honourable exceptions (see the 11.6 per cent and 9 per cent already mentioned), and it is wonderful to see how much more hands-on fathers and grandfathers are these days with little children (a direct gift to them from feminism, by the way). However, even if sons and sons-in-law or grandfathers are willing and have the time, anything they do to help is still seen as a great favour to the primary carer, who is almost always a woman. We still do not expect such work from them in the same way as we do from women. Due to our ageing population, however, many men do end up as carers—but it is often for their wives, rather than for their parents or children. Alzheimer's is not an equal-opportunity condition and is more prevalent in women than men (it sometimes feels like women cannot catch a break). In further cheery news, the number of people living with Alzheimer's is expected to quadruple by 2050.

What is interesting about our attitudes to men and women in relation to caring responsibilities is how entrenched our expectations of women are and, correspondingly, our lack of expectations for men. When my own children were young, I recall vividly how much praise was lavished upon my husband whenever he did anything for his daughters. Ralph has always been a hands-on dad—partly because he wanted to be, and partly because I wanted him to be. However, as I have said, his employer, and the rigid attitudes to the way men are expected to work, continually got in the way of his good intentions. When he did manage to spend time with our kids, I found myself deeply irritated that whenever he did something minimal—like bath a baby, or change nappies, or turn up to a school concert held during working hours (I had to take time off, too)—the response by others to his efforts was positively adulatory. He got praised for doing *anything*. In contrast, as a mother who was also in the paid workforce, if anyone ever commented on my parenting it was to criticise me for something I had failed to do. It is, of course, the same with housework. I know perfectly well that if someone comes to my house and it looks like a bomb's gone off in it (which it frequently did when my kids were small), no-one ever thinks to themselves, 'Gee, that Ralph is a lousy housekeeper.' And don't get me started on fathers who leave work early using the excuse that they are 'babysitting' their own kids. No, old chap, you are parenting them—and about time, too. Many women, particularly those of us who are mothers, live in fear of negative judgement and are only too aware that whatever miracles we may be performing in the workforce, it is by our failures in our duty of care on the home front that we are most harshly measured. My generation may be particularly vulnerable to such judgements because we were so thoroughly trained to expect that the role of housewife and mother was entirely our responsibility. When I was young, it was often quite unselfconsciously referred to as 'women's work'—and not in a good way.

I now believe this tendency to see only the failures of one group while judging the least effort as a remarkable success in another is a very clear indicator of the kind of status we accord to those two groups. I often draw parallels between our attitudes to each gender of parent and our attitudes to types of school, particularly in Australia. Fee-charging schools, it seems to me, are like fathers. They can make just the minimum of effort and will be praised extravagantly for it. How often have you heard a prestigious private school extolled for offering scholarships to a handful of disadvantaged students? Meanwhile, the public school down the road, with a much higher enrolment of such students, none of whom have been carefully vetted before being let through the doors, will go unnoticed for its efforts until something goes wrong. And again, this parallel operates precisely because we have different expectations of the duty owed by the different types of schools, just as we have for male and female parents. We expect public schools to educate all kids, so give them little praise for doing what we see as merely their job, no matter how difficult it may be. Well, so it is with mothers, or daughters, or wives. We do not praise them for caring for the more vulnerable members of our society because it is what we expect them to do. It is their duty.

And women absorb these expectations just as thoroughly as men do. Even if we are feminists, even if we mix in enlightened circles, even if our friends and family would never think of judging us harshly for our derelictions of duty, we do it to ourselves. Even the most self-actualised of us feel more anxiety about our untidy house, scruffy kids, crumpled husband and neglected elderly parents than our male partners do. We see ourselves not just as bad and selfish people but as having failed as women, traitors to our sex. This is corrosive. It must also be acknowledged that the harshest critics when women are perceived to have failed in their duty as mothers, wives and carers are often other women. Perhaps that is because if we have slaved over thankless tasks for years ourselves, we cannot bear the idea that it might have been possible not to do all that dreary work and to get away unscathed. Fortunately, I do think this purse-lipped attitude by women towards women that was so prevalent in my generation, especially when we were younger, is beginning to fade. Women are much more supportive of one another now than they were when I was young, and I thank feminism for that.

The demands on women, particularly when they become mothers, can be overwhelming. We are expected to be endlessly loving and patient with our children. We are meant to spring back to our original svelte shape. We are meant to create and maintain spotless and attractive homes and conjure up healthy and well-balanced meals (that our children will consume joyously) morning, noon and night. Takeaway containers in the bin are a secret source of shame. We are meant to have an interesting and well-paid career. We are meant to be affectionate, supportive and sexy wives, up for a bit of nookie at the drop of a pair of boxers. We are meant to be active in the community, volunteers at the school and concerned and well-informed citizens. We are meant to be dutiful and loving daughters, willing to support our ageing parents so they can continue to live in their own home no matter how frail and incapable they may become. We are meant to be great friends, colleagues and—for our family—informed nutritionists, psychologists, educators, health-care workers, diagnosticians, event managers, cake-makers, present-buyers and party-throwers. Dad brings home his pay packet, but all the other care and maintenance of the family unit, all the other duties required—including what is called emotional labour—are our responsibility, regardless of our own pay packet. This doesn't mean there aren't lots of men who do this labour too; it just means no-one really expects them to. If women fail at any of this—and frankly, it is a standard impossible to maintain for any normal human person—we not only expect to be judged by others, we judge ourselves. Even outsourcing this work by hiring cleaners, ironing companies, gardeners or nannies is frowned upon. Some even describe it as exploiting other women.

Perhaps this is why, as we age, we develop a new and debilitating fear: the fear of being a burden. It makes sense that those of us who have spent our lives looking after others dread needing the same from those we once cared for. And I think it is in our hopes for our children—particularly our daughters—that the feminist revolution has had the most impact on the women of my generation. Unlike most of our own mothers, we did not bring up our daughters to be as dutiful as we were expected to be. We may have found it hard to throw off the ancient expectations of women for ourselves, but we are resentful enough and have learnt enough to want something very different for our daughters. While writing this book I have met many women who are living in very uncertain circumstances, to the point of not being sure of having a continuing roof over their head. Yet the last thing they want to do is to ask their children for help. I know of women eking out an existence on the minimum wage, or the single pension, who scrimp and save every cent so that they will leave their often much more prosperous children something in their will.

This entrenched belief that women exist primarily for the convenience of other people has led to even more sinister consequences. We are only just starting to pay attention to what is being termed 'elder abuse'. According to a report from the Australian

Institute of Family Studies, while hard evidence about the prevalence of such behaviour is thin on the ground, what is available suggests that mothers are most vulnerable to abuse from sons. It is hard to escape the idea that many men have a sense of entitlement when it comes to inheritance. The money and assets were their fathers'; now they expect them to be theirs.

Former age and disability discrimination commissioner Susan Ryan warns about what can happen when a parent is persuaded to transfer their home in return for accommodation in a granny flat and care: 'When the handover happens and the elderly parent is left destitute little can be done typically because there is no proper legal agreement in place. Typically, the older person did not seek independent legal or financial advice.'

And I can see how the expectation we have of mothers that they be unendingly loving and supportive of their children becomes a marvellous lever that unscrupulous sons and daughters can use to talk Mum out of getting any independent advice. Even if a loving mother tentatively suggests such a thing, you can already see the pout of the child who feels such a request means she doesn't 'trust' them. Love is a wonderful thing but it can set some of us up for disaster, particularly when the expectation is that mothers must always be supportive of their children.

The emphasis on women and their duty to love is another reason why so many women find themselves in low-paid 'caring' professions such as nursing, child care and teaching. In fact, Australia has one of the most gender-segregated workforces in the world. Sixty per cent of Australians work in industries that are dominated by either men or women. In general, higher-paying professions are dominated by men and lower-paying professions—many of them the caring professions—are dominated by women. What a surprise.

Yet not all the caring professions are low paid. Medicine is a caring profession but doctors remain among the best-paid workers in Australia. Most medical specialities are dominated by men. General practice, on the other hand, is becoming feminised and correspondingly less well paid—particularly for women GPs, who earn on average 24.7 per cent less than their male counterparts. So what is going on? Why do we so fundamentally devalue caring work when it is done by women? Here is my theory, for what it is worth, and it takes us back to Dutiful Daughters, the home-care service I mentioned at the beginning of this chapter. I think we still expect women to sacrifice themselves to care for others. We expect wives, mothers and daughters to drop everything and care selflessly for the young, the old and the sick. As more women have entered the paid workforce, more of those caring duties have had to be outsourced—to a largely female workforce. My suspicion is we resent having to pay women to perform services we still unconsciously see as their duty, so we almost begrudge every penny they earn. The idea that caring work should be performed by women for love is something that as a society we still seem to cling to, so it's hardly surprising that if they insist on being paid for it we feel they certainly should not earn much. After all, if they are doing little more than their duty, we owe them nothing.

This punitive attitude to 'women's work' costs the people who perform it very dearly.

4

GOLD-DIGGERS, BEGGARS AND THIEVES

If love is woman's full occupation, as Byron said, then it is no surprise that women have a complex and difficult relationship with money. We're not supposed to seek it directly—because that would be selfish and unfeminine. There is even a derogatory name attached to women who are too transparent in their desire to be wealthy: we call them gold-diggers. But we are not supposed to be poor or dependent on a man for financial support, either. Then we are beggars or, especially if we get a decent settlement after a divorce, thieves. Independently wealthy women, of course, are terrifying and—like women who seek power or wield it in other ways, such as in politics or because they are famous or successful in business—are regarded as cold-hearted bitches.

Yet women have a very definite function in our society when it comes to money. Fundamentally, our task in the capitalist economy is to be paid less and to spend more. It doesn't take much financial literacy to work out how convenient that is for a consumer society and the businesses that profit from it. Nor do you have to be particularly brilliant to realise how detrimental that is to our wellbeing, especially in the long run. According to a study by the New York City Department of Consumer Affairs in 2015, products aimed at women cost an average of 7 per cent more to buy than those aimed at men. These include the usual things such as haircuts, clothes and dry-cleaning, but also things you wouldn't expect, such as mortgages, cars, razors and deodorants. Given the gender pay gap is stubbornly stuck at around 18 per cent, the financial odds are stacked against women from day one. Perhaps we're not supposed to mind because of … well … love.

To be motivated by love is to serve others and put their needs ahead of your own (even, it seems, the needs of large multinational corporations to maximise their profits). To be motivated by money, or other kinds of personal reward, is to unequivocally put your own needs first. We send all kinds of messages to women and girls, all through their lives, about how much we approve of them when they do the former and how little we approve when they do the latter. The prime example of our vicious double standard towards women and power (and money is power) is the extremely contradictory treatment of Hillary Clinton. In 1969, when she was a young woman at the all-female Wellesley College, she was the first student to be asked to give the commencement address and was clearly marked out as a person to watch. She was even featured as such in *Life* magazine. Later, as the wife of the governor of Arkansas, Bill Clinton, she was regarded with hostility because she had kept her maiden name on marriage and was outspoken about women's rights. Under pressure, she relinquished her maiden name of Rodham and adopted her husband's (a decision she may later have come to regret).

As the first lady during her husband's presidency, she remained a controversial figure. There was a scandal over her declaring that she was 'no Tammy Wynette', a reference to the country singer's hit song 'Stand by Your Man'. The role of the first lady, after all (until Clinton inhabited it, anyway), was to represent archetypal American womanhood. There was another honourable exception, of course:

Clinton's hero and role model Eleanor Roosevelt, who was also not just first lady but later her country's first ambassador to the United Nations, a body she had been instrumental in creating. Roosevelt excepted (and even she was controversial in her day), the 'first lady' is meant to be submissive, feminine and decorative, a largely silent partner to her powerful husband. Melania Trump almost never opens her mouth. Even an accomplished and successful woman like Michelle Obama was expected to take a mostly supportive role to her husband. Alone among modern first ladies, Clinton followed in Roosevelt's footsteps and turned that assumption on its head. People expressed outrage when her husband declared it was a two-for-one presidency and proceeded to appoint his wife to head the task force looking into health care in the US. In retaliation for her uncompromising self-confidence and assertiveness, opponents made sure there were constant scandals and investigations into her work as a lawyer and her time managing the Clinton family finances. Her investments in a failed real-estate project—Whitewater—and a successful cattle futures scheme drew particular attention. It is important to note here that no wrongdoing on her part has ever been proved. It was almost as if her very canniness as an investor was a crime in itself. Given our ambivalence about the kind of relationship women are supposed to have with money (they are miraculously supposed to have enough, without ever being seen to actually strive for it), Clinton's financial acumen added to our bad impression of her. It was immodest. It was unfeminine. It was clever. Three strikes and you are out.

No wonder Clinton was a polarising figure as first lady. Her popularity waxed and waned; she even copped much of the blame over scandals about her husband's serial infidelity, especially with Monica Lewinsky. Nevertheless, when Bill left the presidency and she stood for the Senate seat of New York, she worked hard to win over her opponents and the public, and her popularity rose. Then, when she fought for the Democratic presidential nomination against Barack Obama, her popularity plummeted and she lost.

When Obama was elected and Clinton accepted his offer of the position of US secretary of state, her popularity once again soared—remember funky Hillary with her BlackBerry? By the time she finished her term as secretary of state, she had a 69 per cent approval rating and was regarded as the most popular woman in America. However, we all know what happened when she ran for president in 2016. Her popularity nosedived as she battled—and convincingly beat—Senator Bernie Sanders for the nomination and then fought—and narrowly lost to—Donald Trump. There were many accusations levelled at Clinton during her campaign to try to discredit her. The most dominant was an entirely spurious scandal about her use of a private email server during her tenure as secretary of state. However, she also copped a pasting (especially from Sanders supporters) about the high fees she received as a celebrity speaker, particularly from large corporations.

The controversy around the money she earned from public speaking (full disclosure: that is how I earn the majority of my income too, not that I can command anything like the fees Clinton can) reminded me of the nastiness that surrounded the then *Today* co-host Lisa Wilkinson's sudden departure from Channel 9. It was alleged that she quit because Channel 9 would not pay her the same amount as her male co-host, Karl Stefanovic. Wilkinson is a prominent and well-respected journalist, and her shock departure grabbed the headlines. Channel 9 management went into damage control immediately and briefed a story that, among other things, implied that the pay rise Wilkinson wanted would have cost ten producers their jobs. Odd, isn't it, that it is only the large salaries paid to women that impact on the jobs of the more lowly paid in an organisation? Apparently Stefanovic's $2 million annual whack had no effect on Channel 9's ability to hire people.

Pardon me for being facetious, but frankly, such a response beggars belief. Channel 9 appeared to be operating under the assumption that women should feel guilty about earning high wages and be ashamed of asking for the same money as a man who does exactly the same job. Wilkinson should have been doing her job out of love. She should have been grateful to get such an opportunity! Indeed, in return for her good fortune she should at the very least have put the needs of others (the poor producers) ahead of herself. Like Clinton, her assertive (and entirely reasonable) behaviour was characterised as selfish and unfeminine. She was also a gold-digger, and there was even a subtle hint that she was a thief who was stealing other people's income and opportunities for her own gain. Stefanovic and the highly paid executives at the organisation were excused any such criticism or the necessity to have such delicate sensibilities because … um … they are men.

Our ambivalence about women and success—in business, in entertainment, in politics or anywhere—remains tenacious. Watching Clinton's popularity seesaw dizzyingly up and down depending on whether she was supporting a man in power (good Hillary) or seeking it for herself (bad Hillary), it was hard to escape the impression that we are still only comfortable with women gaining prominence as long as they remain second in command to a man. Perhaps it was Wilkinson's insistence that she be paid the same as her male co-host, that she was in effect equal to him, that so offended her employers. How very dare she? Julia Gillard's rocky ride to power is another example. As long as she was deputy PM to Kevin Rudd, she was enormously popular; when she took the leadership of the ALP and so became Australia's first female prime minister, she was hated. How dare she do what so many men had done before her and 'stab her leader in the back'?

Women absorb the messages about being modest, self-effacing and self-sacrificing. When I was young, being 'pushy' (guilty), a 'show-off' (guilty) or 'bossy' (guilty) were particularly female failings. I can still remember the hot shame I felt when I was accused of being one or the other (or all three) and felt myself being silently or not-so-silently judged. Even as a child, I never wanted to stand at the back and get hidden in the crowd. I wanted to be up the front, engaged and involved in whatever was going on (except if what was going on was maths—then I was happy to become invisible). My daughters were much the same, and I well remember comforting my elder as she wept over being called a 'pushy show-off' when she got the lead role in the school play. 'Be proud of being ambitious and seeking centre stage,' I said to her. 'What do they [the girls who were bullying her] want to be all their lives? The audience?' Parenting being what it is, she just howled even louder and declared that I did not understand.

Perhaps this discomfort we have with girls who stubbornly seek the limelight is part of the reason we are so exercised about girls doing better than boys in education. We see girls outperforming boys at school as a relatively new phenomenon. Instead of celebrating the achievements of girls, we see it as a 'problem' and dark looks are thrown in the direction of feminism and the so-called feminisation of teaching. We need more male teachers, say the critics, to help the boys escape those biased female ones who favour the girls in their care. Indeed, it has become a regular part of the political cycle for some bright spark to suggest we offer extra incentives (do they mean higher wages?) to men to encourage more of them to enter the teaching profession. (I guess women are once again supposed to do the job for love.)

Absurdly, they are trying to fix a problem that does not actually exist. Boys may do worse at school, but they sure as hell do better than girls after they leave—particularly financially. The real problem is what happens to girls and women throughout their entire life. There is nothing new about girls outperforming boys at school: it has been happening for at least 100 years. Moreover, they don't just outperform boys in the 'softer' subjects, such as English and history—they outperform boys in every subject, including maths and science. My poor performance was the exception in my maths class, not the rule. Perhaps girls outperform boys at school because, once again, they do what they are constantly told to do: work harder. According to most conservative pundits, that is how women can gain merit.

Oh, really? Then why, when they have done exactly that for over a century, do those same pundits see girls' success at school as a problem that must be fixed? Narelle says she did well at school and enjoyed every aspect of learning, to such an extent that she avoided missing any school at all. She wanted to attend university and then be an art teacher. Her parents encouraged her 'to get married, to have children and to stay at home'. Despite her hard work, Narelle did not become an art teacher; instead, she trained as a hairdresser. Now, as an older woman, she is on Newstart. When I asked her what she'd got wrong in her life, she said her fundamental mistake was in not realising 'that hard work doesn't always pay off'. It was true for women then, and it's true for women now.

What has changed since my friends and I were outperforming the boys at school (or indeed, when our mothers and grandmothers were doing so) is that women have started to compete with men where it really matters: in higher education and for high-paying jobs. That is why boys' poor performance at school is at last attracting attention. It didn't matter how well girls did in exams when they were routinely locked out of lucrative work. Now that they can compete with boys—they are beating them soundly at university, for example—it's getting harder to maintain the merit excuse. It was always pretty lame, to be honest with you. What could be more self-serving than the fortunate and the comfortable claiming that they gained their privilege because they simply had more 'merit'?

When I was young, no-one seriously talked about people getting promoted on merit. They didn't have to: prestigious and highly paid occupations were a closed world, reserved for men of a certain class, from certain schools, with a certain skin colour and, often in those days, from a certain religious denomination. Well-heeled Jewish and Catholic boys had a harder time getting ahead than well-heeled Protestant ones, but at least they had a chance. Girls, people from poorer backgrounds and people of colour had virtually no chance and were not expected to aspire to such positions. If they were exceptional they might work their way up through the ranks of the cops, the army, education or business, but such self-made men (and they were virtually all men) were not only few and far between, they were never quite accepted, or regarded as PLU (People Like Us), as my mother used to say.

Indeed, in the 1960s children were still being trained to accept their God-given 'place'. I remember persuading my atheist parents to allow me to go to Sunday school. I wanted to go not because I'd had any kind of religious epiphany, but because my neighbourhood friends all went and I felt left out. My mother, when I asked her, simply shrugged and said, 'As long as I never have to set foot in a church.' It was harmless enough, and I mostly liked the biblical stories and the little cartoons we were given to colour in. However I do remember singing this hymn:

> All things bright and beautiful
> All creatures great and small
> All things wise and wonderful
> The Lord God made them all.

So far, so unexceptional—even charming—and I believe this verse and some of the others are still sung by children attending Sunday school. However, there is a verse—which I remember singing with innocent and uncritical gusto back in the church hall on Bantry Bay Road in Frenchs Forest—that is now skipped. It was still being belted out in the 1960s:

> The rich man in his castle
> The poor man at his gate
> God made them high and lowly
> And ordered their estate.

Little girls singing in Sunday schools in the 1960s didn't notice that the song, class-ridden as it is, was also only about men and creatures. We were used to being left out. I am hopeful that little girls would notice such an omission now.

Even as recently as the 1950s and 1960s, if girls wanted to have a financially secure future, they either had to have been born into a wealthy family or (and the two usually went hand in hand) had to marry well. By limiting our opportunities, notwithstanding how well we were performing at school, we were virtually forced to look upon men as a meal ticket. Yet we had to pretend we didn't, because we knew we would be derided if we did. Hypocrisy, thy name is traditional gender roles. We were all secretly training to be gold-diggers. What other options did we realistically have?

In my youth, to be perfectly honest, nothing much had fundamentally changed since Jane Austen created her hilarious and much-maligned character Mrs Bennet, in *Pride and Prejudice*. Poor Mrs Bennet, ridiculed as she may have been by Austen, was married to a useless husband who was always locked in his study, so she shouldered the responsibility of trying to secure a future for her inheritance-less daughters by snaring well-heeled husbands for them. Those girls literally had no other option, and nor would their mother once her husband died. The estate and income were entailed to a male heir. Her needs were desperate: if her husband died, she and her children would be out on their ears. Interestingly, that is exactly what happened to Austen and her mother and sister. They ended their days living on the charity of Jane's wealthy brother. They became beggars.

While I was at school, women were still routinely dismissed from their jobs when they married. One of my interviewees, Jan, was musing on why she married so young: 'I guess I just wanted someone to love me, as I did not know how to take control of my life with women on such meagre wages and if you married you lost your job.' Gee, it's almost as if women were being set up! Jan's marriage subsequently failed. Even my own mother had hidden her change of status when she was first wed so she could hang on to her job in 1950s London. Almost no-one worked after becoming pregnant, and if you had to go back to work after your children were born, like the number-crunching clerks at my first place of employment, you were pitied. It meant your husband couldn't afford to keep you. Yet women were despised for regarding their husbands as cash cows. Women were not meant to be mercenary, but to marry for love.

And then, as now, many husbands strayed. As a teenager I became aware that the father of one of my close friends had a long-time mistress for whom he seriously considered leaving his wife and family. In the end, he didn't have the bottle and stayed with his long-suffering wife. And suffer she did. I remember staying with this family while my own travelled overseas (ever the show-off, I had a part in the school play that I did not want to miss). I watched this woman beg her husband to call her while he was on one of his frequent 'business' trips (in those days there were only one or two landline phones in a house, and very few phone conversations were completely private). One conversation in particular is seared into my brain. My friend's mother pleaded with her husband to call her after a planned helicopter trip (he was in advertising, so perhaps they were using the helicopter in a shoot). Almost tearfully, she told him she would worry about him until she knew he had landed safely. At the appointed time, she hovered over the phone. It didn't ring. I pitied that woman and despised her arrogant and neglectful husband, but I was also embarrassed and, yes, repelled by her neediness. I did not want to be like her. Nor did her daughters, but despite their desire not to repeat the mistakes of their parents, neither of them has managed to sustain a long-term happy marriage.

A distant relative of mine was also a 'player', in the parlance of the time. His children did not know. I have no idea if his wife knew, but I did. My father and I ran into him being very inappropriately affectionate with a young woman. He did not even have the grace to be embarrassed. My father was, and told me not to tell anyone what I had seen. I never did, until now.

In my childhood, there seemed to be three kinds of women. The majority, like my mother, were wives and mothers. They kept house and cooked and cleaned. In a way, they were the beggars. They had no money of their own and had to rely on the generosity of their husband. Even the houses they cared for so assiduously were almost always in their husband's name. The suburban streets of my childhood were not deserted as they are now: then, they were teeming with able-bodied women and their children. Many of those women were bored out of their well-educated minds—no wonder Betty Friedan's *The Feminine Mystique* was such a worldwide bestseller.

Then there were the 'career girls'—not that they had much of what we would consider careers. In those days they were secretaries, receptionists, salesgirls and clerks. Sometimes they were young women working until they met Mr Right. Sometimes they were mistresses hoping (often fruitlessly) that Mr Right would realise he was married to Mrs Wrong. They were the gold-diggers, waiting to catch themselves a meal ticket either by marrying him (preferred option) or sleeping with him. These women looked much more elegant and sophisticated than our mothers. They were slimmer (never having had kids), wore more expensive clothes, and spent much more effort, energy and time on their appearance—which makes good financial sense, because how they looked was, frankly, what they were selling. Our mothers were selling their fecundity and their child-rearing and housekeeping skills in return for their husbands' support. (You may think I am being cynical, but seeing the number of those young women from the 1950s, 1960s and 1970s who are now, as old women, on the breadline, I prefer to call it being clear-eyed.)

The third group may well have been the happiest, but they were the ones who were most pitied and feared. They were the so-called spinsters and were often teachers, market researchers or the managers of shops. They were older (past their use-by date and so unlikely to marry; they may even have been mistresses once) and their lives revolved around their not-particularly-well-paid jobs. I had a teacher for the last two years of primary school who was very much a spinster. She was probably in her early forties but we thought of her as old and sad due to her honorific of 'Miss'. Unable to conceive of a woman without a man (nothing in our upbringing had prepared us for such a possibility), we spent half our time looking for clues that she was 'in love' with the other Grade 5 teacher, who, despite his lack of marital-status-defining title, we somehow knew was single.

Poor Miss N. I don't think she was happy. I remember being frequently sent to her desk drawer to fetch her a Bex—the drawer was full to bursting with them. And why would she be happy? After all, she had failed at women's whole occupation: love. She was the sad reject, left on the shelf, forced to support herself. It was rumoured she lived with her elderly mother. The world was cruel to single women who earned their own living when I was young. We imagined her cooking over a gas ring, taking another Bex with a cup of tea and having a good lie-down. We did not want to be like her, either. She was a beggar too, but not for money. She, at least, got to work for that. She was a beggar for attention—of which she received very little.

Whenever society or a man was angry with a woman, being a beggar or a gold-digger could quickly be transformed into thievery. Because so few women were able to pay their own way, if they received a settlement in a divorce, hoarded the housekeeping, or complained about how much their husband spent on drinking, gambling, a flashy car or whatever, they were considered to be stealing what wasn't theirs. When I was young all the money we had was earned by my father, and so it was in every other family that I knew of.

Yet we girls continued to do better than our male peers at school. It wasn't until 1969, when I was in my first year of high school, that women in Australia were granted equal pay for equal work, and as I write we are still waiting for that to apply in practice.

Even though women of the generations previous to mine expected to be supported by a man, they still had to be very careful how they talked about and asked for money. And the money was unequivocally the man's money. He earned it, and the pay packet was in his name. If a husband did decide to do the unthinkable and leave his wife for his mistress (I never saw it actually happen), he often tried to prove it was his wife's fault so he would not have to give her much money after the divorce. I remember a salacious little TV program called Divorce Court. I loved it but could only watch it when I was able to wangle a day off school by feigning illness. Then I was allowed to watch telly on the couch with a pillow and a blanket. These are some of my favourite memories. Divorce Court was introduced by actor Ron Haddrick and featured dramatised stories of actual divorce proceedings. The cases presented were all about who was at fault for the breakdown of a marriage. The show was filled with stories of adultery, desertion and cruelty. Some may think it was unsuitable for primary-school-aged me, but I lapped it up and never forgot (as you can see) the life lessons it taught me. It wasn't until 1975 that the Whitlam Government introduced the Family Court and no-fault divorce. (Chillingly, in mid-2018, conservative politicians announced the end of the Family Court, mostly at the behest of disgruntled divorced men. It is to be rolled into the Federal Court, and women and men will be forced to make their case about deeply emotional problems in a much less expert and supportive environment. This development is both retrograde and concerning.) Prior to 1975, divorce in Australia was relatively rare. Numbers rose steadily in the 1950s and 1960s, but by 1970 there was still only one divorce for every 1000 people. Divorces peaked in 1976, the year after the establishment of the Family Court, leaping to a rate of 4.6 per 1000, indicating that there had been plenty of unhappy couples just waiting for a chance to escape one another without having to prove some spurious 'fault'. Today, the divorce rate has settled in at around 1.9 per 1000.

Of course, keeping women almost totally dependent on their husband for their financial security was also a very powerful way of keeping them from seeking divorce. Many women had almost no money of their own and were doled out housekeeping by their husband to cover the cost of running the household. Freda had a financial arrangement with her husband that was typical for the time: she paid the household expenses out of her wages and he paid the mortgage. This division of finances often had a very detrimental effect on a woman's right to half the house after divorce, particularly if the mortgage was entirely in the husband's name.

Some women became very adept at scrimping and saving a little every week in order to stockpile some funds of their own. Entire sitcoms were written around women overspending and the lengths they went to to hide their bills from their husbands. No-one thought such infantilisation of adult human beings (who may even have outperformed their husbands at school in maths) either wrong or unusual. It is good to see how much things have changed.

For women who are now over fifty, however, these were very much the attitudes that we were brought up to accept, and it has taken some longer than others to throw off the guilt and awkwardness we feel about discussing or even understanding money. I am just as guilty as anyone else. I remember when my husband and I had a financial adviser for a while. Whenever he would come to discuss our finances I would try to find an excuse to leave it to my husband. The whole conversation bored me to tears, and I still try to avoid such meetings. Had I married a more unscrupulous man, that sort of lazy, wilful ignorance could have bitten me on the bum—badly. I guess it still could, but after forty-three years together, if he is intending to go off with someone else and leave me skint, he's left his run awfully late.

Women, of course, are just as skilled as men at managing other people's money in a professional sense. They make wonderful accountants, businesspeople, financial advisers and corporate lawyers negotiating mergers and acquisitions. It's just when it comes to putting a monetary value on ourselves that we descend into a puddle of anxious goo. I was part of a panel on the ABC's *7.30* program that featured the very accomplished and respected journalist Sarrah Le Marquand, the editor-in-chief of *Stellar* magazine. During our discussion she was asked about putting a monetary value on her work and confessed that despite all her experience, her seniority and her intellectual understanding of how much she has to offer, she still undervalues herself. She is not alone, and that may be why Lisa Wilkinson's uncompromising stand was greeted with so much criticism by some, but with so much admiration by women. We know just how hard it is to demand what we are worth.

Our hesitation to put a value on ourselves, I believe, is partly because of all the messages we have unquestioningly absorbed, but it is also self-protective. We know how the world reacts to women who ask for what they want. Sensibly enough, we try to minimise the fallout. When women act like women and put other people's needs ahead of their own and when they are modest, self-effacing and submissive, they may win approval but they don't get what they want. When they act like men—put their own needs first, promote their desires, amplify their achievements and ask directly and forcefully for what they want—not only are they criticised, but they also don't get what they want. I had an epiphany a while ago when I realised there is no right way to be a woman. It isn't a trick you are missing: it's that the odds, particularly the financial odds, are stacked against you. Wilkinson lost her fight with Channel 9. Rather than pay her the same as her co-host, the organisation for which she had worked for ten years let her go. Maybe somebody, somewhere, did a quick calculation about how much it would cost to bring every woman up to the same salary as her male colleagues, and decided to cut the network's losses. The BBC is going through exactly this as I write, with female employees of the British TV icon finally coming forward to express their anger about uniformly being paid less than their male colleagues. The stubborn gender pay gap is often explained away as women simply not being as forceful in negotiation as men (aka it's all their own fault) or as willing to ask for more money. However, there is research that indicates women ask for pay rises as often as men do but are less likely to get them.

For those who still believe structural inequality is a figment of feminists' imagination, let's recap some of the ways the financial odds are stacked against women. The gender pay gap sits stubbornly at around 18 per cent in Australia. (It increasers the higher up the ladder you go, by the way.) Female-dominated occupations are less well paid than male-dominated ones. Six out of ten Australians work in an industry dominated by one gender. Australia has one of the highest rates of part-time work in the world: 25 per cent of us work part time. Women make up 71.6 per cent of all part-time workers and 54.7 per cent of all casual employees. Australian women are among the best educated in the world but have relatively low comparable workplace participation and achievement rates. And just to add insult to injury, products marketed to women are more expensive than those marketed to men!

All of these structural barriers matter for all sorts of reasons. It is a terrible waste of talent and potential, and of our investment in the education of girls. But it also has an appalling legacy for far too many women. Our lack of ability to earn what we are worth, our reticence around money, our lingering dependence on a man for our financial security, and our disproportionate burden of child rearing, housework and other caring responsibilities compound throughout our lives. The effects often come home to roost when we begin to get old.

5

WOMEN'S WORK

My generation expected to work—we just didn't expect to get paid for it. Well, not via a pay packet with our own name on it, anyway. We were brought up to expect to be supported by our husband's wages as our mothers and grandmothers had been before us. We expected to repay that support through housekeeping, child care, sex (oh, yes, we did) and reproduction. That was the exchange of goods and services that had existed between one gender and the other for time immemorial. We did not realise—no-one did—just how profoundly it was all going to change. But change it did.

As I keep repeating, the generation born in the 1950s and 1960s is the first in history where most of the women worked for wages for most of their lives. And because money is power, this has changed everything. For many women—perhaps even most women—it has changed everything for the better. For far too many, however, it has not turned out as well as everyone hoped.

It was at school that we first began to get an inkling that we were being offered the opportunity to be more than simply wives and mothers—although we were still expected to be both of those.

We certainly knew that we would go to work for a while between school and motherhood, but the idea of a career of the kind our male peers expected to enjoy was still unusual. When I finished high school in 1974, many more girls expected to go to university than had even a few years earlier, thanks to the Whitlam Government's education reforms that abolished university fees. If tertiary education was free, it was harder to rationalise preventing girls from accompanying their brothers, especially as so many of us had the higher marks. More than that, however, our mothers also began to grasp the chance that was offered to them. It was female mature-age students who radically swelled the ranks at universities during that tiny window of opportunity—my own mother among them. Those of us fresh from school often resented the older women who joined us in lectures and tutorials (what a surprise—older women are always seen as such a downer). They were highly motivated, they were confident, and they were smart. But more than that, they were fired up with the sort of passion that only arises when you feel you have been the victim of an injustice. I am proud now that my mother grabbed her opportunity when she did, but I cannot say I was nearly as pleased at the time. Particularly as she did the HSC the same year as I did and attended Macquarie University with me, doing many of the same courses. She, like so many of the older, wiser and more motivated mature-age students, whooped my arse whenever we competed directly. And it's one thing to get beaten by a woman who reminds you of your mother and quite another to actually be beaten by her.

My sulky, ungrateful whinges aside, those mature-age female students got their degrees and went on to invade the world of work and change Australia forever. Looking back, they helped my generation beat the path.

It is a no-brainer that if you educate people you increase their expectations about what their life could hold, so it is no coincidence that the increased numbers of women entering universities coincided with the first stage of what was then called women's liberation. In

1970, there were 269 male university students to every 100 female ones. By 2014 that ratio had completely flipped, and there were just eighty males to every 100 females. That, in and of itself, is a revolutionary change achieved in just over four decades. In fact, the tipping point where women first began to outnumber men came way back in 1987.

Yet the revolution in women's education has still not been adequately reflected in the workforce. Women make up 46.2 per cent of employees although they are 50.18 per cent of the population. Their workforce participation rate is only 59.3 per cent while, despite males' underachievement in education, the male workforce participation rate is 70.4 per cent. For women of my generation, even such relatively low rates of workplace participation were a positive step forward, and it was a change that happened in front of our eyes. In 1954, when my mother was twenty-four and working as a secretary, only 29 per cent of women were in any kind of paid job. By 1998, when I was forty-one and working as a copywriter, 58.9 per cent of us aged between fifteen and sixty-four were in the paid workforce.

Despite women voting with their feet over the last half-century and entering the paid workforce in ever-increasing numbers, they still tend to be concentrated in lower-status industries and at the lower end of the pay scale. Even more depressing is the fact that previously high-status, well-paid occupations tend to fall in both status and pay when they become female dominated. General medical practice, marketing and human resources (the latter of which once meant a board position) spring to mind.

It is commonplace to point out that it is the other job women hold down—the ubiquitous 'second shift' in the home—that leads them to sacrifice pay, seniority and job security for flexibility. Yet despite the fact that this is now so thoroughly discussed, acknowledged and written about that it has almost become a cliché, we still do nothing to fix it. To be fair, things have improved since my mother was slogging away raising four children in the 1960s. Then, women did an average 30.4 hours a week of housework. And that, according to ABC TV's *Back in Time for Dinner*, is a vast improvement on the amount of housework my grandmother was doing in the 1950s: a staggering seventy-seven hours per week. *Back in Time for Dinner* took a 2018 family, the Ferrones, back in time to experience what life was like in Australia in the 1950s, 1960s, 1970s, etc. up to the present day. Keeping up with those housework demands had the thoroughly modern Carol Ferrone in tears during the week her family spent living as they would have more than half a century ago. No wonder: the shock would have been profound. In 2018 women do about 14.2 hours a week of housework. Men have improved—a little—since the 1950s. In 1965, they might have kindly lifted their feet so their wife could vacuum more easily under them, but they only did two hours' work around the house every week. By 1995, that had doubled to a grand total of four hours. I don't want to depress you, but a recent study by the Texas-based Council of Contemporary Families says that this figure has not changed since then. Men still average only four hours of domestic work a week. (Yes, I know, not all men, but these are statistical measures. That's how they work: they look at the average. That means some wonderful men—like my husband—are doing much more, but it also means that some are doing much, much less—like nothing.) So if men still aren't generally pulling their weight, why have the hours women spend on domestic duties fallen? Mostly it is to do with improved labour-saving devices and an increase in outsourcing the chores, but I bet it's also because we're all sensibly getting a little less picky. I can't remember the last time I dusted, for example. It's not something that ever crosses my mind, and I rationalise cobwebs on the ceiling as natural fly and mosquito repellents and let them gather dust in all their glory. Another reason that hours spent on household labour may have fallen is because women are having far fewer children than they used to. In 1965 the birthrate per Australian woman was 2.98; in 2016 it had fallen to

1.79. There's nothing like kids to up the amount of housework that needs doing.

Women may have been taking matters into their own hands as far as reducing the work they do around the house in response to increasing the hours they work outside it, but it is hard to look at Australian policy settings around women, children and work and not feel there is something deliberate going on.

For example, one reason women may be having fewer children is that the cost of child care is eye-wateringly expensive. More than a woman's total after-tax salary may be eaten up by paying to have her children cared for, and while it is all very well to claim that child-care costs should be seen as a family expense, as I have already argued, if it is a choice between paying the mortgage and Mum going back to work, she'll stay home. Recent changes to the child-care rebate have made child care more affordable for those with lower incomes, which is an entirely good thing. However, those bright, high-achieving women who have kicked major arse (most of it male arse) at university are often the ones who find they have to haul themselves over innumerable obstacles—such as the cost and availability of child care—to get back into the workforce after they have had children.

Child care is not tax deductible, for example. It used to drive me batty that I could claim my laptop or even my dry-cleaning as a work-related expense, but the part-time nanny I employed to mind my kids (I had their name down for a place in all the nearby child-care centres but did not make it to the top of the list until both of them were in high school), without whom I simply could not have earned an income, was not considered a legitimate deduction. I have long argued that until we regard child-care costs in the same way we do holiday pay, sick pay and superannuation—as work-related expenses rather than welfare—the pay gap and the far lower rates of female participation in the workforce will remain.

Infuriatingly, it isn't just the lack of tax deductibility that creates a barrier. As writer Nassim Khadem put it recently in the

Sydney Morning Herald, 'Australian women experience high effective marginal tax rates when moving from three to four days a week to full-time work due to the loss of family and child benefits.' As she points out, these policy-based barriers mean many women remain in part-time work and on lower wages than they otherwise would. This structural (and deliberate) impediment compounds into a loss of opportunity and lifetime income for an entire gender. And if the barriers discourage a woman from returning to work at all until her children go to school, as Khadem points out, we know that the longer she stays out of the workforce the harder it is for her to get back in. Society then has the gall to wonder why so few of our talented, highly educated girls rise to leadership positions. Talk about damned if you do and damned if you don't. We still tend to blame women for their relative lack of achievement. They are deficient in confidence, we are told, naturally less ambitious, and they fail to 'lean in'. Bullshit. They are being consciously and deliberately hobbled for all sorts of reasons, including old-fashioned, often religion-based ideas about women's 'role', plain misogyny and, of course, the fact that it means a lot less serious competition in the workplace for men. Indeed, the family tax benefits, the loss of which help make it so expensive for women to return to full-time work, were put into place by John Howard. He referred to himself as the 'father' of family tax benefits. You remember him? He's the guy who said women will never reach fifty-fifty representation because of all their caring responsibilities. He failed to mention a few structural barriers put carefully in their way by … well … him.

All of these hurdles and impediments combined with a stubborn unconscious bias against women and their abilities—despite how well they do in education—is the reason women lose that much-quoted $1 million of potential earnings over their lifetime in comparison to men. This situation is grossly unfair and limiting if you are a woman who has managed to earn a relatively high income, but it is devastating if you have earned a low one. The cumulative effects of this loss on women as they age and become less able to get paid work are why so many of this generation are living on the edge of poverty. They are directly responsible for the fact that women retire with half the super of men and a major contributor to the fact that one in three women retire with no super at all.

And it is not as if women do not work at least as hard as men or, arguably, even harder (see above the hours we spend on housework). However, if a couple lived according to traditional gender roles with the man in charge of the finances, no matter how hard the woman worked she would still risk missing out. Lorna says of her two failed marriages that despite the fact that she always worked for wages, 'all money was controlled by both men and doled out. Luckily women of my era are used to not having money; we had none when we were young and none when we got older. Somehow I feel that to the government we were only here to populate the country, with no rights and no future. Talk about past your use-by date.' Regarding it as 'lucky' that you are used to having very little is not much of a reward for a lifetime spent working hard both at home populating the country and at work contributing to GDP. Tragically, however, we still have trouble regarding women's work as real work at all, especially when much of it is invisible.

When I was juggling being a part-time ad writer and being the major carer for my two small daughters while my husband had a job that took him away every second week, a colleague asked me to think of an unusual but motivating prize for a consumer competition aimed at mothers. I was asked in my professional capacity as what the ad industry calls a 'creative'. My answer was immediate and heartfelt: what I wanted was a producer for my life.

The reason I was so quick to identify the best and most motivating prize I could think of (I have no idea what they eventually decided upon—a trip to Paris or something, no doubt) was I had recently returned from a blissful five-day business trip to New Zealand to shoot a series of commercials. It was the first time I had been away from my children for any length of time and I was both anxious about leaving them and raring to go. I anticipated the delights of a luxurious hotel room, on-demand movies (still a novelty in the 1990s) and room service. What I had not thought about but deeply appreciated was the way the agency producer managed all the minutiae of our trip. She always had a Cabcharge to hand and had booked the taxi and the restaurant. She reminded us of where we needed to be and by when. She even made sure we were awake on time, and if we needed anything, anything at all, she sprang into action. As I watched her take care of our every need, I realised that I was enjoying it so much because in my 'real' life (well, that was how I thought of it while I was swanning about Wellington pretending to be important) it was me who did all that work for my husband and children. It was me who remembered birthdays and bought presents and arranged celebrations. It was me who booked restaurants, arranged babysitting, made sure there was enough food in the fridge and cupboard, took the cat to the vet and the kids to the doctor, and called the tradespeople when anything broke down. Nobody may have noticed me doing all that stuff, but it was work and I always had a list of outstanding jobs nagging away in the back of my mind. The list was never completed. No sooner was one birthday done and dusted than another loomed on the horizon. No sooner was one broken-down utility fixed than another started playing up. No sooner were one week's groceries bought than they got eaten. I was spending my life in a low-level simmer of irritation at the sheer level of shit it was just assumed I would take care of. All unpaid!

I was not alone in that frustration. They even have a term for it now, although they didn't while I was struggling with it. They call it 'emotional labour'. Author Annabel Crabb (who also, coincidentally, hosted *Back in Time for Dinner*) termed it 'the wife drought' in her book of the same name. Writer Gemma Hartley asked her husband for a house-cleaning service for Mother's Day but, as she explained in an article in *Harper's Bazaar*, it wasn't just a clean house she was after. What she really wanted was someone else (aka her husband) to make all the mundane decisions involved in arranging for such a service. She wanted her husband to 'make the calls, get multiple quotes, research and vet each service, arrange payment and schedule the appointment. The real gift I wanted was to be relieved of the emotional labor of a single task that had been nagging at the back of my mind. The clean house would simply be a bonus.'

None of this mental and emotional work (they call it 'admin' if you get paid to do it) gets counted in surveys about how many hours each gender spends on housework. Add it all in, and I bet it blows us back to 1965 and the thirty hours a week our mothers were doing, or even the seventy-seven hours our grandmothers (and poor Carol Ferrone) broke their backs over.

While women today have fundamentally changed their expectations of what their lives will be like, nothing else seems to have changed to accommodate them. The workplace has not changed. It still expects employees to fit the so-called male worker model, whose only real responsibilities are at the office. The home has not really changed, either. The day-in, day-out work of parenting and home and personal maintenance remains stubbornly intransigent despite all the whizz-bang labour-saving devices. What has changed is the expense of buying a house, paying a mortgage, running a household and a car (or two), bringing up kids and paying all the bills that go with them. As we all know, it now takes two incomes to simply keep a family's head above water, particularly in our major cities. The earner of one of those incomes, usually the woman, still shoulders the lion's share of all the other unpaid work required. She pays a high price for this not just in terms of exhaustion, but also in terms of loss of time (and energy) to devote to her paid work. This means she often works part time, or even if she works full time gets overlooked for promotions and pay rises. It is a circular bind that women of my generation and our daughters have found themselves caught up in. The sheer weight of the unpaid work women do impacts on their ability to find higher-paying work. Their lower income then leads to both partners accepting that he should work longer hours and she should take on more of the housework, which impacts on her ability to get paid work, which … and round and round we go. It's a vicious cycle that gathers speed as women age, until it becomes a tornado.

What we are also just becoming aware of is how overtly hostile many workplaces are to women, and the extra layer of psychological effort required to simply survive in many male-dominated industries. The recognition that this exacts a cost from women as they try to put their talents and skills to good use and earn a living has been a long time coming. However, there appears to be a growing glimmer of understanding since the world began to listen in shock to the outpouring of revelations of sexual harassment of women, often in their place of work, following the scandal around the conduct of Hollywood movie mogul Harvey Weinstein. While the idea of the casting couch is nothing new, female actors, directors, writers and producers are now coming forward in droves to tell stories of the sexual services they have been asked to perform to get the role, the job, the script read or the chance to pitch. Some young men are also revealing how they have been similarly preyed upon, but—so far, anyway—also entirely by powerful men.

The problem with this sexually predatory behaviour is not just the misery it creates. It is that many of the women faced with such a Hobbesian choice (have sex with me or forget your career) have given up their dreams, their profession and, yes, their career. They have literally been driven out of the industry. Perhaps these are the sorts of decisions that were previously used to illustrate how little 'ambition' women had, or that opting out when the going got tough was simply their 'choice'. For most women, a choice between sexual abuse and achieving their dreams was no kind of choice at all.

It is my view that this sexualisation of so many workplaces—and hey, I worked in ad agencies—may be unconscious for many men. But that makes it no less deliberate. As my years in the advertising industry have taught me, if you want to know why a certain behaviour persists, follow the benefit. The message being sent to women as they entered the male-dominated environment of paid work in greater numbers was that this was not their place. They were not welcome. They had no right to be there, and if they insisted on doing so, they must put up with whatever humiliating, sexist crap the guys decided to dish out.

It is not only the women who dream big and attempt to enter highly sought-after, highly competitive industries who find that the workplace can be a profoundly hostile environment. Women working in all sorts of places have come forward with similar tales. We have long heard stories about the female paramedic or firefighter or copper bullied unmercifully by her male work colleagues until she leaves. The stories of the sexualised bullying of young women recruits to the army and, particularly, the navy have led to court cases and much soul-searching in our defence force. A surgeon caused headlines a few years ago when she told female interns that it might be easier just to give the male members of their profession a blow job than complain. She was being ironic, but she was also making a point about the way some of her colleagues abused their power over ambitious young women.

What is not often thought about is how much this male workplace hostility impacts on women's ability to make a decent living. Perhaps this is why Australia has such a gender-segregated workforce. Faced with the clear message that their presence is not just unwanted but deeply resented and, possibly, dangerous, many women have cut their losses and retreated to friendlier, if (not coincidentally) lower-paid and lower-status female-dominated occupations. But even those who choose female-dominated careers are not immune. Nurses suffer horrendous levels of abuse and violence at work, even to the point of being murdered. According to a 2015 study, 86 per cent of remote-area nurses reported experiencing violence or aggression while at work in the past year. Many female school principals report higher incidences of bullying and intimidation, particularly by male parents, and some now always have a male teacher or deputy accompany them to parent interviews.

It seems women attempting to earn a living in any occupation can suffer this kind of misery at work. The cliché of the mechanics' workshop plastered with nude pictures sends a message to any woman who might aspire to work in such an environment, even if she is merely employed in a typical female role such as answering the phone or doing the accounts. The men who distribute internet porn in their place of work are sending their female colleagues an equally clear message: this is not your place, it is ours. Female wait staff who must put up with lecherous patrons and predatory colleagues and bosses are faced with a level of stress and difficulty that men generally do not have to worry about. And it all takes its toll. Women who work in such male-dominated environments (and I know—I was one of them) learn to shrug their shoulders and roll their eyes. They learn to keep silent in the face of completely unfunny, foully sexist jokes that make all the blokes roar with laughter. They become adept at scraping one another off the floor of the ladies' when all the laughter gets too loud and the humiliations too numerous to ignore.

Let's not even go into the pre-eminently anti-female world of sport. I have long believed that sport is a ritualised form of warfare and that in these (thank God) more peaceful times (at least in the West), sportsmen have taken the place of what was once the warrior class. Nothing can be more antithetical to women, the givers of life, than the warrior, who is a taker of life. I have dealt with the hyper-masculine world of sport by having absolutely no interest in its pursuits. Nevertheless, I have always had an admiration for the women who have decided to take the bit between their teeth and make sport their chosen career—often, it seems, as journalists. The shit they have copped is legendary, and publicity around the latest sports 'hero' or boofy wannabe commentator insulting, harassing or downright assaulting a female sports journalist trying to do her job has become so routine as to be almost expected. Whole books have been written about it. Trouble is, there are bucketloads of money invested in sport. It's a lucrative and well-paid industry. If women stick to a less hostile environment, such as the arts, they are once again relegated to an industry that must perpetually beg for funds—unless, of course, it's Hollywood, and then they come up against Weinstein world. Are you seeing a pattern here? I hope so, because it's a bloody obvious one. But let me spell it out for you. Where there's money, there are men. If women want to be part of highly paid industries (even though they will still be paid less), they must be compliant and ally themselves with the men. Lots of women aided and abetted Weinstein, for example, and the female apologists for appalling male behaviour at Fox News are numerous. Whatever tactics they use, women in male-dominated industries have had to learn to survive while being under constant low-level attack.

Thanks to #MeToo, all is not lost, however. Even in the blokey arena of sport, women are finding male allies. Veteran US sportscaster Robert Lipsyte has written a very insightful essay about his experiences since the 1950s watching men bully women in the workplace—coincidentally the entire lifespan of the generation of women this book is about. He lists many examples, from the playground of his elementary school in the 1940s to the newsrooms of the 1950s, to the TV studios of the 1980s, right up to the present day. He describes a powerful executive producer in the 1980s and the way he would routinely berate, scream at and insult the women who worked for him. Lipsyte tells of meeting this man—called Shad—for the first time in the company of his (much lower down the food chain) female producer when they were being briefed on a new show that would involve them going on the road. He says that Shad described the young woman standing beside Lipsyte as a 'crazed slut' and said they would have to watch her constantly while they travelled: otherwise, she would 'embarrass' them. Lipsyte says he was 'flabbergasted' and once they'd left the meeting he asked his female colleague if she was okay. 'Oh, he's like that,' she answered. 'Forget it. It's like dues for working here and getting the good stories.'

Every woman who has ever worked in a male-dominated workplace will recognise the way Lipsyte's producer had learnt to swallow the insults and justify her humiliation as simply the price she had to pay for holding an interesting job—a price, I would like to remind you, that men rarely pay. To Lipsyte's credit, his essay explores why he did not stand up for the women he saw being treated so appallingly, and how fear and workplace (and society-wide) norms kept him silent despite his genuine horror at the behaviour. Powerful bullies frighten everyone, not just their immediate victims, so people of goodwill such as Lipsyte often resort to under-the-radar attempts to help the victims.

I had a similar experience at an advertising conference many years ago. It was an annual event built around awards for the best newspaper ads of the year. It was called after the first English printer, the Caxtons, and was attended predominantly by people who, like me, worked in creative departments. It was a testosterone-charged event. Despite that, I attended it regularly and enjoyed myself. Over the years I had developed highly sensitive antennae for the men and situations to avoid at such gatherings, and I believed I could give as good as I got and keep the bullies at bay. I'd also won a few of the awards, and that did gain me—even though I was just a chick—some grudging respect, or so I thought. By the 1990s, the event had begun to attract more female delegates. There had always been a handful, but now their numbers were approaching about a third. It was interesting to see how hostility and tension increased as a result. We were invading the blokes' territory. One year there was a running joke about the number of 'lesbians' who were at the conference. Hardy har har, these blokes were giant wits (not).

At the last of these conferences I ever attended, one of the very few female creative directors in advertising (they remain a rarity—must be due to that famous female lack of ambition, confidence, talent and willingness to lean in) described the intense pace and length of her typical working day. Her point was, as a woman in her thirties, how impossible it was to imagine fitting a child into her life (yet another female-only workplace hurdle—fathers have no such difficulty). Her brave contribution was controversial and caused much discussion, most of it—from the blokes, anyway—angry, dismissive and defensive. I was concerned about the messages the growing number of young female delegates might be receiving. During the final question-and-answer session, I stood to make a comment. I pointed out that while it was difficult for women to juggle parenting with a career as an advertising creative, it was not impossible; there were women in the room who had managed to be mothers and have a successful career, and the women here should not be discouraged. I listed some of those women as examples (there weren't many, but there were some) and included myself. Quick as a flash, one of the blokes, a man I had thought of as a friend, responded: 'I don't think you could say you have had a successful career, Jane.' There was a deathly hush as everyone looked at me. Not a soul spoke in my defence. My brain was on high alert and I knew I was under direct, public attack. I also knew that if I fought back and tried to justify myself, I would be doing precisely what the bully wanted. Instead I said, 'Fair enough, but that still leaves the other women I have named.' And then I sat down, overwhelmed by shame and humiliation. I wished I had not said, 'Fair enough', but at least I had not gone on the defensive. Moments later someone handed me a note. I read it. It was from a man in the audience. He said he agreed with me entirely and that his wife was going through exactly the same thing in her work as a psychologist—could she have kids and a career? Instead of feeling comforted by his note, I was furious. I scribbled a reply: 'Thanks, but don't tell me—get up and tell the audience.' Needless to say, he did not. I struggled through the rest of the last day of that conference with a smile plastered to my face, not a soul offering a word of support.

I never attended again, and am pleased to note that the conference is now deservedly defunct.

I know why that man—a man, by the way, with a much poorer track record as a creative than me—spoke to me the way he did. I know he was using me to send a message to all the other women in the audience. And that message is the same one sent by girly calendars, internet porn, sexist jokes, being labelled a 'crazed slut', all-male golf days, sexualised bullying, the casting couch, and all the insults, scorn and ridicule that women must put up with in male-dominated workplaces. The message is this: the workplace is ours. The public sphere is ours. Earning a living, and the plaudits, admiration, status, recognition, financial security, independence and, yes, decent superannuation that come with meaningful work, belong to us. You are not wanted here, and if we must have you we will make you suffer for it. So think twice before you get any ambitious ideas.

Mind you, I have to hand it to the patriarchy. It has been a brilliant and comprehensive strategy to keep women under control, to create so many hurdles and levels of difficulty—both overt and covert, both in the workplace and in the home, both through the tax system and the lack of services—that women must expend much of their energy just overcoming them and have little left over for battling for promotion and higher wages. Exhaustion is a feminist issue.

6

SLAGS, SLUTS, GOSSIPS AND STACEYS

All work and no play may make Jane a dull girl, but what sort of fun were my generation of women encouraged to have? You can find a clue in that rich repository of cultural norms: the advertising of the time. The 1950s was the period of labour-saving devices. After the war, women who had entered the workforce in large numbers to replace the men who went off to fight were encouraged (and/or forced) to vacate those jobs, go back home and make room for the returning blokes. By and large, they did. Mass-production techniques had vastly improved in efficiency during the war due to the necessity of rapidly producing weapons and armaments (World War II was as much won on the factory floor as it was on the battlefield—thanks, ladies) and were now churning out consumer goods to service growing households. Baby boomers, all of whom are now well over fifty, are not called baby boomers for nothing. Post the war, women hung up their military uniforms, their factory overalls and their Land Army dungarees and went home and had babies—lots and lots of babies.

The image of the beaming housewife was everywhere during my childhood. She smiled at us not only from ads, but from sitcoms such as *Father Knows Best*, *Leave It to Beaver*, *The Patty Duke Show*, even *The Addams Family*, in which matriarch Morticia was also a homemaker—albeit an eccentric one. Even the sitcoms that were built around female stars (Duke doesn't count—she was a teenager at the time), like *I Love Lucy* and *The Donna Reed Show*, were all about happy little homemakers. Their joy was in the new labour-saving devices flooding off the factory conveyor belts.

This joy over household appliances was not all contrived. Going from a hand-operated wringer washing machine (not to mention a copper) to an automatic washer and dryer saved women real, back-breaking labour. I remember my own mother patiently feeding sopping-wet items through the wringer one at a time before hanging them on the clothesline. This was hard work, not to mention dangerous, as fingers could get crushed—particularly when large, heavy items such as sheets and towels were fed through the spinning rollers. Washing day was a full day for a reason, especially if, like my mother and so many other women of the time, you had four or more children. For women of my mother's and grandmothers' generation, washing day was the worst day of the week. No wonder they felt liberated by automatic washers and dryers.

Electric irons were a similar godsend. So were vacuum cleaners, floor polishers, Mixmasters (no more creaming the butter and sugar endlessly despite aching hands and elbows) and, a decade or two later, the blessed dishwasher. I will never forget my mother's joy when she got one of those. No longer having to wash every dish, glass, pot, pan, knife and fork for six people, three times a day, really did feel like freedom. And having more free time no doubt allowed women to get out of the house and seek an education, go into the workforce and have more fun.

Fun and women has often been seen as a problematic concept. There is a limited repertoire of behaviours that 'good' women are meant to enjoy. Caring for their children was meant to be fulfilling—although, having raised two, I can say that the good times are very few and far between the drudgery. If you believe the ads of the time, women got satisfaction out of sending their husband to work in the whitest of white shirts, though that never seemed to motivate my own mother. They were allowed to enjoy cookery but daren't eat too much in case they 'lost their figure'. Even spending time in the company of female friends and neighbours was denigrated as 'gossiping'. Society generally approved of women when they enjoyed themselves by shopping, because encouraging women to spend is good for the economy. Mind you, there was often a little sting in the tail: shopping has always been considered self-indulgent. And, of course, they were never allowed to forget they were spending someone else's money. Women were also allowed to take pleasure in adorning themselves even if, once again, they were (and still are) often mocked and belittled for doing so. Their interest in their appearance is taken as proof that women are essentially trivial, superficial, vain little creatures, or it certainly was when I was young. Yet little consideration was ever given by those who did the mocking (mostly men) that it was only by being attractive to men that women in those days could make some kind of decent life for themselves and gain any kind of financial security. When few women earned their own income, a preoccupation with their appearance wasn't foolish—it was literally a survival skill. For many women, it still is.

Illustrating the damned if you do, damned if you don't dichotomy that so bedevils women's lives, women who took pleasure in more intellectual pursuits—reading, the exchange of ideas, and politics—were routinely warned to keep their brains to themselves in case they frightened men away. 'If only she was a boy' was a common reaction to clever girls when I was young. Brains, according to conventional wisdom, were wasted on girls because intelligence in women was not regarded as an asset but a deficit.

My 86-year-old mother still bitterly recalls an entry in the autograph book she had as a ten-year-old. Autograph books were all the rage in Manchester in 1941. (They made comebacks in popularity throughout my childhood too, but I don't know if they even exist today.) A friend of her mother's wrote this on one of my mother's pages: 'Be good, sweet maid, and let who will be clever'. My mother, being clever rather than good, recognised this for what it was: a rebuke. If only the term passive aggressive had been around at the time, she may have been able to understand why the entry made her feel the way it did.

Sadly, this fear of female brainpower still seems to exist. A number of studies have shown that if a man sees a woman as 'too smart' (I am assuming that means smarter than he is), then that is an actual turn-off. For women, it is the opposite. We are attracted to high achievers. But before we get too self-congratulatory, it's probably because they tend to earn more money than less brainy blokes, and what our male partners earn has a disproportionate impact on our own financial future, even today. However, what is even more dispiriting is that it is not just in romantic relationships that women with brains are seen as a problem. Bizarrely, even at work a woman's intelligence is regarded with suspicion. A recent study by Ohio State University revealed that when a woman's résumé showed she'd had a high grade point average at school and college, when applying for a job she was actually *less* likely to get an interview than if her marks had been lower. Ah, merit—if only women had any.

Back in the 1950s and 1960s, women who would rather read a book or newspaper than keep a spotless house (like my own mother) were judged harshly. The house I grew up in was almost always a mess, and I still recall feeling embarrassed and defensive when schoolfriends came to visit and made no secret of their disapproval. I knew they were criticising my intellectual mother, who saved her own sanity by skiving off from the housework and doing what she enjoyed. Women were allowed to have some fun, perhaps, but only after they had done all their duty.

Attitudes to women and fun may have loosened a little over time, but we are still not permitted the same licence as our male peers.

Women and girls still find themselves much more harshly judged than men if they get drunk, for example. It is routine for society to turn up its collective nose at women out on 'hens' nights' (how I hate that term), particularly if they are loud, raucous and three sheets to the wind. The judgement of the out-of-control woman is very real and can be very damaging. In Sarah Ferguson's powerful 2015 documentary about women escaping domestic violence, *Hitting Home*, an abusive man facing trial for his brutality tried to claim, when he gave evidence from the witness box, that his wife's horrific injuries were self-inflicted. The injuries were impossible to deny because they had been photographed by police and submitted to the court. However, the accused husband denied inflicting them as his wife had alleged, instead claiming that his wife had injured herself after coming home drunk from a 'night out with the girls': 'Isabella is a great woman, except when she drinks.'

You can see what the husband was trying to do. He was exonerating himself while shifting the responsibility for any bad behaviour onto his wife. She went out to have a good time, which in itself, he implied, was irresponsible. She came home falling-down drunk, he explained more in sorrow than in anger. He knew that we judge a drunken, out-of-control woman very harshly. He was hoping that, if we believed him, we would sympathise with the put-upon, long-suffering husband and condemn the selfish, self-indulgent, lying wife. A man will often excuse bad behaviour by claiming he was drunk at the time. For a woman, such an excuse just compounds her crime.

I have seen first-hand this method of blaming the woman who 'drinks' and so is selfish, out of control and, literally, having too much 'fun'. In my own extended family, in the midst of a messy marriage break-up, a husband who had for years been having a blatant affair attempted to excuse his behaviour by saying his estranged partner was a drinker. I'd seen her enjoy a couple of glasses of wine on occasion, even quite regularly, but I had never seen her remotely drunk. Apparently, any sort of imbibing of alcohol—even to moderate levels—can be used to impugn a woman's moral character and thereby minimise any bad behaviour by the poor man who is saddled with such a failure of a wife. No wonder he hit her, the story goes, or had an affair—after all, she drinks! Frankly, even if she got drunk as a lord every night of the week, that still wouldn't excuse violence or betrayal.

The fact that a woman is drunk is routinely used as an excuse to sexually assault or rape her. Sexual assault victims are still often questioned about how many drinks they had, implying that the rape accusation is a case of morning-after-the-night-before remorse. Even if we believe the crime was committed, we often seem to take a 'Well, what did she expect?' attitude to female victims who have had a drink or two or five. Girls are routinely schooled to curtail their drinking, police where they walk, and think carefully about what they wear and who they spend time with, in ways boys are not. After the 2018 rape and murder of (sober) 22-year-old Melbourne comedian Eurydice Dixon as she walked home from a gig through a park, police warned women that they needed to have 'situational awareness' and take responsibility for their own safety. Say what? She was walking home from work at night and did everything women are told to do, including texting a friend to let them know she was almost home. The outcry by women about this knee-jerk victim-blaming saw Victoria Police apologise for the insensitivity of their language.

Coerced apology aside, while we furiously criticise women for doing something as unexceptional as expecting to walk home unmolested at night, wagging our fingers at them for not keeping themselves safe, we applaud risk-taking in boys. We even see extreme drunkenness as proof of masculinity. Maybe that's why we see the same behaviour in girls as such a failure. Men are encouraged to let off steam, but women are expected to always remain in control—even when threatened by a murderous stranger who is much bigger and stronger than they are.

Perhaps our fear of the woman out of control and—particularly—under the influence, and the shame we feel about female drunkenness (it goes back centuries, by the way—that's why gin was once called 'mother's ruin': it was an attempt to shame women into good behaviour), are linked to our awareness that her inhibitions are down. Maybe that's partly why we are so suspicious of any claims she may make about being attacked (if she survives, of course). But perhaps it is even more basic than that. A woman might not put other people first when she is pissed. She might tell us what she really thinks about her life, about the work she has to do, or even what she thinks about you. We train women to be nice and to protect our feelings. Drunk people don't do that. They often get angry—and anger in women is deeply disapproved of and feared. Controlling how much you drink is unequivocally a good thing, especially for your health, but to restrain your intake for fear of being judged and shamed is not the right reason to do so.

Not all fun involves risk-taking behaviour, of course. Women have always taken a lot of pleasure in the company of other women. It is certainly the place where I have experienced much laughter and even more emotional support and encouragement—not to mention wine (with nobody counting how many I have). Contrary to the 'women competing nastily with one another to catch a man' stereotype so beloved by misogynists, women have honed their ability to create wonderful, life-enhancing friendships for longer than most people realise. Christine de Pizan published her work extolling the rights of women, *The Book of the City of Ladies*, in 1405. Even 600 years ago women fantasised about ways to be with one another and free from the control of men. I think the companionship and understanding of other women are literally what has enabled many of us to keep going. That's why mothers' groups are so ubiquitous and why women have taken to the internet with such alacrity—it has given us even better ways to connect with one another. Feminism, in essence, is itself a giant female support group, where women (mostly) offer each other support and encouragement—literally, pass on courage to one another. Perhaps that is why abusive men so often separate their female partners from their friends and families, a behaviour so common that it's one of the hallmarks of abuse. The abusive family Susan grew up in was a typical example: 'He removed my mother from her family, especially the women, who were all close and very supportive. She had no friend or family networks in the same state. My mother was a very petite woman; my father had done national service. I clearly recall at least one day where she was walking around the house naked with a black eye.' Separate your partner from other women and she is much easier to victimise.

Girls develop intense friendships at school, and, yes, when they are young they can be horrible to one another (especially between Grade 4 in primary school and Year 9 in high school). And don't they cop a bollocking for that! We are very quick to denigrate little girls as 'bitches' and judge their squabbles and jealous spats harshly. I have a different take. I think little girls are learning about relationships and put a lot of time and effort and energy into doing so, and like anyone learning something new, they make many mistakes and experience many failures before they become good at such a sophisticated skill. But most women do eventually become very good at friendship, and the solace offered by women to women is wonderful. I think little girls, by the way, put so much energy into learning how to do relationships not because they are biologically hardwired that way, but because they can see from the adult women around them that relationships will be the business of their life and the source of both the most joy and the most difficulty.

If you were cynical, you could say we are merely taking Lord Byron's prescription literally—relationships (aka love) being women's entire occupation. But despite it being seen as a 'soft' skill, our preoccupation with relationships has important lifelong benefits. Indeed, I often feel very sad for little boys. Far from agreeing that boys are somehow naturally less 'complicated' or 'bitchy' than girls, I think that boys don't put the same energy into learning about relationships for the same reasons that little girls don't put the same energy into STEM (science, technology, engineering and mathematics) subjects. They can see for themselves that it is not what is expected of them. The cost to little boys, however, of not learning about relationships, emotional intelligence and self-awareness in the way that girls do is much higher, I believe, than even the loss of income girls incur by not being attracted to technical subjects. (Anyway, as I pointed out in the previous chapter, if women were dominating technical occupations, those occupations would be lower paid.) Men and boys (with many honourable exceptions, of course) suffer throughout their lives from their lack of emotional intelligence, and also miss out on a lot of fun. Male friendships tend to be competitive rather than confidential. They tend to be forged around doing something together—sport, work, drinking at the pub—rather than just shooting the breeze about the experience of being human. Women bond over their shared weaknesses and vulnerabilities, men over their shared strengths and competencies. Trust and intimacy are only built by letting another human being see who you really are, warts and all—not hiding behind your 'got it all together' mask. I sometimes wonder if the difficulty men have in revealing their true selves is one reason why male suicide rates are so high. Living behind a mask of competence when you actually feel anything but must be exhausting and profoundly lonely. I applaud initiatives like the Men's Shed movement, which aims to combat depression among men by encouraging them to bond over shared projects. Perhaps those who came up with the idea noticed that female friendships can protect women from the kind of bleak emotional isolation that so many men seem forced to live with. The ABC TV series *Man Up*, where (deceptively) boofy bloke Gus Worland explored the deadly price of the emotional repression that boys and men hide behind, was also a heartening sign that men are themselves beginning to rebel against what novelist Tim Winton has referred to as the 'uniform of misogyny'.

Maybe the rigid, emotionally repressed male culture that is still so prevalent in Australia also explains why many men are so reliant on their wives emotionally. Their wives are not as vulnerable (unless deliberately isolated, as Susan's mother was), because they also get emotional succour from their girlfriends. Being asked to carry the full—but unacknowledged—emotional responsibility for your male partner may be one reason why so many divorces are instigated by women and why studies show married women express lower levels of marital satisfaction than married men do, while expressing higher levels of satisfaction with the number and quality of their friends. Perhaps marriage (despite the claims made for it in my mother's heyday) is just more rewarding for men than it is for women—and not just emotionally, either. When women marry they increase their workload while men decrease theirs, particularly if they have children. Marriage has long been known to help men live longer, but being single or married makes almost no difference to women's health or longevity. There is some evidence that it may even have a small detrimental effect.

Being entirely responsible for another adult's emotional wellbeing is hard enough when you love them. It is hard enough when there are just the two of you, but it is no fun at all once a woman also takes on the responsibility of the physical and emotional care-taking work of motherhood. I have heard many women explain their decision to leave a marriage by saying that their husband had become just another child to look after rather than a support. They were, in other words, tired of all the work—physical, emotional and psychological—they had to do alone. Marie was inspired to leave her abusive marriage by advice given on a TV show: 'I used to watch *Beauty and the Beast* and will always remember the beautiful Maggie Tabberer saying "Get out, girls" when talking about a bad relationship, especially an abusive and controlling one.' But not all women leave their marriage because it is abusive, controlling or just exhausting. Some of them leave because it is no fun anymore—and fair enough, too.

Which brings us to sex. It is meant these days to be fun, even for women. I sometimes think how hard it must have been for women to enjoy sex in the past when there was no reliable contraception and obstetrics was next to useless. The consequences of sex could literally be fatal, and were for many women. Women have died horribly in childbirth throughout human history, and still do in many developing countries. Reliable contraception and the huge advances in maternal care and obstetrics didn't just liberate women so they could enter the workplace: they also enabled them to enjoy sex without fear. Mind you, even then, new barriers to women's enjoyment were hastily erected. Freud built a beauty when he discounted the clitoral orgasm in favour of the so-called vaginal version. Many women were left wondering whether they were having the 'right' kind of orgasm—that is, if they were lucky enough to have one at all. It wasn't until very recently that couples were able to do much more than flail about in the dark. It is quite astonishing to realise that medical science knew little or nothing about the clitoris until 2009, and it wasn't until then that we started to understand what a major, complex and sophisticated organ of pleasure it really is. As evolutionary psychologist Edward Clint points out, it isn't just interesting to know how the clitoris works: it is vitally important for women's health, particularly women who have undergone the horror of female genital mutilation (talk about wanting to prevent women from having fun). As he says, how can you repair or remediate an organ you don't understand? Women might also ask quietly how you can expect to stimulate the clitoris and create pleasure in your sexual partner when you have only the vaguest idea what it is and where you might find it. Even for women themselves, the lack of information about the one organ in the body created purely to give its owner physical pleasure, and the shame and taboo around what many women still call 'down there', have their own limiting effects on women's ability to enjoy themselves in bed.

How can shaming women about their own genitals help them experience any pleasure? Yet shame them we do and, according to gynaecologist Jen Gunter, it is mostly men who do the shaming, telling their sexual partners that their genitals are 'too wet, or too loose, or too gross'. She believes there is a reason some men say things like this to their partners. 'While I admit this is anecdotal data,' Gunter says in an article in the *New York Times*, 'my years of listening to secret shame about healthy vaginas and vulvas seems to suggest it is largely, if not entirely, male partners who exploit vaginal and vulvar insecurities as a weapon of emotional abuse and control.' In other words, let women enjoy sex too freely, allow them to feel pride instead of shame in their bodies, and who knows where it might end?

Society is not just gripped by puritanical horror about what women being able to have sex without any consequences may mean in garden-variety dysfunctional relationships. There is also an existential fear of it more generally. And, once again, I think it is driven by the fear of women being out of control—male control and patriarchal religious control, in particular. I think this is why so many fundamentalist religions have such a contradictory set of beliefs around sex. They oppose sex education, they oppose contraception and they also oppose abortion. Yet we know that the best way to prevent unwanted pregnancies (the kind that often end up being aborted) is to provide comprehensive sex education to kids, and easy and cheap access to contraception, including the morning-after pill. It is rational to think that those who oppose abortion will therefore want to do whatever they can to minimise unwanted pregnancies. But no, that does not seem to be their agenda at all. Given this contradiction, it is arguable that what they fundamentally oppose is the idea of people being able to have sex purely for pleasure with no fear of consequences—and by 'people', I mean women. This taps directly into the religions' terror of a lascivious, sex-sodden society with no boundaries or punishments. Their God is a vengeful God. He (and he is very definitely a He) is about command and control. These people see children as a punishment, as a control mechanism. If you 'open your legs', as I have heard some vociferous right-to-lifers put it, you deserve whatever you get. For control freaks, the fear of women's unfettered (literally, 'without chains') pleasure is profound.

It is so profound that it is also becoming deadly dangerous. On 23 April 2018, a 25-year-old man drove a rented van into pedestrians on a sidewalk in central Toronto. He killed ten people and injured fifteen. At first, many assumed it was an Islamic State–inspired attack (that group doesn't approve of female autonomy much either), but it turned out the driver—I do not intend to add to his notoriety by including his name—was actually a follower of a shadowy movement whose members call themselves 'incels'. Incel is a portmanteau of 'involuntary celibate'. Before he committed his crime, the van driver posted praise of another incel who had randomly massacred six people and injured fourteen others with an automatic firearm in Isla Vista, California before killing himself. The shooter left a manifesto and a series of YouTube videos spewing hatred and bile towards attractive women who he claimed had oppressed him by refusing to sleep with him. Apparently, in incel world, women's bodies do not belong to them but are objects of pleasure for the use of others. The Toronto killer, it seems, had the same infantile motivation. Since these attacks, much has been written about the incel community and its members' obsession with violent tactics either to force women to have sex with them (mass rape) or to punish women for refusing to have sex with them (mass murder). This seems to me to be an extreme manifestation of the attitudes that regard women as vehicles for the gratification of others and not as sentient beings in their own right, entitled to seek pleasure for themselves as long as—and this is the bit the incel nutjobs entirely miss—it doesn't hurt anyone else. When women gain control over their own lives—a vital ingredient in the ability to experience pleasure and enjoyment—the most inadequate people in our community become particularly resentful and afraid. They seem to see pleasure and power as a zero-sum game. If women are allowed any, then they will miss out.

This murky soup of seething undercurrents, taboos, judgement, ignorance, shame and fear around women and their sexual pleasure is nasty, sticky and toxic. It produces terrorists like the Isla Vista and Toronto killers, whose stated aim is to terrify attractive women ('Staceys', they call them) and the attractive men they sleep with ('Chads') and all the rest of us who go about having sex occasionally ('normies'). One of the things that many of the current crop of mass murderers (whether their choice of weapon is gun, bomb, knife, acid, truck, van or car) have in common is a hatred of women and, often, a history of domestic violence. There are a lot of very angry men out there, and we ignore them at our peril.

But it's not just the extremist and terrorist violence that misogyny can trigger that puts women's lives at risk. Internalised shame can be a killer too. Shame can lead and has led many women, especially young, poor and vulnerable women, to have unsafe and illegal abortions, particularly in countries with draconian abortion laws. And even among those of us fortunate enough never to face the sullen, murderous fury of an incel, or be forced to risk an unsafe abortion, shame about our bodies and our right to enjoy them carries health risks.

The intractable taboo around women's genitals can keep us silent when we experience symptoms 'down there'. I really thought I was beyond such false modesty, but a decade ago, when I began to experience an intense itch on my outer labia, I found I was wrong. Even though I knew I shouldn't, I put up with it in silence. I was too embarrassed to tell anyone about it, even my doctor. God knows why, but my symptoms made me feel ashamed, almost dirty. I guess the ancient lessons I absorbed in my youth about how disgusting my genitals were had lodged themselves somewhere in my reptilian brain. Eventually, I am glad to say, the intensity of the itch and my rational self (I kept giving myself a good talking-to about how silly I was being) led me to a dermatologist. It was dermatitis, and a cream was all I needed to keep the itch at bay. I was lucky but also stupid. I had put up with years of discomfort for no good reason.

I am not alone in this, either. The silence around our 'front bottom' (I remember a childhood friend calling it that for lack of any other words) means women have always felt unable to talk to their doctor about any such symptoms. Not just poor and downtrodden women, either, but all women. After Queen Victoria died it was discovered she had a prolapsed uterus (not surprising after bearing nine children), a condition she had never complained about or even mentioned. It must have caused her great and silent discomfort for years. It is sad when women put up with years of pain and misery for no good reason, but our reticence can have much worse consequences than that. Silence can be fatal if cancers of the genitals go undetected for too long. And, yes, persistent itching can be a symptom of something sinister. I was an idiot.

Idiotic or not, many women put up with all sorts of uncomfortable symptoms—such as stress incontinence—without complaint. Mostly this is due to shame, but there are other reasons too, including the horror of untested 'treatments' that have been foisted on women for centuries, including in our own supposedly more enlightened times. The current legal wranglings about vaginal mesh treatments for prolapse are a case in point. For too many women, when they did finally confide their symptoms to their doctor, the cure turned out to be worse than the disease.

Irritating, painful and debilitating health issues inevitably increase with age, but all is not lost. Getting older for women can also bring with it many gifts, particularly when it comes to enjoying ourselves. If we have managed to stay with the one partner, the intense and dramatic moments of the relationship have most likely (although not always) become fewer and farther between. We may no longer be 'in love' but may have replaced that heady experience with a deeper, more lasting emotion that combines companionship, shared memories and trust. If we re-partner at an older age, we often choose more sensibly. After two failed relationships and fifteen years alone, Nancy found a new partner late in life. She says, 'I am now in a partnership that is beyond wonderful.'

If we have had children, they are mostly grown and more or less responsible for themselves. We may not have achieved all our dreams—we could even have some regrets—but for the first time in a long time, we have some time on our hands. For some of us, being the first generation to earn our own money for most of our lives means we now control some disposable income. We can even have some fun, and we are doing that. The more fortunate women over fifty could also be on the threshold of an age of indulgence. I don't say that with any sense of disapproval, by the way. I am all for having fun. Life is for the living, if you ask me. However, not everyone agrees.

To return to the vexed issue of alcohol for a moment, there has been recent unease about the amount of it older women are drinking. While there are legitimate health-related reasons for the concern, it is hardly surprising that women who are finally free of so many responsibilities may want to stop being so bloody dutiful and constrained. As someone who enjoys a glass of wine, I am certainly not going to preach to anyone about how much you should or should not imbibe. What I do think is that enjoyment is important however you find it, because without joy there is no mental health.

Many among this generation of older women are discovering the joys of less responsibility, more time and their own money. They are enjoying being women who, while they could be out of the control of others, are most decidedly in control of their own life. I love the famous poem 'Warning' by Jenny Joseph about ageing and women that talks about older women wearing outrageous, unflattering hats and unsuitable, clashing colours like red and purple. It is all about age giving you the freedom to do exactly what you like regardless of what others think. I once saw a group of older women meeting up on the old Pyrmont Bridge, and it suddenly struck me they were all wearing outfits of purple topped by outrageous red hats. I almost cheered. The refusal of this generation to quietly and sweetly disappear might be irritating to the young, but I would caution them about complaining too loudly. The young will get old far faster than they ever thought possible, and I bet they won't want to go quietly either.

The newly cashed-up and assertive older woman is why events like writers' festivals are exploding. It is why arts workshops, tourism, cookery classes, Pilates, yoga, reading groups, book clubs and older women's dance groups and choirs are popping up everywhere. This generation of women are demanding their right to have fun, often in the company of those with whom they have had the most fun throughout their lives: other women. In my view this is an entirely good thing and one reason, perhaps, that women, despite all the extra work and responsibility they shoulder, and all the hoops they must jump through, still generally outlive men. Most women who have married will eventually end up as widows.

However, there are far too many women of this generation who are not finding much joy in their older years. These are the women who must worry about keeping a roof over their heads and do not have the resources to have much fun—most of which costs money. These are the women too young for the old-age pension, not sick enough for the disability allowance, who must eke out an existence on Newstart, forced to apply for jobs they know they have no chance of getting. These are women who have put other people's needs ahead of their own, who have helped others to have fun—and, no doubt, got some joy out of that—but who have ended up with no-one to care for them and for whom having fun is the least of their worries. Poverty in older women is a feminist issue.

7

INVALIDS, LIARS, HYSTERICS AND MADWOMEN

Women have been seen as 'the weaker sex' for at least a couple of thousand years. This irrational idea (if you have ever watched a woman give birth, you will know that weakness is not the defining characteristic of the female body) has profoundly influenced the way men think of women and how women think of themselves. Much of this belief is because most women are smaller and less well-muscled than most men. In that sense, I suppose, we generally are 'weaker'. Somehow, in what appears to be typically human fashion, we have decided that this difference in height, weight and upper-body strength is indicative of other perceived weakness, including intellectual, psychological and emotional weakness, and ability to endure. We therefore see women as more likely to be chronically unwell, less likely to possess a superior intellect, emotionally unstable and psychologically fragile. When I was a child watching those TV series where the hero invariably had to rescue the useless heroine, I sensed even then that the idea of feminine weakness and fragility had a great deal to do with making men feel big and strong by comparison. In other words, we had to be seen as weak so men could fool themselves into believing they were not.

When the generation of women who are now over fifty were young, this gigantic female conspiracy to protect men from any knowledge of their own human weaknesses and vulnerabilities led to a culture of deceit. In my own family, my maternal grandmother kept my grandfather chronically unaware of what was actually going on. My mother's father was a stern disciplinarian, especially after he returned from serving in World War II. My mother has very few fond memories of him. He was a stickler for his two daughters eating everything on their plate. My mother found this impossible and developed a method of sneaking her unwanted food into the crevice created by the folded leaf of their extendable table. As a child, she just accepted that her food then magically disappeared, but as an adult, particularly when she became the parent of a fussy eater herself (me), it suddenly dawned on her that her mother must have been silently conspiring to deceive her father. My gentle and outwardly utterly compliant grandmother must have known what her daughter was doing and quietly cleaned up the food without ever saying a word to her husband. In traditional marriages I think this sort of kindly-meant deceit went on all the time. In the 1944 film *Meet Me in St Louis*, the eldest daughter, Rose, is expecting a telephone call from a boy at dinnertime. The only phone is in the dining room (the film is set at the turn of the previous century) and the family is aware that the (ahem) head of the household will not approve of the call. He is also, like my grandfather, a stickler for having the evening meal at a certain time. The entire family and household staff conspire to create a cover story that compels them to have their meal an hour earlier. The father character even complains, when he eventually finds out what is really going on, that no-one ever tells him anything. He is quite correct. Almost every plot of the hit TV series *I Love Lucy* revolves around Lucy's unsuccessful efforts to keep her husband in the dark about some madcap scheme she knows he will not give her permission to undertake.

This idea that a grown woman needed 'permission' may have caused the problem. Deceit is the inevitable response to such control.

It is my observation as a parent that those who exercise a rigidly strict and authoritarian discipline over their children, particularly as they become teenagers, unwittingly create a situation that encourages their children to lie. That is because people who are not supposed to aspire to or exercise power directly will lie and manipulate to get what they want. They know that if they come straight out and ask, they will not only be unsuccessful but may also get into strife just for making a direct request. My authoritarian grandfather often admonished his daughters by saying, 'She who wants doesn't get.' As you can imagine, they quickly learnt to stop asking and start manipulating. Many years ago, before I had my children, I used to moonlight as a group leader with Relationships Australia (then called the Marriage Guidance Council). I remember in one assertiveness training group that I co-led a woman participant saying she had been so thoroughly trained not to ask for what she wanted that she had lost any sense of her preferences. She said that even if someone asked her if she wanted tea or coffee, her automatic response was to wonder which one the person offering the refreshment wanted her to want. Talk about making life more complicated than it needs to be!

This tradition of avoiding speaking directly to one another in relationships between men and women no doubt contributed to the false assumption that women were morally 'weak' and deceitful by nature. It may bear some of the responsibility for the stubborn belief among so many—both men and women—that women are more likely to lie. It may also help explain some of the difficulty women have in the workplace in getting higher wages. So many of us have been trained since birth not to ask for things directly, and so many others have been trained to believe that women who ask shouldn't get. The anxiety that women feel at the idea of asking for more pay is not a weakness, even though that is often how it is painted. It is a survival technique in a world that believes that just by wanting things and asking for them you are being selfish, demanding and—crucially—unfeminine.

A male teacher in the US wrote an article recently about why he believed so many teachers in his country are walking out of their schools protesting their pay and conditions. He doesn't believe it's simply because both said pay and conditions have become so bad as to be intolerable—although they have. He says it's because teachers are mostly women and, thanks to the #MeToo movement, they have finally woken up to the fact that they have been systematically abused and taken advantage of because they are, as he puts it, a subordinate group. The author, Seth Nichols, argues that as a male teacher in a largely female world he has watched the workings of what he calls 'the female code of honour' and learnt that women will do almost anything to be seen as good nurturers. He uses simple examples from his own life as a teacher. If a female teacher needs a whiteboard, he says, she will figure out a way to get one using her own money if necessary. It will never cross her mind to ask the school system to pay for it. She has been trained not to ask for what she wants but to solve the problem at her own expense for the benefit of the kids. A male teacher like him, he argues, simply expects the school system to pay for it. He also points out that US teachers are now being asked to take a bullet for their students rather than politicians taking on the potentially difficult (but probably not fatal) task of fighting the National Rifle Association. This may (one sincerely hopes) be a step too far, even for professional nurturers. If Nichols is right and #MeToo is causing ripple effects such as this, then it's not before time.

If you consider, however, the burdens that women have shouldered disproportionately throughout history (not least spending their lives making sure the men around them feel big and strong), you are left with the impression of considerable strength rather than the opposite—and so it is, I believe, when women age.

Contrary to conventional wisdom, ageing is often easier for women than it is for men. We have never been able to take our bodies for granted in the way that men do, especially when we are young. Youthful, strong, healthy women still have to deal with menstruation every twenty-eight days, and deal with it silently with a smile on their face. When I was young, everything about menstruation was kept a secret from any men in the household. At my school, us girls had a code word for the arrival of our periods. We called it, for some unfathomable reason, George. I do like the nascent feminism that went with calling such a female event by a masculine name.

Menstruation remains the great unspoken. There is an old saying that Ginger Rogers did everything Fred Astaire did but backwards and in high heels. What we never mention is that she probably did a lot of it while bleeding for five days a month as well. Whether a woman has painful periods or relatively easy ones (it's never completely discomfort free), she carries on with her life regardless, from, on average, the age of thirteen until the age of fifty-two. If she gets a break it's because she is either pregnant or lactating (yippee …?), both of which are even more uncomfortable and awkward than menstruation. The upside of this—albeit a small one—is that ageing offers women some very real compensations. The first of these is that we don't get periods anymore, and there is simply no downside to that. Indeed, for many women, menopause is when we start to get control of our lives and our bodies back. It's when we stop being life-support systems for other human beings. Thanks to our biology, some things get better as we get older. Of course, menopause is not a picnic for everyone, and peri-menopause (the period of time when a woman's fertility begins to wind down) can be particularly unpleasant, often involving copious and unpredictably irregular periods that go on for years. However, once we are through 'the change', for many women, life improves—whether with the help of hormone replacement therapy or not.

For men, ageing is the opposite. For the first time, for most of them, their bodies will no longer do what they want them to do. Women are used to having bodies like that.

But the physical cost of shouldering the burden of gestating, birthing and caring for the next generation is high. Few women who have given birth do not suffer some lifelong consequences, be they mild or major. For most of us there may be a little stress incontinence, but for some there can be prolapses—of vagina or uterus—and quite severe incontinence issues. Not only can these be painful and disabling but they also remain taboo. It's not like having bunions or arthritis, which are horrible but can at least be publicly complained about and acknowledged. Excuses will be made for you if you suffer from conditions such as these, but women's intimate health issues must be suffered in silence. The result is that many women withdraw from life altogether if their pain is unendurable; or they seek desperately for a solution, making them vulnerable to sellers of snake oils. The despised female invalid from Victorian times may well have been suffering from just such literally unspeakable conditions, particularly as Victorian women had such high rates of pregnancy and birth. Indeed, Queen Victoria's undiagnosed prolapse may well have contributed to her possible addiction to laudanum (mostly an opiate) towards the end of her life. Many women were no doubt similarly self-medicating. Many still are today.

Even today, despite such astounding breakthroughs in medical understanding and treatments, sometimes the cure is worse than the disease. The scandal over the mesh implants and slings used to treat prolapse and pelvic-floor problems is a result of not just women's desperation but also the astonishing lack of rigour around medical interventions for what are still sometimes euphemistically called 'women's problems'. Female patients have been complaining for years about the crippling pain and misery that accompanied receiving these implants. They have also often been astonished to discover too late that in many cases the devices are virtually impossible to remove. These women have been given a life sentence of severe pain. It has also been revealed that many of the devices that were in use for over two decades were launched and marketed despite undergoing no clinical trials at all. Australia has now banned the use of these products, and there are various class actions in courts around the world as women sue the health system and the manufacturers for the consequences of their lack of care.

Endometriosis is another example of a female condition that is often dismissed and minimised. Medical practitioners, unable to find any cause for a female patient's often extreme pain, have preferred to default to the 'crazy woman' explanation rather than accept their own lack of knowledge—this despite the fact it is estimated that somewhere between one in five and one in ten women suffer from this debilitating condition. The figures are vague because endometriosis is so often misdiagnosed and unreported.

The cures offered to women for their 'special' problems have long been suspect, from various kinds of snake oil peddled by the unscrupulous (and yes, this still goes on—just look at some of the unproven but expensive lotions and potions recommended by 'alternative' health practitioners and 'wellness' bloggers) to the fact that until terrifyingly recently most medical research was carried out on men and just extrapolated to include women. The consequences of this cavalier attitude to women's health can be fatal. Women actually die from heart attacks more often than men precisely because they exhibit different symptoms and so are fatally misdiagnosed. There is even evidence that women's pain is taken less seriously than that experienced by men and that it is less aggressively treated than men's pain unless women can prove they are just as sick. This is despite women reporting suffering more pain, more often and for longer. The phenomenon is now so well understood in the medical community in the US that it has its own name: Yentl syndrome.

Women's reproductive systems have long been seen as a source of their supposed gender-wide weakness, and not just because they can sometimes go wrong, or even because childbirth was so dangerous to women for most of human history. That might have been reasonable, even helpful. But no, our reproductive organs have instead often been directly linked with madness. Even the word 'hysteria' (for centuries an almost exclusively female ailment that seems to have magically disappeared from medical textbooks in the last few decades) comes from the Greek word for uterus. The very first recorded example of a diagnosis of hysteria is found in the oldest medical document in the world, the Ebers Papyrus from 1600 BC, where it is described as the spontaneous movement of the womb through the human body. This belief in the 'wandering womb' and the damage it could wreak remained a staple in the way doctors diagnosed women for centuries. Just about any malady could be explained by it. Better a demonised woman, it seems, than a doctor admitting his (and they were all men) cluelessness.

To cure the imaginary disease of hysteria, women were locked up in mental asylums or purified with fire (I bet that was fun), endured clitoridectomies, were raped, were told to abstain from sex, and were dosed up with God knows what. They put up with pelvic massages (I wonder which medical practitioner came up with that idea) and were psychoanalysed by men entirely hostile to the idea of anything female. Our wombs made us crazy, apparently. No-one ever thought it might be the kind of life our wombs condemned us to live—unless we remained completely celibate—that was the culprit. Nor that it might be the ghastly treatments women were expected to put up with from the medical profession that drove us mad. How sane might you be after being 'purified by fire'?

No doubt Susan was seen as crazy and weak when she had a series of nervous breakdowns as a teenager on the anniversary of the birth of the child she'd had at age sixteen. She had been persuaded to give the child up for adoption but received no support or counselling. The GP who did try to help her was deemed 'too expensive' by her abusive father and she was left to struggle with her grief alone. She says as a result she 'became more promiscuous with boys … it was a form of approval that did not involve screaming and rage'.

Of course, outspoken and unruly women have always received short shrift, whether they were diagnosed with a wandering womb or not: scold's bridles, ducking stools, the stocks, Bedlam, the workhouse, the attic (madwoman in residence thereof), the lunatic asylum, the psychiatrist's couch, the frontal lobotomy, electroconvulsive therapy, enemas, diets, ice baths, douches, drugs, exercise regimes, restraints and force-feeding have all been used to tame women who were deemed to be 'out of control'. As I have written, girls of my generation were threatened with 'The Girls' Home' or being charged with being 'in moral danger' if we were seen as getting out of line. It is undoubtedly the source of much modern-day domestic violence and abuse that many men still see having a wife who is not completely docile as an affront to their identity. Like the gorgon-style mother-in-law, the hen-pecked husband was a staple of comedy when I was a girl.

It is difficult not to see the wholesale demonisation of women as the weaker sex, as the ones most susceptible to madness and incapable of rational thought, as psychological projection by one more powerful gender onto another. You can see how it works. Instead of men taking responsibility and ownership of their craziness (we're all a bit nuts), vulnerabilities, irrational fears and weaknesses, they could simply project those things onto the women in their lives and punish them for the parts of themselves they didn't like. What is amazing is that more women did not actually go mad faced with such unrelenting ignorance, disapproval and lack of compassion or understanding. And there is another, more pragmatic reason for demonising women. Susan's adoptive father behaved in a very sexually inappropriate way with her, once climbing naked into her bed (she screamed until he left—crazy bitch) and on another occasion punishing her by throwing her to the ground and leaping on top of her while he was wearing only a towel. Obviously, if you can convince the outside world that the women and girls you are abusing are crazy liars, then you lessen the risk that you will be stopped and held to account for your behaviour.

I also hear the echoes of this ancient belief in woman's 'natural' irrationality in the scorn and ridicule that are used to try and shut women up, even today. There is a particular belittling tone to the laughter that often greets a woman's attempts to be heard, especially if she is debating men about women's rights. Instead of being listened to respectfully, women who speak up are much more likely to be scoffed at than otherwise. Our experiences are dismissed, our view of the world ignored or openly disbelieved, and our feelings discounted. The number of men on social media lecturing women about their responsibility to 'keep themselves safe' (aka do not move through the world the way men do) in the wake of Eurydice Dixon's murder is just one recent example of this disrespect. As women are currently explaining … and explaining … and explaining … no-one is more alert to danger than a woman walking around after dark. Just to add insult to injury, a man—later revealed to be an acquaintance of friends of Ms Dixon via his work as a comedian—took it upon himself to desecrate the temporary memorial of flowers and candles left by mourners where her body was found. He painted a large penis over it (I kid you not) in defence of men's rights, or so he claimed. It seems even in the face of their actual death, women's pain and fear can be ridiculed if they are deemed to be offensive to men.

It still takes a great many of us insisting before we can get our experiences taken seriously. It wasn't until a male comedian gave credence to the accusations against Bill Cosby—made over decades by sixty women all telling a very consistent story—that anyone paid any real attention.

That said, women of my generation have been witness to a very profound change in how much female voices can be heard. Indeed, it is probably true that Cosby could only have been convicted at this moment in history. Prior to that, and there had already been a previous court case where he was acquitted, I doubt such a unanimous verdict would have been possible. (Women are liars, didn't you know? Even sixty of them.) I give social media full credit for this revolutionary change. The 'Destroy the Joint' hashtag back in 2013 (full disclosure: I was involved in the original social media storm) was successful because it changed the tone of the way women reacted to the kind of scorn and ridicule they have been putting up with for centuries. The movement that followed the hashtag condemning shock jock Alan Jones's fact-free contention that women in power were 'destroying the joint' created real consequences for such insults in Australia for the first time. The outcry that followed his original statement might have burnt itself out if he hadn't followed it up by claiming that then prime minister Julia Gillard's much-loved father had 'died of shame' because of all the lies she had told. (Are you seeing the theme here?) In response, the #DestroytheJoint movement got serious and the radio station employing Jones began to lose advertisers, who withdrew in response to the protest to the extent that Jones lost his Mercedes when the car manufacturer also withdrew its sponsorship. Thoughtless, nasty and cruel sexism actually cost some powerful men and the companies they worked for real money. That was a revolution, all right, and it isn't over yet. In fact, consequences for sexism may just be getting started.

The 'Me Too' hashtag existed before the revelations about Harvey Weinstein. Originally created by three black US feminists as a means of supporting sexual assault survivors, when it was needed it was ready and waiting, like #DestroytheJoint. #MeToo gained momentum once the numbers of women sharing their stories about Weinstein and other famous and not-so-famous men became too large to ignore. Many men were astonished by how widespread experiences of sexual abuse and harassment are among women, and that may well be why the movement has had such an effect. It has revealed to men of goodwill just how dangerous the world can be for the opposite sex. The scales have finally fallen from their eyes.

Of course, that is also what did Cosby in. There is power in numbers, and social media has given women, people of colour, LGBTQI people and other groups unmediated access not just to the public conversation but also to one another. And this solidarity is starting to bite.

At the time of writing, Australian Greens senator Sarah Hanson-Young had taken Australian Liberal Democrat senator David Leyonhjelm to court for defamation. He yelled that she should 'stop shagging men' in response to a remark he claims she made about all men being rapists, although he now cannot remember exactly what she said (?). These remarks are protected by parliamentary privilege because they were made while both Hanson-Young and Leyonhjelm were in the Senate debating whether restrictions on pepper spray should be loosened to help women protect themselves in the wake of the Eurydice Dixon murder. Leyonhjelm was in favour; Hanson-Young was against.

Leyonhjelm went on to make similar statements about rumours regarding Hanson-Young's sex life outside the safety of parliament on Sky News, obviously daring her to take him on. She has. As I write, she is crowdfunding for the coming court case. (I am one of the trustees of the GoFundMe account because I believe strongly—see #DestroytheJoint above—that behaviour like Leyonhjelm's, aimed at shaming and silencing women, will not change until there are real consequences for it.) Leyonhjelm is crowdfunding his defence.

Like Leyonhjelm, many who would resist the legitimising of female voices and experiences are fighting back, and among the arguments they are using to discount #MeToo are the usual ones that imply women can't be trusted and probably lie and/or sleep around. Opponents of #MeToo claim to be concerned about it becoming a 'witch-hunt' (a revealing use of language), or they ask why the women speaking out took so long to tell, why they didn't fight back, and why they didn't 'just say no'. Of course, the mere fact those questions get asked contains the very reasons why women don't report, fight back or 'just say no' in response to abuse. Namely, the women do not think they will be believed (they know we are easily convinced that women lie), they often absorb the blame themselves (why did he pick on me, we all wonder—yes, #MeToo), and they don't want to cause grief or difficulty for others. They also fear that they will be thought of as malicious, crazy and, yes, hysterical. Or even promiscuous and immoral. And they may be genuinely afraid while they are being abused that if they resist too strongly they may be hurt, humiliated or worse.

There are other just as damaging fights over whether women's experiences of their lives can or should be taken seriously. The stubborn contention by many, including some women, that the gender pay gap does not exist despite all the evidence to the contrary is one that has a particularly harmful effect for women as they age. Denial about the reality of the wage gap directly increases the risk women face of ending up living in poverty. Another, equally dangerous counterargument is the constant chant of 'not all men' (hello, Senator Leyonhjelm) whenever a woman dares to speak up about abuse or sexism. It seems our first duty before voicing any anger about being treated badly is to soothe the hurt feelings of the men who, according to them, never do such things. Apparently, women's lives must always be about men first and their own experiences second. Even when women—or serious researchers—write about male violence against women, we must defend the shocking statistics. Little is as well documented as the fact that in Australia, about one woman a week is killed by her intimate partner (dead bodies are hard to hide), but this seems to cut no ice with those who simply refuse to believe. Too often women and men who want to draw attention to this appalling situation must first fight those who want to pull the focus back to men by arguing that men are the victims of domestic violence too. They are, but in much fewer numbers and generally with much less debilitating consequences. It is a fact that men are more likely to be victims of violence than women but—and this is vitally important—this is almost exclusively at the hands of other men. Men are not most often murdered by their intimate partner, whereas women are. For women, the tragedy of Eurydice Dixon notwithstanding, the riskiest place on the planet is not a deserted street after dark or a bar or pub, but their own home.

According to 2013–14 figures from Victoria Police, 87 per cent of all homicides were committed by men, 98 per cent of sexual assaults were committed by men, 83 per cent of non-sexual assaults were committed by men, 90 per cent of robberies were committed by men, and 92 per cent of abductions were—you guessed it—committed by men. No wonder most of us don't feel afraid when we hear the telltale clip-clop of high heels following us down the aforementioned dark and deserted street. We know we are in less actual, physical danger from a woman than we are from a man, and yet women are still thought of as the crazy, irrational ones. Riddle me that, Batman.

Almost the worst conundrum of all this is the fear and disapproval of the 'angry woman' or, even worse, 'angry black woman'. If we dare to access our feelings of rage about the cards we have been dealt simply because of our gender, our sexuality or the colour of our skin, our very anger is often categorised as extreme, irrational, undignified, unreasonable and, yes, crazy.

When I first set out to tackle the subject of women over fifty and the quite devastating statistics about their vulnerability to poverty and homelessness, I tried to interview a number of women in that situation. Some of them responded with great honesty and generosity, and their stories have enriched this book. But some reacted with fury. This surprised me at first, and it was uncomfortable. I am no better than anyone else at dealing with someone else's anger towards me. Anger as an emotion is a protective one, used to make others back off. And back off I did. On reflection, I began to understand. These are women who have been betrayed by a society that has done nothing but make them promises that weren't kept, and sent them double messages. Why should they trust any of us, including me, who, after all, wanted to interview them for my book? They are entitled to feel furious. They are entitled to tell people like me to fuck off. Frankly, it is an entirely sane and reasonable reaction to the dilemma in which they now find themselves. Many of these women have done what was expected of them all their life. They have been faithful to the lessons they were taught at their parents' knee. They tried to have good marriages and raise well-adjusted kids. They tried to take an often unsatisfactory education and hold down some kind of job to contribute to their family and to support themselves. They put other people's needs first, as they were trained to do, and their reward has been poverty, insecurity and misery when they grew old. Who can blame them for being pissed off?

I have noticed elsewhere the increasing fury of older women. Recently I facilitated a panel of feminists at a writers' festival. This is work I do often. Our topic was women's voices. The panel was fierce and funny and I opened the last ten minutes or so to questions from the floor. When our time was up and I closed the event to warm applause, the panellists and I all felt that the session had gone well. Then an older woman approached us, shaking with fury. She directed her first remark to me: 'You ran that panel just like a man.' As you can imagine, that set me back on my heels a bit. 'You weren't interested in hearing from any of us—it was just the sound of your own voices you were interested in. You're just the same as men.' I later found out that she had been at the back of the room waiting to ask a question, but unfortunately the lighting in the venue was very poor and I had not been able to see the microphone set up at the rear, only those at the front. That does not mean, of course, that even if I had seen her she would have got to ask her question. It's the nature of these sessions that only a few members of the audience get called upon. Mostly when that happens people shrug and move on or they come up and ask you afterwards. However, if you have felt unheard all your life, if you have been asked to constantly put others' needs ahead of your own, and if you feel you are running out of time as you age to ever have your questions answered, your point of view listened to and understood, I can understand how angry you might be when—even in a feminist panel all about the silencing of women's voices—you still do not get heard.

What is also interesting to me is how often this fury is expressed by women towards other women rather than towards men. When I see a woman challenge a man in a forum it is usually done politely, or at the very worst with some wry humour. I have only ever faced shaking fury from members of my own gender. I get this, too. If you feel powerless, it is far too terrifying to confront the powerful—aka, particularly for women of a certain age, men. It is safer to confront not just other women but women you suspect are sympathetic. The chance of your anger having damaging consequences for you is less. You can judge for yourself from what I have written here whether the women who let loose the full blast of their anger on me were correct in trusting me to understand it and deal with it usefully. I certainly do not think they were crazy.

The demonisation of female anger as ugly and deranged has had a debilitating effect on all women, and it is really heartening for older feminists like me to see how younger women are accessing their fury over how they have been treated via the #MeToo and #TimesUp movements. Watching Uma Thurman respond through gritted teeth when she was asked about the Weinstein revelations was an exercise in how careful women must be with their fury. Thurman said in a measured way that she was too angry to talk about it and needed time to gather her thoughts. It took her from October 2017 until February 2018 to do so.

Thurman's revelations of the way she was mistreated on film sets are terrible, of course, and demonstrate once again how vulnerable even powerful and successful women are in a male-dominated world. However, it was her feeling that she needed to be calm and measured before she would be taken seriously that was most interesting to me. When women are discounted, disrespected, underpaid, ignored, humiliated, groped or assaulted, just like anyone they will feel angry about receiving such treatment. If they also feel they cannot directly express their anger, if from an early age they have been trained not to show such a challenging and intimidating emotional response, then the risk is they will take that emotion (which exists, whether it has permission to or not) and turn it inward against themselves. Internalised anger often becomes depression. When Thurman had to put up with disrespect, sexual bullying and humiliation—right up to having her safety put at risk in a car for the sake of getting a shot, against her better judgement—she had to keep her feelings to herself. And that can make you feel as if you really are going nuts. It's not female anger that is insane—it's the inability to express that anger. But, women are becoming much better at showing their fury and refusing to automatically cede space. At a recent festival of ideas held in Adelaide, the facilitator of a panel about #MeToo opened the floor to questions and a man in the audience, among a sea of hands, got the nod and the mic. He began by saying, 'I have two questions, actually …', but got no further. He was immediately cut short by the women in the audience: 'Only one question, only one!' they shouted. The times, they are a-changing. More and more women are beginning to own their anger and, yes, own up to it. *Nanette*, comedian Hannah Gadsby's internationally successful one-woman show, is about her decision to stop using comedy to express her rage about the way she has been treated as a woman, a lesbian and an outsider. Instead, she lets us see her pain, her grief and her rage front-on and in the raw.

And then, of course, there is the phenomenon called 'gaslighting'. Taking its name from *Gaslight*, a 1944 movie starring Charles Boyer and Ingrid Bergman, it is the means by which someone, usually a woman, is manipulated into doubting her sanity. In the movie, Boyer's character tries to convince Bergman's character that she is crazy so he can have her committed and gain access to her money. As I write this, Donald Trump and his cronies are engaged in gaslighting America. It involves convincing someone to doubt the evidence of their own eyes. In *Gaslight*, Boyer's character does this by continually turning the gas lighting up and down. Trump is a master at it, denying that he has said what he has said despite recordings, videos or millions of witnesses, or asking others to accept that a small crowd was huge or that another president's achievement was really his.

In less exalted circles, gaslighting is something that many women experience in both their personal and professional life. It is a common tactic in fights, particularly the 'but you said …' / 'I never said any such thing' style of argument. Gaslighting really can make you feel as if you are going mad when your perception of reality is consistently denied. It is a common tactic in psychologically abusive relationships. The fact that we are very easily led to believe that women are more likely to be liars, or crazy or hysterical or exaggerating, is, in and of itself, a form of gaslighting. When you tell someone their experience of the world is not real, their emotions are not valid, you make them feel as if they are losing their mind.

Far from women as a species being vain, flighty or irrational, overemotional, hysterical, lunatic or morally weak, what strikes me about women and their history is just how damn sane we have managed to stay.

8

VESSELS OF REPULSION

Being ladylike was not a goal for young women in the 1970s. We ditched the hats and the gloves, the strings of pearls and the modest, pastel-coloured twin-sets. We no longer went to the hairdresser weekly for a permanent wave or to get our hair set. Thanks to the pill, we discovered sex, big time. Mind you, we still had to navigate our way through a forest of contradictory expectations. Like our mothers and older sisters, we continued to be expected to police male sexuality, but we were also being covertly encouraged to do the opposite and 'come across'. The worst thing you could be called in my era was a 'prickteaser'. The Beatles even wrote a rather nasty song about it. The double messages were overwhelming. Our parents, teachers, and political and religious leaders fulminated about morality from bully pulpits, official or otherwise. They feared, rightly, that female sexuality was off the leash.

When the women of my era were young, we were often considered to be vessels of temptation. Young women always had been, of course, but now we were flaunting it in a way that women had never really done before and were beginning to claim some sexual agency. The miniskirt shocked people, even in its early days when it was only a few timid inches above the knee. When in the late 1960s and early 1970s it rocketed crotchwards to become the micro-mini, the usual suspects had apoplexy. And it wasn't just our skimpy skirts that caused outrage. I can still remember beach inspectors (invariably pot-bellied older white blokes—well, leathery brown blokes, really—wearing themselves rather skimpy speedos) who were empowered to measure girls' bikinis and ban their wearers from the beach if their garments did not meet the regulation inches.

We were constantly being told to cover up on the one hand while being covertly encouraged to reveal as much as possible on the other. Schools, particularly those that charged fees, drove themselves potty trying to lengthen girls' skirts and shorten boys' hair. Indeed, the last time public schools were vastly more popular than private ones—at least among students—was during the 1970s, when their relaxed attitudes to hair length and uniforms were more in tune with the spirit of the times.

This fear of women's bodies is as old as civilisation. Paradoxically, it is a fear that actually has nothing to do with women or their bodies. It does, however, have everything to do with men and their complex relationship with their own sexual desires. Masculinity as an ideal can send as many contradictory messages to men as femininity sends to women. Masculinity demands that men always be in control, able to overcome any weakness and, of course, lug swooning heroines out of danger with ease. Yet in truth, men are just as emotional as women, just as subject to doubts and fears, and experience the desire for intimacy just as intensely as any other human. These needs when demonstrated by men can be seen as a weakness and a cause of shame. Boys are rigorously groomed from a pitifully tender age to reject and overcome such feelings. Men, it seems to me, are often afraid of their own softness and need for love and affection. The tale of Delilah destroying Samson's strength is a wonderfully Freudian metaphor (long before that bloke was even dreamt of) for the fear men have that women can get under their skin and weaken them by sensing that they are nowhere near as strong and invulnerable as they like to pretend. Much of misogyny, perhaps, is really projected dislike of the parts of themselves that men have been taught to reject. It simply can't be a coincidence that those very qualities are the ones most likely to be identified as stereotypically feminine.

Women have paid a high price for this fear (men have, too). It has affected every element of their lives and the control they are permitted to have over their own bodies. The male anxiety around women's bodies has dictated what women can wear, where they may go, whom they can marry and what they can do with their lives.

It sometimes seems as if women's bodies do not belong to them at all. They belong to the entire culture, and often represent its values. I remember being in an advertising industry discussion at a conference back in the 1990s. A bunch of experts (all men, of course) were earnestly discussing the rise of what was then called global advertising—a relatively new phenomenon at the time. In the 1950s, 1960s and 1970s, most of the TV and print ads we saw were written, produced and created in Australia. Then, along with the increase in free trade and the weakening of tariffs, came deregulation of advertising content. Suddenly, a great many ads were being written, produced and created in places like the US and the UK and exported globally. Sometimes they might change the accent of the voice-over or photoshop in a cricket ball instead of a baseball, or change the eye shape of the talent from Asian to European. Sometimes they didn't even bother to do that. Anyway, to return to the conference, the experts were gung-ho about global advertising and the resulting economies of scale. Some took it a step further and declared it showed that the world was becoming much more homogenous and connected because an ad for Coke in Japan or Saudi Arabia could work just as well in Australia. They were even a bit evangelical about it, waxing lyrical about the brotherhood of man, blah, blah, blah. The experts were all men, but even in the audience, there were very few women. After listening to this for a while, I could stay silent no longer and said, 'Ads aimed at men may be able to be much the same the world over, but that does not apply to women. If you try to sell skincare or lingerie in the same way to women in Muslim countries as you would in Australia, you'll face all sorts of cultural problems.' As was usual when I spoke to male experts about the situation of women, they looked at me with confusion. They had never thought about how what they were talking about would affect women, notwithstanding the fact that (she repeated wearily) the world over, 80 per cent of ads are aimed at them.

I saw this extreme difference in how cultural values are expressed through women a couple of decades later when my husband and I were on a stopover in Kuala Lumpur. We were breakfasting in a large international hotel. Malaysia, as a Muslim country, attracts many tourists from the Islamic world as well as from the West. That's why the enormous buffet restaurant in the basement of our hotel was host that morning to representatives from so many varied cultures. What struck me, as I gazed around the huge room, was that regardless of country of origin, the men and the children were all dressed more or less identically. KL is hot, so they were all wearing variations on shorts, cargo pants, T-shirts, shirts, sandals and thongs. What the men and children were wearing in that restaurant was indistinguishable from what was being worn on the streets of Brisbane, LA, Rio de Janeiro or Bangkok that day.

For any female over the age of twelve, however, the opposite was true. Their clothing could not have been more varied. The women were wearing a vast array of garments, all sending a clear message about the culture they belonged to. There were women wearing the full burqa or niqab, including face-covering (it was a little confronting to watch them lift their veil so they could sip coffee or take a mouthful of food), and there were women dressed in hijabs and modest but not all-enveloping clothing. There were women sporting colourful African dresses and turbans, jewel-tinted Indian saris and slinky, body-hugging cheongsams. Other women and girls, many of them Caucasian, ranged from those dressed in cut-off jeans (revealing virtually all of their bottom) and tiny spaghetti-strapped tank tops or sarongs over bikinis, to women wearing clothing virtually identical to that of their male companions. It struck me then that if you ever wanted to know how little ownership women have over their bodies and what they can dress them in, all you had to do was look around that cosmopolitan but oddly depressing (for this feminist, anyway) restaurant.

It seems that because we all started life inside a woman's body, we still feel we have some form of tenant's rights. This cultural assumption of once-removed ownership has led to the complicated and conflicted way that women view their own bodies. We often spend a great deal of time trying to see ourselves as others see us. When we were beautiful, nubile and young, we gained power and acceptance by seeing our desirability reflected back to us through men's admiring eyes. Yes, it could be confronting, even scary, but it was also exciting. And frankly, when my generation was young it was often the only sort of unequivocal approval we were going to get. Our currency, as we were often told quite unashamedly, was our attractiveness to men. The equation was simple: the more men who wanted us, the more valuable we were.

If a woman becomes pregnant, and most womb-owning women still do (only 24 per cent of women currently of child-bearing age will never have a baby), that is when the rubber really hits the road (if you'll excuse the expression) as far as the peculiar attitude society has to women and their bodies. All of us who have ever got about in public with a prominently pregnant belly have experienced complete strangers feeling entitled to come up and give our tummy a pat—something they would never dream of doing when we were just ourselves, rather than a container for a baby. This idea that a woman stops being the sole owner of her body when she conceives a child may also be behind the heat that is generated by the abortion debate.

What really seems to be at issue is whether the woman controls her body, or whether the rest of us do.

On 25 May 2018, Irish citizens voted in a second referendum on abortion rights. In the run-up to polling day, Irish author Anne Enright argued that the first referendum, passed in 1983, had invented a new kind of person or, as she put it, 'a new category of rights-holder'. This was because the eighth amendment enshrined the 'right to life of the unborn' in the Irish Constitution. She also pointed out that as the amendment also acknowledged what it called the equal right to life of the mother, it had transformed the pregnant woman from an individual human being into one side of a relationship: a mother. Her view is that the 1983 amendment established an odd equivalence between woman and foetus. 'Pregnancy was a binary state, in which two souls temporarily shared the same blood supply,' she wrote. 'The question of who had it first was neither here nor there and the fertilised egg was a grown adult, temporarily inconvenienced by being a few hundred cells large.'

This relegation of the original owner-occupier of a woman's body to just a tenant-in-common during pregnancy is yet another way we make female bodies more complicated to own. The disapproving looks a pregnant woman will receive if she smokes a cigarette, orders a drink or even dares to sip coffee are all clear indications that she is no longer regarded as a free and equal adult entitled to make her own decisions (right or wrong) about her own body. When women fight for their right to choose whether they will take a pregnancy to term or not, they are really staking a claim about their prior right to their own sovereign territory—namely, their own flesh. For a society to take it upon itself to decide what a woman may or may not do when she becomes pregnant is quite literally to colonise her body. No wonder feminism understands that the first and most essential of a woman's rights is to retain power and control over the body she occupies.

Women of my generation were taught to use our bodies to attract men. Then we were taught to use them to produce children.

What we were not taught was to use our bodies for our own benefit, or even our own pleasure. As ten-year-olds in 1967 my best friend and I attended what was called a 'Mother and Daughter Talk'. We knew it was about sex—whatever that was. What we were told blew my tiny mind. The woman who stood on the stage in the Frenchs Forest Public School assembly hall that evening is indelibly fixed in my mind. I can see her now. She is smallish and roundish, with tightly permed grey hair crushed under a woven raffia pillbox hat. She has the embellished cat's-eye glasses so beloved by Australian suburban matrons in the 1960s that they have been mercilessly pilloried by Edna Everage ever since. She is also excruciatingly embarrassed by her mission, and so desperate not to give us permission for licentiousness that she manages to give us—well, me, anyway—totally the wrong impression. She informs her prepubescent audience that when a husband and wife love each other 'very, very much' (she can't emphasise this enough), the man takes his penis and puts it in his wife's vagina and rubs against her until the sperm comes out and then it mixes with the mummy's (she becomes the tenant-in-common instantly, apparently) egg and makes a baby.

I was so shocked by this disgusting idea that I only half-believed it. The next morning at breakfast I confronted my parents. 'You didn't do that, did you? I asked them, pulling a face. My mother went bright red. 'How do you think I got you lot?' she replied. I had my answer.

What I now thought happened was this: sexual intercourse (as the woman had called it, forming the dangerous words as if she was holding them at arm's length) was like an inoculation, and about as much fun. You did it once when you got married (holding your nose), and then the number of children you conceived after that—whether it was one or twenty-one—was entirely a matter of luck. I can remember my horror when I read the 'Dear Del' advice column in a women's magazine and a reader inquired whether having sex 'once a year' was unnatural. Unnatural! Of course it was, ten-year-old me thought. Such unnatural frequency was deeply perverted.

Indeed, it was only through persistent reading of Dear Del and her advice that I began to realise that people did this disgusting thing quite frequently, and often enjoyed it.

I'd always known that it was good for men to admire women and think them beautiful. It was what all the midday movies told me, and every princess in fairytales was described that way, but it was only after that Mother and Daughter Talk and a good dose of Dear Del that I realised why. Little girls grow up knowing they are meant to be beautiful. Fecund young women enjoy a spurious kind of power. Pregnant women get an inkling that this power may be a con trick—but what happens to women when they get old? It is all very well for me to be chirpy about not getting periods anymore (though I stand by the absolute liberation of that), but how does it feel to go from vessel of temptation to vessel of repulsion in what is often a few short years? If—as so many women do—you have invested your self-worth in the physical appeal you have for men, the loss of it can feel terrifying.

No matter how annoying we may find the barrage of sexualised remarks and admiring noises that younger women routinely experience as they go about their business, for my generation (I am hoping it is different for the current one) the loss of it was sobering. Despite second-wave feminism, we had absorbed the idea that our value to men equalled our actual value. Once that was gone, once we began to experience the invisibility I wrote about in Chapter 2, we could feel literally devalued. Our value to our children, if we had any, might delay the realisation for a couple of decades, but once they had grown up and become independent (meaning we had successfully completed our job), we were—as far as society is concerned—past our use-by date. This is not simply a Western concept, either, or even the fault of a throwaway, consumerist society (though that certainly doesn't help). The dismissal of older women seems endemic to many cultures. The more misogynistic a culture, the more theocratic, the worse the fate of older women can be.

Since the defeat of Islamic State forces in Iraq and Syria, evidence of the attempted genocide of the Yazidi population has been uncovered in many mass graves. Most contain the bodies of Yazidi men and boys; however, at least two graves predominantly contain the bodies of older women aged between forty and sixty. Younger Yazidi women and girls (some horrifyingly young) had a value as sexual slaves, but their mothers and grandmothers had no value at all and so were simply and ruthlessly disposed of.

This is an extreme example of the attitude that sees women as existing only in relation to their sexual or reproductive value to men. A less extreme example is the revulsion that accompanies the idea of an older woman being the sexual partner of a younger man. No-one turns a hair when an older man—usually a rich and powerful one—trades in his ageing wife for a younger model (I'm looking at you, Rupert Murdoch; oh, and you too, Donald Trump), but when, very occasionally, it happens the other way around it is regarded at best as a curiosity, and at worst as revolting. President Emmanuel Macron of France is forty years old. His much older wife, Brigitte, triggers complicated responses, including Trump's astonished 'You're in such good shape … beautiful' exclamation when he met her in Paris. Trump was clearly amazed that he could (almost) fancy a woman who was only seven years his junior. Ah, if only men could see themselves the way we see them. Worse, it appears the US president genuinely felt that he was paying 65-year-old Madame Macron a compliment!

Indeed, when we admire older women who 'look good for their age' we are often incredibly and unconsciously patronising. Even elegant older women such as Helen Mirren and Judi Dench have their appearance dissected in tones of surprise. We can see the difference in attitudes to the sexuality of older men and older women in the way Hollywood casts its films. In 2015, Maggie Gyllenhaal revealed that she was turned down for a movie role because at thirty-seven she was deemed 'too old' to play the love interest for a 55-year-old man. US website GraphJoy has plotted the average age gaps between leading men and their female co-stars. The site found that since he turned thirty-five Denzel Washington has averaged an age gap with his leading ladies of over fifteen years, while Tom Cruise has averaged an almost thirteen-year difference. Apparently it is fine for men to continue being sexy into their dotage (Washington is sixty-three, Cruise is fifty-five and Harrison Ford—average age gap fourteen years—is seventy-five), but older women? Yuck! Indeed, as the male star starts getting older, the age gap between him and his female co-stars gets wider. In the 1999 film *Entrapment*, Sean Connery was forty years older than his romantic lead, Catherine Zeta-Jones. Whatever happened to Zeta-Jones, by the way? Oh, of course: she's now closer to fifty than thirty—over the hill for a woman.

Is it any wonder, then, that older women also have a complex relationship with their sexuality? We are perfectly well aware that we have gone from being desirable to being repulsive. Yet many of us still enjoy and want sex. Young people may hate to think about their parents being sexually active—and let's not mention their grandparents—but chances are many of them still are. In fact, once the exhaustion and lack of privacy that accompanies parenting small children is over, couples often get the opportunity to revive their sex life—a sex life that may continue for a very long time. A US study into the sex lives of over 3000 people aged between fifty-seven and eighty-five found that a quarter of 85-year-olds reported having sex at least once in the previous year. Those who continued having sex into their senior years were generally in better health. The bad news is that older women were less likely to remain sexually active than older men, but, according to the study, this was also because they were more likely to outlive their husband. In other words, they lost their partner rather than their interest.

Becoming a widow—something that is much more likely for women than men (42 per cent of men over eighty-five are widowed, compared to 77 per cent of women of the same age)—has an obvious, profound impact on your sex life. Women are also less likely than men to remarry after being widowed, even if they lose their husband relatively early. A French study found that a 65-year-old widower and a 45-year-old widow both have a 7 per cent chance of remarrying or, to put it more discouragingly, a 93 per cent chance of remaining single for the rest of their lives.

It is interesting to speculate about why it is so much harder for women to re-partner than it is for men. And this gap is characteristic whether the woman is single due to divorce or because her partner has died. According to the Australian Bureau of Statistics (ABS), the remarriage rate for divorced men is fifty-four per 1000 such men in the population, but there are only forty-one remarriages for every 1000 divorced women. Is it because we regard older women as intrinsically less attractive and desirable than older men? Are men simply able to seek new partners from a much wider range of women than the other way around? Are they more likely to marry younger women who have never been married before because the men's sexuality remains more acceptable than that of their female contemporaries? And, as they grow older, if they have managed to accrue more status and wealth than their female peers, does this also help to maintain their desirability as life partners? Divorced and widowed women are fishing in a much smaller pool: men who are older than they are. They are also routinely judged much more harshly for their appearance, and are more likely to have lost wealth and status as a result of losing their male partner than the other way around. Once again, the decks are stacked against women.

Nevertheless, it is also possible that once a woman finds herself single again, she may decide she is perfectly happy to remain that way. Many of the studies I quote in this book indicate that men get a lot more out of being married than women do. No doubt some women make a deliberate choice to stay single. Being a vessel of repulsion has its upsides.

Financially, however, women tend to do better if they are married, particularly if that gives them access to their husband's (usually larger) superannuation. And for women with no superannuation or income, most often because they made caring for husband and children their entire occupation (hello again, Lord Byron), the widow's pension offers very cold comfort indeed. It is means-tested, and the current maximum for a single woman with no children is $545.80 a fortnight, which is the same as the notorious Newstart comparable rate. If a widow remains single and gets the Widow Allowance (as it is rather condescendingly called) for nine months in a row, then it will rise to a princely $590.40 per fortnight.

The appallingly low rate of Newstart is apparently justified because (as its Orwellian name implies) it is meant to act, in the words of Coalition federal member for Goldstein Tim Wilson on ABC TV's *Q&A* in May 2018, as a 'trampoline', not as a 'hammock'. In other words, Newstart is kept deliberately low to act as an incentive to get people off welfare and into work. This may be arguable when you are twenty-five, thirty-five or even forty-five, but it starts getting awfully tough when you are fifty-five or above. How you can justify a widow's pension at such a paltry rate is harder to fathom. Is it meant to act as a disincentive for her to stay unmarried and an incentive to force her back—at whatever age—onto the marriage market? It strikes me as yet another example of how we trap women in a sticky web of contradictory expectations. Conservative politicians and pundits thoroughly approve of women who make home and hearth the centre of their existence, yet I haven't heard any of them raising any kind of fuss about the plight women who have done just that find themselves in once they are widowed. And, as we have seen from the stats, most women who stay married will become widows eventually. Five hundred and ninety dollars a fortnight is not much of a thank-you for a woman who has spent her whole life caring for others.

Most of the panel on that episode of *Q&A* were sympathetic to the idea that the Newstart rate ought to be raised, but, as so often happens in these discussions, people automatically assume that it is predominantly young people who find themselves on the dole. Of course this is true, up to a point. Youth unemployment is frighteningly high, especially in disadvantaged areas and in the regions. However, the group that almost never rates a mention is women over fifty. I was in the middle of writing this book at the time that *Q&A* episode went to air, so the plight of my generation was very much at the front of my mind. I tweeted the following in direct response to Wilson's ideologically doctrinaire comment about trampolines and hammocks: 'Many women over 55 are stuck on Newstart, forced to apply for jobs they are never going to get & leaving them terrifyingly vulnerable to homelessness #QandA'. Seventeen hours later my words had been retweeted 598 times and liked 1236 times. What struck me forcibly, however, were the many heartfelt responses I received from older women, including widows. Here is a sample, reproduced with permission of the authors:

> Yes, I am one of them. 64. 2 years ago I was a happy wife, respected employee of family business … Now, I'm the rubbish left over when the taxpayer died. Had to move 2.5 hours away from anyone familiar, just to get a house I could afford. 10 job apps a month in a country town (8/5/18 12.30 p.m.) @prudinx

From other responses I received, it seems some unscrupulous employers are using the few government incentive schemes that encourage them to hire older workers, such as Restart, to gain the subsidy but not commit to the worker:

> My mother was put off the day before her 3 month trial and govt incentive to employ older ppl ran out. She was gutted. Always received high praise for her work. This sort of rorting must occur but ppl too embarrassed to report. (8/5/18, 2.38 p.m.) @percivalsmum

Here is another:

> A single mum (54 years young) who spent quite a few years on a sole parent pension. I've got a decent job now, but will never own my own house, not much superannuation and a job loss away from being homeless. My future is frightening. (7/5/18 10.09 p.m.) @alicia_papp

And then this response to the one above:

> I'm hearing you Alicia 100 per cent. My boys will go. My ex husband has a ripper of a life. I raised 3 sons, worked, studied, struggled a lot. No super (well barely any) renting forever. What do we do? (8/5/18 12.10 p.m.) @rachelQuayle08

Anyway, you get the picture. I received numerous responses to my initial tweet, all of them saying very much the same things. There is an entire cohort of older women out there living in a state of anxiety about what their future may hold. And their fears are entirely realistic.

Many of the women I interviewed for this book have felt at risk of homelessness, have been homeless in the past, or are homeless now. 'Come August I will have been homeless for three years. I've been living in the car for five months,' says Susan. Women do all sorts of things to keep a roof over their heads. Pat ran a semi-boarding house for young people, an experience she found draining. And no wonder, because with homelessness comes terrible vulnerability, especially for women. Nerida faced a psychotic live-in manager at the only share house she could afford: 'I had to flee after he backed me into a corner, about to take a swing at me.' And, as she has since discovered, using public toilets can also be dangerous: 'A guy tried to jump me at the amenities one evening. Apparently he's a well-known sex pest.' When you are living in your car, forced to use public toilets to keep yourself clean, it is almost impossible to maintain any semblance of grooming, let alone look (or smell) attractive. The face of poverty is never a pretty or an employable one.

Every year Anglicare does a snapshot of housing affordability on a certain day. In 2018, it found there were 67,000 rental properties available in Australia on 24 March. Of those, three (no, that is not a typo—three) were affordable for people living on either Newstart or the Youth Allowance. I dare say if you were on the Widow Allowance things would not be much better. Older women have every right to be afraid.

These grudging, parsimonious and reluctant payments send a clear message to their recipients, male or female, old or young, black or white. You are a bludger. You are a loser. You are unwanted. You are worthless. Once, no doubt, all these women were young and full of hope, sure that they would find a man, settle down, have children and be loved and supported all their lives—the old 'happily ever after'. Tragically, it very rarely works like that.

Like all human beings, women internalise society's attitudes to them: never more so, perhaps, than as we age. If we are treated as superfluous to requirements, it's hard not to feel there is some truth in that. Our flesh—the only thing we were taught we had that was of any value—has let us down. It has become old, infertile, ugly and irrelevant. Women often feel tremendous shame about how their bodies look—all through their lives, of course, but particularly as they grow older. That is why there is such a lucrative market in anti-ageing products and in botox and more drastic forms of cosmetic surgery. Given how much we punish women for getting older, it's hardly surprising that many fight ageing with real desperation, frantically trying to stave off the inevitable. Some of this may have beneficial results. Despite their naturally higher percentage of body fat, women are less likely to be overweight than men. According to the Heart Foundation, 28.8 per cent of women were overweight in 2014–15 compared to 42.4 per cent of men. However, when it comes to obesity this gap narrows dramatically. Twenty-seven per cent of Australian women are obese compared with 28 per cent of men. Women also increase the amount of exercise they do as they age; men do the reverse. Fewer women are as physically active as their male peers when they are aged between fifteen and twenty-four (52.8 per cent of men are active compared to 47.7 per cent of women), but those figures flip in every other age group, with more than 50 per cent of women doing regular physical activity compared with around 40 per cent of men, until the over sixty-fives, when men and women start to do almost the same amount—46.7 per cent of men versus 47.1 per cent of women. If vanity or fear of the consequences of looking old drives women to stay more active for longer, that is a good thing.

However, the shame many women feel about their appearance, and—particularly—the failure of their body to match the idealised, youthful versions we are constantly bombarded with, has a detrimental effect on women's confidence about and willingness to engage in sex. If part of the thrill of sex (or, as it was chillingly referred to when I was young, 'the chase') is to see desire for you reflected in your partner's eyes, then it is understandable that many older women are terrified of being naked with a new partner and of letting them see what they really look like. No wonder so many older women prefer fucking with the lights off.

When society constantly tells you that you are past your use-by date, at best sexually invisible and at worst sexually repulsive, it is no wonder so many women literally hate and despise their own bodies—a feeling that is, as I said earlier, not helped by the peculiar double occupancy of pregnancy. We punish ourselves for not taking care of a body that many in society consider we do not really own. Now that is a major form of gender-wide gaslighting.

9

LOSS AND LAMENTATION

In theatre, opera, legend, folktales, fairy stories and country and western music, it is always the women who weep. It is they who are left to mourn the men who risk their lives either on the battlefield, at sea, in the hunt, or—these days—in the rat race, the concrete jungle or the vertiginous corporate ladder. There is even a particular kind of enclosed turret at the top of older seaside houses called a 'widow's walk', designed so a woman can pace its length while searching the horizon for her husband's returning vessel. Part of the reason for this bitter tradition may be that women generally live longer than men—if they survive the travails of childbirth, which most of them, of course, do these days. Men still predominantly go to war, to sea, to hunt, while women sit at home and wait, or so the story goes.

But it is not all myth and folklore. Women are much more likely to experience the loss of a partner and spend their later years alone, either as widows or divorcees. Given how much women of my generation and those of the generations that went before us were taught that men were their entire destiny, it is ironic how rarely this turns out to be true. Most women will outlive their husbands. According to the 2016 census, of people aged over eighty-five, 63 per cent are women and only 37 per cent are men. The single pension ($894 a fortnight) is disproportionately relied upon by women.

Yet despite how common this fate is, the widow—like the spinster—has always been a problem for society. We just don't like the idea of women without a controlling man (see the co-hosts of just about every TV breakfast show you can think of). Jane Austen's mother and her two unmarried daughters, Jane and her sister, Cassandra, were left homeless and dependent on the kindness of male relations—her wealthiest son—when their husband and father, the Reverend George Austen, died, taking with him his parish and the home and income that went with it. Once upon a time, when the main breadwinner died, when men really were the only possible financial plan a woman could have, the loss left many women cast into poverty. Given Austen's personal experience, it is not surprising she is the most practical and wryly realistic of the so-called 'romance' writers. She completely understood that marriage was an economic transaction for women at least as much as it was a romantic one. Genteel widows and spinsters living on next to nothing are staple characters in Austen's fiction. They are the forgotten people—forgotten by everyone, that is, except Austen, who was one of them.

In today's world, elderly widows remain vulnerable. Elder abuse is something that we are just starting to turn our attention to. What we are discovering, now that we are bothering to look, is yet another indication of how the disadvantages of being a woman in a patriarchal society accumulate over a lifetime. According to a 2015 study commissioned by Seniors Rights Victoria, the most common type of elder abuse is financial, and it is most often perpetrated by sons against their mothers—40 per cent of sons are the perpetrators versus 27 per cent of daughters. The most common scenario seems to go like this. The father dies and leaves his estate to his widow. Her children, particularly her sons, resent this and feel that the money is 'wasted' on their elderly mother and ought to be put to 'better' use by them.

Perhaps there is even an assumption that the ownership and management of assets and property are more naturally the province of men, particularly if the family has been a traditional one, where Dad held the purse strings. It is not uncommon in older couples that when one partner dies the other is left helpless, particularly when faced with tasks they never had to bother with while their spouse was alive. For widowers, it may mean they do not know how to shop or cook for themselves or how to operate the washing machine, dishwasher and other kitchen appliances. My husband and I bought and renovated a very run-down house a couple of decades ago. It was sold to us by an elderly bachelor who had lived there all his life with his ageing mother. After her death he lived on alone in the house for a decade or so. It became obvious as we began the renovation that no housework at all had occurred since her death. The son had simply let the dirt and decay accumulate around him. I suspect this may not be uncommon in houses occupied by elderly men living alone. Women face a different and even more devastating ignorance. Many of them have left all the finances to their husband. An elderly aunt of mine, once widowed, had no idea how to write a cheque or use a credit card. She had no idea how much money she had or didn't have. Such financial illiteracy can leave older women very vulnerable to all sorts of people, including their own children.

At the 5th National Elder Abuse Conference held in Sydney on 19–20 February 2018, Australian Banking Association (ABA) CEO Anna Bligh spoke about the dilemmas tellers face when they suspect a son, daughter or carer is draining the bank account of an elderly customer. The tellers often realise pretty quickly that something is wrong but have no protocols to follow or legal avenues to turn to, especially if the carer has power of attorney. According to Bligh, there are moves afoot to do something about this. The ABA is proposing that whistleblower protections be extended to include bank staff, and has released some guiding principles about how that could best be done. Not before time, either.

However, elder abuse is not just restricted to being cheated financially. It also includes emotional, psychological, physical and sexual abuse and neglect. According to the same Victorian study, women are 2.5 times more likely than men to be the victims of some kind of elder abuse, and not simply because they generally live longer. Recently two brothers aged thirty-nine and forty-two were charged with the manslaughter of their 73-year-old mother. The older brother was actually a member of the Australian Federal Police. Their mother died in hospital after being discovered at the family home suffering malnutrition, dehydration, bedsores and blood poisoning in a urine- and faeces-covered bed. The brothers stood to inherit $1.5 million from her.

Not all neglect and abuse are this extreme, but it does seem particularly unjust when the person who cared for you when you were small and helpless is left to waste away in a pool of excrement because you can't be bothered to return the favour. Perhaps many of us never quite get over the idea that our parents should care for us rather than the other way around. Women, particularly of my generation, were brought up in a world where they were the domestic servants for their husbands and children. When I was young I literally never saw it the other way around, and the habits and assumptions of a lifetime can be hard to break. Moreover, if as a society we have never shown much respect for women and their bodily, economic and emotional autonomy, it's not surprising we fail to do so as they age.

Of course, the most likely abuser a woman encounters in her life is not her sons or an unscrupulous carer, but her male partner. Far from the popular, conservative (if paternalistic) belief that heterosexual marriage offers the best 'protection' for women, domestic violence remains the leading health risk factor for women aged between eighteen and forty-four, higher than smoking, obesity or abuse of alcohol. Domestic violence, by the way, is also the most common precipitating event that tips women—of any age—into homelessness.

Yet despite horrifying statistics like this, most women still marry. Hope springs eternal despite so much evidence to the contrary. However, even if love triumphs and a couple manage to build and sustain a relatively contented relationship—and, contrary to the doom and gloom, you still have a 75 per cent chance of staying married, so the optimism is not entirely misplaced—there is a price to be paid.

Loneliness is something that we do not discuss enough, and it can become a particular issue as people age. The loss of a spouse is always devastating, even if it is by choice and through relatively amicable divorce. But the price for a happy and long-lasting relationship is inevitably grief for one of you, unless you die together in a car crash or something. It was the Queen who said that grief is the price we pay for love, and she is spot on. To lose a life partner after decades together must literally feel like the loss of a part of your own body, and the readjustment that is required is very challenging, particularly if you lose your partner when you are old. Perhaps the Queen was pondering her own future when she made this remark, as she and Prince Philip have now been married for seventy-one years and she famously fell in love with him seventy-nine years ago, when she was thirteen. However, perhaps it is better that women are more likely to face this loss, as there is evidence that it may be harder for men to adjust to being widowed than it is for women.

Australian men over eighty-five have the highest rate of suicide of any population group. They kill themselves at the rate of 39.3 per 100,000 compared to women of the same age, whose suicide rate is 5.7. As the rate of depression appears to decline in old age—although this is disputed—and assisted suicide as relief from a terminal illness has been discounted as a cause, the reason why so many elderly men suicide remains uncertain. I can't help wondering if losing a spouse has a much greater detrimental effect on an older man than it does on a woman. Women are often their husband's only emotional support, whereas women also get a great deal of support from their female friends.

The emotional and domestic labour that women do for their family continues into old age. This may be hard work, as I have pointed out, but it also maintains a routine for women and can give them a sense of remaining useful. Husbands and kids may come and go, but the washing needs doing, the food must be bought, carpets hoovered and the bed made regardless. When my grandmother entered her nineties she was no longer able to do the elaborate (and much appreciated and enjoyed) baking she had done for decades. However, whenever we visited her she had a ready supply of store-bought biscuits and cakes to tempt our tastebuds. She never gave up the tea trolley laden with sweet treats that had been a ritual part of visiting Granny since my earliest memories. The rhythm of her days continued unchanged until a day or two before her death at ninety-two.

It is also worth remembering that 70 per cent of divorces are instigated by women. Perhaps this is evidence that marriage may be experienced as more of a burden for wives than it is for husbands. If that is true, it is easier to understand why once a man's wife has died he loses much more than simply her company. And we do know suicide rates are higher among the divorced, separated and widowed and lowest among the married. One other possibility is due to the fact that Alzheimer's disease is more common in women than men and carers have a higher risk of suicide. Worse, men are more likely throughout their lives to successfully kill themselves than women, even though men are less likely to suffer depression or have suicidal thoughts. The fact that men often complete suicide rather than simply attempt it is down to the very different methods each gender chooses. Women are more likely to overdose on medications; men are more likely to hang or shoot themselves. Yet despite all the information we have and the many plausible theories, no-one as yet has any real idea why suicide spikes so dramatically among elderly men.

There is much emphasis these days on the need for people to age 'in place', by which is generally meant the family home. This is something that a great many older people themselves are also very determined about. There is a real fear of ending up in a nursing home. As our population ages, an entire industry is developing around the housing needs of older Australians. Retirement communities are popping up all over the place where wealthier and healthier older people can live independently while surrounded by their peers. Despite intermittent scandals about very high fees on entry and very low refunds on departure, and complicated contracts that seem almost to have been designed to confuse the vulnerable, many people find this style of living a bulwark against loneliness, particularly after the death of their partner. There has also been an increase in graded care communities, where residents can start out in independent units but if and when they become frail can move into higher levels of support. These may well be the way of the future—for those with the money, anyway.

Regardless of these residential innovations, many people fear another loss as they age: the loss of their own home. Hence the increasing number of government programs designed to help older people stay in them for as long as possible. The idea is that older people will benefit if they stay in their local community—something that may be all very well if their community has also stayed with them. The trouble is that it often doesn't. There is a natural turnover in established suburbs. People tend to buy into them when their children are young and then move out, or downsize, when their children have finally left the family home for good. A new, younger generation then moves in to replace them. What this means is that many older people, often women, are left in communities where the houses may remain the same (apart from relentless gentrification, renovations and extensions) but the people who live in them have all changed. Suburbs become dormitories, where most of the inhabitants return only to eat and sleep and the houses are empty during the day. This means the lone elderly person still rattling around in her big family home may have an even more profound sense of loss and isolation. Once this was her street, her community, her kids, her neighbours, her friends and her generation. Now, it can feel like she is surrounded by strangers busy with their own, very different lives.

It is inevitable that we will experience more grief and loss as we age. Our relatives, peers, colleagues and friends age alongside us, and increasing age increases the chances of death. Not all of the things we lose are due to death, however. In our middle age we may watch our parents enter old age and deteriorate before our eyes, succumbing to physical frailty and mental decline. The life journey of parent and child is a fascinating one (worth a book on its own, perhaps). Once, our parents loomed so large in our lives that they represented the whole world to us. As we get older and emerge from infanthood into childhood and from adolescence into adulthood, we leave that dependence on our parents behind. They inevitably decline in importance to us as we make our own way in the world and turn our focus to our own children, if we have them. Indeed, it is a parent's job to make themselves redundant. When they begin to suffer the 'insults of ageing', as writer Helen Garner calls them, their decline is, of course, a harbinger of what may happen to us as we continue to follow in their footsteps. To care for an ageing and bewildered parent—a duty usually shouldered by daughters—is to stare our own possible future in the face. For those without children, or who are estranged from them, while we may not suffer that unavoidable reminder of our own fragility and mortality, it is impossible not to wonder who will care for us when we grow old.

Ageing tests us with losses in other areas, as well (it was Bette Davis who said ageing wasn't for sissies). As I discussed in the previous chapter, women more rapidly lose their sexual appeal. Susan Sontag expresses perfectly why that loss, common to both genders, affects women so much more than men. She points out that Western culture allows men to have two standards of beauty, that of the boy and then the man, while women only have one standard, that of the girl. As she says, the beauty of the boy and the girl is very similar, featuring smooth skin, a slender body and more vivid colouring. But as the boy becomes a man, we accept the inevitable weathering that occurs in both face and body and even continue to find such signs of maturity attractive in their own way. We give no such leeway to the girl when she becomes a woman. To grow older for a female is to become less desirable. No wonder women try to hold back the clock every way they can, or, indeed, that the vast age gaps between male and female movie actors cast as romantic leads in films are so unexceptional—as long as it is the woman who is years younger than the man, of course, and not the other way around.

Nevertheless, all of us lose the strength, agility and robustness of youth. The stress of fighting gravity takes its toll, and for some, old age does not last very long. I have sometimes felt that every one of my decades has been marked by events that celebrate—or mourn—rites of passage. In my childhood it was yearly birthday parties and the relentless upward climb through grades at school. In my adolescence, outrageous parties characterised by noisy music, illicit alcohol and drug use, and experimenting with sex (yep, the 1970s were fun) marked my transition from childhood. Then came the decade of twenty-firsts, university graduations and, later, weddings, followed by baby showers and christenings. After that, sadly, divorces and, more happily, school reunions. This was followed by my own children's rites of passage—birthday parties, school and uni graduations, weddings and baby showers all over again. Now, as I enter my sixties, I am noticing an increase in funerals, and I guess that is only going to get worse (there are a few silver and golden wedding celebrations in there too, just to lighten the mix). Grief and loss are the next great lessons I am going to have to face. In only a few decades, very few of my generation will be left.

Perhaps one of the reasons we fear ageing so much is that it forces us to face the reality of our own mortality. I am always conscious of just how many older people support voluntary assisted dying, and how regularly the audiences at events debating this issue are filled with silver heads. (I am also well aware of the irony of how rarely any older people are included on the panels at such events.) It makes sense that control over how and when we die should feel so vital to the old: to the rest of us, death remains (we hope) theoretical. To those in their seventies and above, it is the next great adventure. Ageing makes you viscerally concerned about the manner of your dying, not just the inevitability of it. As we age and watch others we care about face their own final moments, we begin to see just how awful they can be. Who can blame the old for wanting to minimise their own suffering? But I think the fears the old have about dying are not just the desire to reduce pain, indignity and discomfort. I think their fears are very much about losing control. The old are relentlessly patronised by the young, and that loss of authority is experienced as a loss of power. The old are not stupid: they can see they have lost status and importance, and they know that puts them at risk. Many of the elderly dread dying because they fear that the way they die may be taken out of their hands and they will be helpless in the face of interventions, decisions and procedures that others decide for them, be they relatives or the medical profession. They dread, quite rationally and reasonably, that things will be done *to* them, rather than *for* them. And when I say 'them', I mean 'me' and 'us'.

As we age, we must face the loss of our youth with all the physical benefits that confers, and the loss of parents, friends, colleagues, peers and—possibly—our partner. We must also face the loss of respect, status and, often, our profession, our job and, far too frequently, our income. We also face the loss of control, and something that social researcher Hugh Mackay rates as the single most important need that must be met before we can live a satisfying life: the desire to be taken seriously. As my father said to me wistfully one day after he had turned eighty, 'I have lost my relevance. The future is no longer any business of mine.' Perhaps this is another clue about why so many elderly men find life increasingly insupportable.

In my own life, aged sixty as I write this, I have been fortunate. Most of the funerals I have attended so far have been for the parents of close friends or for elderly relatives, most of whom have lived long, rich and interesting lives. Of the two losses I found hardest to bear, one was the death of a vibrant 38-year-old woman who I worked with for a few years. She died, as far too many young people in Australia do, of melanoma. She left behind two very young children, and that was gut-wrenching. The other was a close friend who died suddenly of a cerebral haemorrhage two days after he had cooked us a fabulous meal at his home. The shock of that was profound. He also left behind a young child. All of us know what it is to lose people we care about. Some of us are much luckier in that respect than others. However, as you get older the loss of friends becomes an unavoidable price you must pay for your own longevity. There is a lovely—possibly apocryphal—story about an elderly Marlene Dietrich chatting with her old (in every sense of the word) friend Noël Coward. She was bemoaning how many of her friends were dying. Coward replied, 'Frankly, my dear, these days, I am relieved if my friends make it through lunch.'

Despite the inevitable losses, however, to live a long time is in itself a win. When we do eventually die, whatever kind of life we may have lived, we will not have missed out in the way those who were snatched earlier did. It was the writer Christopher Hitchens who said as he was dying of cancer at sixty-two that he felt like he was being forced to leave a fabulous party much earlier than he wanted to. He knew lots of lovely things would now happen without him.

Hitchens was an atheist, like me, and so his regrets were about the joys of the earthly life he was being forced to leave prematurely. For those with religious faith there may be compensations around the idea of dying: the chance of once again meeting loved ones who have died before you, perhaps, and the hope of living eternally in paradise with your god. I am aware that such beliefs offer very great comfort to many as they face their own demise, but they fill me with dread. The idea of eternal life has always made me feel very, very tired (imagine it just going on and on and on and on …) and also trapped—after all, death offers us a means of escape, even if mostly we have no inclination to choose it. To lose the option of death means no way to escape at all. The downside for the religious, however, is different. For them there is also the fear of judgement and of being found wanting—even, perhaps, a fear of hell. Hence the need for end-of-life religious rituals offering forgiveness and cleansing, such as the last rites. The atheist has no such hopes or fears. They suppose that they will merely cease to exist. Such a fate is often incomprehensible to believers. I have been asked many times by the religious what I think happens after death. I tell them that I believe what will happen after my death is exactly what happened before my birth: I will return to the oblivion from which I emerged. As I don't remember that as being in any way unpleasant, death holds the same fear for me as it did for Hitchens—namely, the fear of missing out (FOMO). Otherwise, I am relaxed about it. The manner and timing of my dying, of course, is another thing. Like everyone else I hope it happens peacefully, in my sleep, in my own bed, a few decades from now. I am also sadly aware that this is very unlikely. Only 10 per cent of Australians die in their own home. Seventy per cent of us will die in hospital, and far too many of us will suffer the indignity and pain of unnecessary interventions at the end of our life. CPR is legally required if there is no advance care directive on file, and horror stories have emerged of broken ribs and painful bruising on frail, elderly patients subjected to the procedure. Over half of them will die anyway. No wonder the elderly become so much more exercised about controlling their fate as they approach the end of their life.

Old age, however, precisely because we have all experienced losses, is also a time of triumph. I have often noted how many people become rather proud of their advanced years after they turn eighty. Rather than pretending to be younger than they are, they start to drop their venerable age into every conversation: 'I am eighty-four, you know, my dear,' and so on. I remember thinking when I turned sixty last June that while I could still die too young, I could no longer die young, and there was a sense of achievement in that. Of course, the proviso about the pleasures of living to a grand old age is that we retain the economic independence and physical and mental health needed to be able to continue to participate in and enjoy the party. To live year after year in the half-light of Alzheimer's or dementia, to live in a painful body that is crumbling around you, to live in continual fear of poverty or homelessness, or to live dependent on those who resent you, wish you were dead or may even physically, emotionally or financially abuse you, is another story altogether.

The loss of relevance, status and a sense of a stake in the future are all hard lessons, but it is probably the loss of job, profession and income that have the most profound day-to-day effects on us all as we age, particularly, of course, for women. Once, when the retirement age was sixty-five and most of the people who were given the gold watch were men, people lived for only a few years into their retirement. Indeed, our superannuation and pension systems were designed when life expectancy for men (the only gender anyone thought about then in terms of retirement) was sixty-eight. The money put aside by governments for the aged only had to last them a few years. Now, people may survive many decades after their paid working life is over. And the loss of relevance can be hard to take, particularly for men. For women, particularly women living alone, it can be the loss of income and community that bites the hardest, particularly if mobility becomes an issue.

However, not every story about ageing is a sad one. Many people do manage to live satisfying, productive and, yes, even sexually active lives through the decades. Christine and her husband survived what she described as some 'wobbly' times in their marriage and are now enjoying an active retirement: 'We started off paddling canoe marathons together in double kayaks, and now ride a tandem bike.' They are also taking on a challenging project: 'We are owner-building a major renovation/extension of our current house, and ironically, while it does my head in because it feels like it will never be done, and it eats up weekend recreational time, it's the work we do together on it that also binds us.' My own parents, aged eighty-seven and eighty-six, are a wonderful example of ageing well. Both (touch wood) remain fit and active. They would no more paddle a kayak, ride a tandem bike or owner-build than fly to the moon, but they see every play and film and are leading lights in their local branch of U3A (University of the Third Age).

While much is lost as we age, if we are fortunate we can gain both a bit of wisdom and the time and confidence to put it to good use. Here are some examples of the wisdom (some of it very hard-won) offered by the women I interviewed for this book.

> 'Don't leave it as long as I did (after having children) to get back into the workforce. Find a way to keep your hand in.'

> 'Get in control of superannuation now, particularly with casual jobs. Roll it over into one account. Try and understand it better than I do.'

> 'DON'T JUDGE OTHER WOMEN FOR THEIR LIFE CHOICES. [Caps as written] Whatever you decide to do, you're not superior. It might be better for you, but it's not "better". You have no idea what someone else's marriage and life situation are like. If you ever feel you need to discuss your decision, don't frame it so that the women who made the opposite choice feel like shit about themselves.'

> 'You are a human being with every right to social collateral, independence and self-determination. How you think, what you value and what you enjoy are much more important than whether you are "fuckable".'

'Do not accept abuse or bullying in any form to stay in a relationship or job. If one doctor, police officer or HR rep won't believe you, find another that does.'

'Make sure you are financially secure and that you ensure you put super away.'

'Go live your life, we moved the Victorian thinking [I am quoting verbatim here—I think my correspondent means we have moved on from outdated attitudes to women], use your common sense and brain, and never regret anything you do. It's all experience, hindsight is a great thing.'

'Treat women as equal, we can do anything a man can do except lift heavy objects. We are all citizens of this country and without women they lose their greatest asset.'

10

PAST OUR USE-BY DATE

The 55-year-old woman was a regular panellist on a popular TV show and had been for over five years, since the show launched. When it went into its next season, despite her personal popularity (particularly, it must be said, among women of a certain age), she was told she was no longer wanted. They needed to 'freshen' the line-up, the producers said. She knew perfectly well what 'freshen' was code for.

Then there was the very experienced and skilled presenter, writer and journalist who'd had to take time out from her busy career to care for her ageing parents. When she returned to the fray and attempted to pick up where she had left off she was told—without embarrassment, to her face—that the conference she used to work with regularly wanted a younger 'feel', and then that the editor's job (that she could do on her ear) needed someone no older than forty 'at the outside'. This second casual dismissal of her talents and experience came from a bloke well into his fifties, by the way.

Then there was the highly successful and admired management team (all blokes—yes, it happens to them too as they age) who had steered the company from debt-ridden to highly profitable over more than two decades. Just when they should have been enjoying the fruits of their labours, they were all made redundant to make room for 'generational change'.

Oh, and there's the woman who auditioned for a TV show only to be told that another woman had also auditioned and that they 'cancelled each other out'. Both women were over fifty, you see, and you could only have one of those per panel. Never mind that there was almost twenty years between them in age: one older woman is just like another, apparently.

Then there were the nine workers all made redundant as the consequence of a restructure. All nine were women over fifty. Coincidence? I doubt it.

When it comes to the workforce, employers have been shamed out of openly discriminating because of race or gender. There is also legislation outlawing these practices. Employers may still make such discriminatory decisions, of course, but they now know they have to pretend they're not. Only when it comes to age is it still perfectly acceptable to be overt about the fact you don't want someone—no matter how highly qualified—simply because you see them as too old.

And this attitude is not exclusive to employers. I remember reading a pompous little article from a young man telling baby boomers to 'get out of the way' (his way, I think he meant). There have been a number of books published on a similar theme. The general thesis seems to be that we've (boomers) had our time and it is the next generation's turn. The article that got my goat appeared about ten years ago, when I was only fifty. I was so infuriated by it that I took the trouble to contact the author. I pointed out that female baby boomers had largely put their careers on hold to devote their time and energy to bringing up entitled little shits like him (I didn't quite use those words, but that was what I was thinking), and if he expected us to put our lives on hold again for his generation, he had another think coming. To his credit, he did reply with a mea culpa. He had not thought about the different life trajectories of female baby boomers (or women of any generation, in fact) and agreed that it was a bit rich to expect us to put our hopes and dreams aside yet again for the benefit of the young. It is extraordinary to me how often I have to point out to otherwise quite thoughtful and intelligent men that they have not taken into account how their idea, policy or program might affect women. We're only slightly more than 50 per cent of the population, after all.

Sometimes women of a certain age are discriminated against as a job lot. A few years ago I was chatting to a board member of a very successful regional arts festival. I congratulated him on its success, and he responded by saying that, yes, it had all been going very well, but their next task was 'to change the audience'. 'Change the audience?' I repeated his words just to make sure I had heard them correctly. 'Why? What's wrong with the audience?' This man (aged about forty-five, from the look of him) pulled a smelled-something-nasty face. 'Well, they're all older women …' Let's forget about the rudeness of saying that to me, an older woman. Let's not mention the lack of business nous that would allow you to openly despise your customers. His unselfconscious response remains the most egregious representation of ageism and sexism I have ever witnessed. No wonder older women struggle so hard to take up any space in our community. Even their money and appreciation are seen as undesirable.

Losing your job and being unable to find another one, not being offered interesting opportunities in your field, being despised in general, are bad for your income, of course, but they are bad for all sorts of other things as well, including your mental health. As I write this, I can't help remembering—a little guiltily—an ad agency I worked at in the 1990s, when I was still in my oblivious forties. There was a lovely older bloke who no longer worked at the organisation (I have no idea whether he'd left voluntarily or not) who nonetheless used to appear in the lunch room a couple of times a week. He'd arrive mid-morning and often hang about till mid-afternoon, just shooting the breeze with whoever was around. He wasn't miserable or bitter.

On the contrary, he was always cheerful, enthusiastic and interested in what you were doing. He'd often share experiences with you from his days running important accounts. He was a little old-fashioned: smartly moustachioed and bow-tied, and the sort of guy who stood whenever a woman entered the room and pulled the chair out for her. He was a throwback to the *Mad Men* days of yore, but in the nicest way. Younger (and employed) staff would often make gentle jokes about him behind his back. Never to his face, I am pleased to say—everyone was very kind to him. It was hard not to be: he was charm itself. However, we all felt vaguely sorry for him and, if we had only admitted it to ourselves, a little uneasy. Was his inability to let go of his job, his obvious sense of being at a loose end, going to be our fate too? Looking back on it, I see a man with skills, talent and energy to burn desperately trying to find an outlet for them. I wish I knew what happened to him. I hope it was good.

I defy anyone to reach their mid-fifties without having been left open-mouthed by suddenly being the recipient of assumptions based purely on your age. If you haven't, you are either extremely lucky or extremely rich and powerful. For the rest of us, it hits us like a slap. However, considering the baby boomers never give up anything without a fight (hello, are you looking at me?), this is perhaps why there is such a stirring of new energy around ageism and the determination of many older people, not least older women, to fight any attempt to dismiss us as past our use-by date. For many women, our fifties are just when we are revving up again.

All stereotyping and discrimination against any group in society is fundamentally stupid, but ageism has to be the dumbest of all. After all, every time a younger person discriminates against, disrespects or dismisses someone purely because of their age, they are shooting their future self in the foot—if they are fortunate and live long enough to get old, of course. The increasing likelihood, however, is that most people—particularly the economically fortunate—will reach what are patronisingly referred to as their 'senior years'.

The average lifespan for a woman in Australia today is 87.3 years. One hundred years ago, in 1918, it was 63.3. That means women today can expect to live twenty-four years longer than our grandmothers did. However, it sometimes feels as if nothing about our society has caught up with that fact. For example, the average age of 'retirement' (voluntary or not) is currently 58.8 years for men and 52.3 years for women. Yet if you, like me, were born after 1 January 1957, you are not eligible for the old age pension until you are sixty-seven. If you have superannuation (and remember, one-third of women currently retire with no superannuation at all), you can access it between the ages of fifty-five and sixty, depending on when you were born. Nonetheless, given so few of us have much put aside for our old age, if so many women leave the workforce—either voluntarily or not—a good fifteen years before they can access the pension, what on earth are they living on? Not all of them can be depending on the financial support of their husband, particularly considering the rates of divorce and widowhood.

There is a particularly cruel irony in this, given how much more difficult it becomes to stay employed and get a new job, or even new contract work, as we age. The way governments are increasingly expecting older Australians to support themselves financially and the way the workplace airily sheds those same older people are fundamentally at odds. No wonder the fastest-growing group among the homeless are women over fifty-five. Since 2011 there has been a 10 per cent increase in homelessness for women, particularly older women. And in 2016–17, for the first time since records started being kept, more women than men sought assistance from specialist homelessness services. Far too many older women are facing a perfect storm of disadvantage.

I have spoken to women over fifty who have been made redundant and now find it almost impossible to find other work—of any kind, no matter how skilled they are. Teri's story is typical: 'I became a full-time carer for my mother. Since her passing I have been unable to gain employment. Being on Newstart is extremely difficult. I am unable to afford rent and live with both my children in order to survive.'

Too young for the age pension, too well for any disability support, these women are condemned to try to exist on unemployment benefits. Forget the appallingly small amount of money they receive or even the increasingly punitive, guilty-just-for-needing-it hoops they must jump through. All unemployed Australians must now put together a 'jobs plan' and meet a set of what are called 'mutual obligations'. If you are over fifty-five, these include thirty hours per fortnight of paid work, self-employment, approved voluntary work or a mix of these. Imagine how soul-destroying it must be every fortnight to rack your brains as to how you can put all that together when the workplace has already told you, in no uncertain terms, that you are surplus to requirements. We toss these women aside and then we rub their noses in their irrelevance. If they fail to fulfil their (ahem) mutual obligations they can be judged to be 'in breach' and lose their income entirely for a time. Our cruelty sometimes knows no bounds. The women I have spoken to tell me their stories with tears in their eyes.

Perhaps that's why so many older people, both men and women, take their redundancy payments, if they get them, or their super, if they have any, and buy themselves a job by purchasing a business or a franchise. Older Australians are increasingly taking on other people's ironing, mowing lawns, packing supermarket shelves, doing nannying work and cleaning houses. All of which is all very well—as long as their health holds out.

And that's the rub. Our very occupation can have a compounding effect on our health as we age. This can be a particular problem for men who have worked in physically demanding occupations. A lifetime spent as a brickie or plumber or builder can mean an old age spent struggling with arthritis, painful joints and a bad back. However, many female jobs are physical, too. Nursing is notoriously hard on the back, and child care can exert an immense physical toll. Years hunched over a computer can have excruciating consequences. Repetitive strain injury, carpal tunnel syndrome and other conditions resulting from overuse of our fine motor skills are the most common workplace-related injuries, costing the US economy over US$20 billion a year in workers compensation payments.

The way we earn our income can negatively affect that very same income in later life. Expenses inevitably go up in unexpected ways as we age due to deteriorating health, but if we are forced by economic necessity or government regulation to work long hours at whatever occupation we can get, meaning one that is often low-skilled, low-paid and physically demanding, there is an extra catch 22. Judged as too old and past our use-by date for the work we can do, we may be compelled to undertake work our ageing bodies can't do. Which means our health may be directly affected by our work, starting a vicious downward spiral. The terrific Ken Loach film from 2016, *I, Daniel Blake*, was all about the descent into just such an economic and bureaucratic hell of a 59-year-old carpenter. Diagnosed with a heart condition, he is advised by his doctor not to work until he can get the necessary surgical treatment. Unfortunately, the British welfare system, now as heartless as its Australian counterpart, will not accept his doctor's diagnosis. Blake becomes captive to a system that refuses to believe him or his doctor on principle. The punitive and suspicious attitudes that now characterise welfare systems in the West (thanks, neoliberalism) mean that everyone seeking help is assumed to be guilty until proven innocent. Australia experienced its own version of this during the recent Centrelink robo-debt collection debacle, where welfare recipients of all kinds, from the very young to the very old, were sent letters demanding repayment of often large sums that the agency claimed the recipients had been overpaid. Vulnerable people all over the country went into meltdown in response, with many unable to discover whether the sum they were accused of owing was correct or not. In the Loach movie, the effects of this punitive attitude towards the unfortunate were fatal.

Even if you are not relying on welfare or a menial occupation to survive, ageing itself can get expensive. GPs understandably are aware that the odds of developing life-threatening conditions increase exponentially the longer we live, so they do their job and take precautions. Anyone over sixty can tell you how much of their time is taken up with medical tests and specialist appointments of all kinds. Our health system is pretty good, but Medicare generally does not keep up with what doctors—particularly specialists, pathologists and radiologists—charge. The gap between the Medicare rebate and the actual cost can be a huge hurdle for people on low or fixed incomes, even if they get some kind of pensioner discount. If they are fortunate enough to have paid employment and so are ineligible for any support, they may have to save for weeks to afford a medical appointment. Also, as people age, they find they are prescribed a bewildering array of medications. Once again, Australians are a great deal more fortunate than the ageing citizens of places like the US, for example, thanks to the Pharmaceutical Benefits Scheme, which helps insulate us from the true cost of drugs. Like many foreign tourists, I was gobsmacked when I travelled to the US and had to seek medical help when I wrenched my back lifting a suitcase (I always pack too much stuff). It cost me well over US$500 for one visit to the doctor and for the medication he gave me. I got it all back through travel insurance, but it did make me wonder how on earth Americans manage, particularly those on low incomes. I dare say many of them, particularly the ageing poor, don't.

My parents are well able to support themselves financially and are now in their late eighties. They are both also hale and hearty. Nevertheless, the number of pills they must take each morning has to be seen to be believed. They have those daily pill organisers to keep their medications under control. Obviously, given my parents' vigour, whatever they take is doing them good, but none of their pills are free. How must it be for elderly people who do not have the financial good fortune my parents enjoy? Do they simply do without the medication they need so they can pay the gas bill? A 2017 Productivity Commission report said that 900,000 Australians put off going to the doctor because of cost, and 7.6 per cent (that's almost two million of us) do not buy the medications they are prescribed because they are too expensive. Not all of the Australians putting off needed medical treatment will be elderly, of course, but it is a safe assumption—given the pernicious intersection of increasing medical requirements due to age and lower incomes for the same reason—that far too many of them will be. And dental care is even more inaccessible for too many people. A school principal I know who has always worked in schools in disadvantaged areas says that if you want to know what the socioeconomic status of an area is, don't look at income or taxation data, just look at the state of the local residents' teeth. Yep, even in prosperous Australia.

There is an increasing body of research that reveals that where you reside, how educated you are and how much you earn have a real impact on how long you can expect to live. And this is just another example of how the divide between the women over fifty who are fortunate and those who are not is exacerbated. Poverty directly affects lifespan. Not just your own lack of income, either: the poverty of your neighbours also affects how many years you may have left. A Dutch study done in 2000 found that people who lived in neighbourhoods with high levels of unemployment, disability and poverty had a higher mortality rate than those who lived in neighbourhoods with lower levels of these things. So if you are forced to sell your house to provide yourself with an income and must therefore move to a less expensive area so you can afford the rent, that's another way that becoming impoverished in old age can directly affect both your health and your longevity.

If you find yourself unable to pay the rent even in a crappy area, according to another Dutch study, conducted between 2001 and

2010, homelessness has a greater impact on women's life expectancy than it does on that of men. Life expectancy for a homeless man at age thirty was eleven years lower than that of the general population. For women at age thirty it was 15.9 years lower. There is some (very) small comfort for those who find themselves on their beam end, however, and it is that this difference decreased with age.

A similar lethal effect of homelessness has been reported in Australia, although the study that showed this only looked at men. A 2014 Tasmanian study into men staying at a homeless shelter in Hobart discovered that the average age of death for those who had passed through its doors was forty-eight.

Remember earlier in this chapter when I referred to the average life expectancy? Well, as with all averages, that means some people will live longer than average and some people will have much shorter lives. According to a 2015 report, life expectancy for wealthy baby boomers has increased but life expectancy for those who are poor has not and may even be declining slightly. Wealthy male baby boomers can expect to live for 88.8 years; the poorest for 76.1. For women, the richest can expect to reach almost ninety-two, while the poorest are unlikely to make it to their seventy-ninth birthday. These are US figures, but it is unlikely that Australia is very different, particularly given the shameful stats regarding the life expectancy of Aboriginal and Torres Strait Islander people. Indigenous Australians can expect to live an entire decade less than the rest of us: Indigenous men have a life expectancy of 69.1 years and Indigenous women 73.7. Indigenous Australians generally still experience more disadvantage across the entire spectrum of their life, from before their birth until their (usually much earlier) death. Nevertheless, anyone who is living in poverty, regardless of their background, has their health negatively impacted. In fact, low socioeconomic status cuts 2.1 years off an Australian's life. To put that into perspective, like domestic violence and its effect on the health of women, that's more of an effect on lifespan than obesity, excessive drinking or high blood pressure. Of course, one of the other consequences of doing it tough is what health professionals refer to as 'co-morbidities'. What they mean by this is that people living precarious lives tend to have a complex web of other, related problems too. For example, disadvantaged people are more likely to smoke than other Australians. Fifty per cent of Indigenous Australians are smokers, as are 70 per cent of homeless people, as many as 90 per cent of people with a mental illness, up to 91 per cent of those with drug and alcohol problems, 60 per cent of young people deemed 'at risk', and 46 per cent of single mothers. Forty-two per cent of low-income smokers say they prioritise buying cigarettes ahead of food. All forms of addiction, including gambling, are possibly ways of self-medicating for those living marginal and difficult lives. They provide an escape from reality, a moment of relaxation, and are a source of (relatively) affordable pleasure.

There may be another, hidden morbidity that results from homelessness, and it ranges from self-harm to suicide. The homeless man with the bottle of fortified wine in a brown paper bag is so ubiquitous he has become a cliché. We may even automatically assume that to be homeless is to be an alcoholic, and blame homeless people's shorter lifespan on their consumption of booze (as we censoriously sip our chardonnays and sav blancs). However, if the caller who rang a recent radio program about older women and homelessness is anything to go by, there may be another even more drastic way out. The caller was herself an older woman, and she rang to tell us that she had been homeless in the past and was once more facing the loss of her current residence. This time, however, as she said in a steely voice, she was not afraid. She was certain that she would never spend another night without a permanent roof over her head. If what she feared came to pass and she was evicted, she said calmly, she would simply kill herself. Death was vastly preferable to living on the streets.

It is hard to blame the woman who rang the radio program for contemplating such an extreme solution. After all, there can be no more emphatic way to tell a person that she is past her use-by date than to cast her out onto the streets—twice. This woman, as she confided later off air, was educated and had worked part time for most of her life in relatively low-paid occupations—a very typical work history for a woman of her (and my) generation. Redundancy in her fifties and then a series of health crises had eaten up what little super she had, so she had sold her house to live off the capital. Unable to find even the lowest-skilled work, she quickly ate through the equity she had in her house and found herself unable to cover her costs. No-one, it seemed, much cared. Past her use-by date in every way possible, she came up with a plan to avoid what she saw as the very worst fate. She already knew what it felt like to experience the terror, shame and misery of having no fixed address. Fortunately, thanks to the radio producer and announcer and her courage in sharing her story, the radio station got her details, contacted the social housing provider in her state and managed to find her a permanent and affordable home.

Sadly, few such stories end as well. In 2017 I emceed a conference run by the Shellharbour City Council. Shellharbour is a coastal area about 100 kilometres south of Sydney. The conference was about women and homelessness—a growing issue in the area. Many older women move to areas outside major metropolitan cities because housing is more affordable there. Unfortunately, once they move they may also find that transport and lack of a familiar community are a problem, particularly if they are single. And being single and older are two of the major risk factors for women tipping into homelessness.

What made this conference unique—and a great privilege to be involved in—was that the delegates were not researchers, housing providers or community workers: they were the women themselves. The conference featured a series of panels that enabled the women in the room to directly question those paid to work in the area. The stories, which began to flow thick and fast, were heart-rending. One woman stood up and told us that she had never, until that moment, shared her story honestly with anyone. She had put on a brave face to her family and friends for, as it turned out, twenty years. Her story was typical. She had married young, had a high-school education and worked in an office until she had children. Then she stayed at home caring for her family, depending on her husband's pay packet for support. Then their marriage broke up. They divorced and she got custody of the kids and the house, but not much else. She went back to work part time in a low-skilled, low-paid job. The kids grew up and left home. She got retrenched and left her job with a small redundancy and the pitiful amount of super she had managed to amass given her low pay, part-time hours and relatively short time in the workforce. Unable to find another job because of her age and lack of skills, she sold up and moved to a cheaper area, Shellharbour. As rents and living costs rose she very quickly worked through her savings—what she'd made from the family home after paying off the remaining mortgage. She had been facing housing stress for decades and had had her name down on the list for affordable housing in the area since 1998. In 2017, she was still waiting. She wept as she told us her story and confessed to her shame over her poverty and insecurity, but, like the other women in the room, she was angry too. She had done nothing wrong. Indeed, she had done everything society had told her to do, and this was her reward.

Her courage inspired others to tell their stories. Many were similar to hers, but some women in the room had run businesses or been employed in managerial positions. They saw themselves as archetypal members of the middle class and had never expected to find themselves eking out an existence on Newstart, skipping meals to pay the rent. Even some of the women who had organised the conference, who were part-time community workers, had found themselves no longer able to rent apartments on their own and had returned to the living style of their youth—namely, share houses. Others rented out rooms in their own home to help keep up the payments. Some had made a profession of house-sitting or pet-minding and spent their lives moving from place to place.

Most women try to keep such precarious living situations a secret because they are ashamed. Hence the reason why this is still a relatively invisible problem. We see many more homeless men on the streets than we do homeless women. Researcher Yvonne Hartman and her colleague Sandy Darab from the School of Arts and Social Sciences at Southern Cross University published a report in 2013 called 'Understanding single older women's invisibility in housing issues in Australia', a subject they began researching in 2011. In 2016 Hartman said that many women won't seek help until they are desperate because 'they are ashamed that they don't have anywhere to live and are reluctant to go to service providers until they're in a bad way … By then they have multiple and complex problems and it is much more difficult to help them.' The women who poured out their hearts at the Shellharbour conference back up her research in every particular, as do the women who have trusted me with their stories for this book. Some of them, like Elaine, have been struggling with housing stress and homelessness for so long they have developed skills at navigating their way around whatever support is on offer: 'In three years I have dealt with ten different agencies. Over the holidays I got three weeks respite. I use every food bank and support agency I possibly can, to ensure I keep the car.'

A car, by the way, that doubles as her home.

11

INVISIBILITY V. INDEPENDENCE

There is no point avoiding the truth: the third stage of life is primarily a process of letting go. When it ends, our final task is to let go of life itself. Accompanying that process is an inevitable decline. You can slow down that decline with exercise, diet, keeping active and engaged, medical interventions, even plastic surgery, but you cannot stop it. Of course, that decline can also be hastened by many things, not least poverty, the neighbourhood you live in, stress, lack of social connection, insecure housing, and everything else that accompanies disadvantage.

But the third stage is not all a tale of woe. There are compensations that accompany growing older. Not everything gets worse—some things may even improve. As we age, if we are fortunate enough to hold on to our marbles, our outside may get worse but our inside can get better, stronger and more resilient. The years we have lived, the events we have survived, the blows we have recovered from and the perspective we have gained simply by staying alive are assets, not least because they can help us weather the difficulties of getting old.

When we were young we did not know what we know now. We did not know, for example, that everything passes. When I was young and struggling with an anxiety neurosis, I can remember how awful it was to believe that everything I was feeling and experiencing would last forever. If I felt scared, depressed, bewildered and lost (I often did when I was young; I rarely do now), I thought I would always feel that way. If I had insomnia (I often did when I was young; I rarely do now), I thought I would be forever unable to sleep. If I was humiliated, I felt that everyone was talking about me, pointing fingers and pouring scorn; now I know most people are not interested in me and have not noticed the faux pas or thoughtlessness that has made me squirm inside. And even if they have, they won't for long (I was once the butt of a social media pile-on—it only lasted a couple of days, then evaporated in a puff of angry smoke). Now I understand that bad experiences pass, as do good ones. I am no longer afraid of flying, and all my other irrational fears (once, I had plenty) have gone too; I think, eventually, they just bored me. I am even far less afraid of pain than I used to be. I have experienced so much more of it now and realise that it also passes, but, even if it doesn't, fighting it only makes it worse. All of that—I think we call it wisdom—takes time. You have to live for quite a while before you start to understand much about the business of living.

So with longevity comes a sense of perspective, for most of us. Indeed, apart from the anxiety that often accompanies forms of dementia, almost all mental illness is most intense when we are young. The prevalence is greatest among people aged 18–24 and the illness generally becomes less debilitating as we age. That fact alone ought to give us pause before we accept the conventional idea that youth is always carefree and old age always careworn. The opposite may be true more often than we realise.

The young, particularly those of this current, very protected generation, are untried, and they know it. I sometimes think that to be young is to be insecure for just that reason. The young do not yet know how strong they are (much stronger than they think, in my experience); the old are tested and true. We have learnt, often the hard way, how to minimise unnecessary misery—there being quite enough of it that you can't avoid—and maximise enjoyment. We know what battles are worth fighting and which ones we can afford to let go. We usually (I may still be working on this one) know when to speak up and when to keep quiet. We know what we can't change and what we can.

Not everyone gains wisdom as they age, of course. There will always be some older people who appear to go through life with both eyes firmly shut. A young fool often (though, thankfully, not always) becomes an old fool. But the opportunity to learn the lessons taught by just living through six or more decades is open to anyone who cares to notice it.

For women I think the lessons are harder to avoid, perhaps because we are less protected from them as members of what remains a subordinate group. Far from the loss of our sexual attractiveness being all downside, it brings with it unforeseen gifts. Invisibility has its advantages. If they are lucky enough to be financially secure, older women often find themselves able to exercise independence in a way they haven't for years. What women gain as they age, ironically enough, is time. This may seem an incongruous gift, given that when we grow old we have more time behind us than we have ahead of us, but it is a real one nevertheless.

For women, freed at last from the inexorable demands of our biology, if we have the money we now also have the time to do the things we have always wanted to do. Even if we don't have very much money, as long as we have secure housing and a regular income that covers our expenses and can be relied upon, we may now have time to enjoy our friends, our gardens, our hobbies, our families and our community. The ranks of volunteers are often filled with the recently retired. Many older people, both men and women, grasp the opportunity this extra time offers them to get active about the issues they really care about. A friend of mine from the advertising industry, now in her seventies, is an indefatigable and very effective campaigner for those, like her, who suffer from chronic pain. Indeed, older women with time on their hands are a resource the value of which we have yet to properly understand. These are women who, like my friend, are highly skilled and effective. They are also self-confident, having survived in often-hostile, male-dominated workplaces for decades. They are now free to take those skills and use them for the benefit of others—for good, if you like, instead of evil. Some of them famously sit outside proposed gas fracking sites cheerfully knitting while politely denying access to those who would exploit the environment. Known as Knitting Nannas Against Gas (KNAG), they began as part of the Lock the Gate Alliance and now have forty chapters all over Australia and have expanded into the US and the UK. Whenever I picture the dilemma faced by local coppers trying to move these savvy (and deceptively sweet) older ladies along, I am reminded of the quiet power of the old and the wise.

Older women are prominent among those who fight hard and doggedly for the rights of the refugees locked up indefinitely on Manus and Nauru. They use their increasingly powerful skills and networks to give voice to those who might otherwise be forgotten. Perhaps when you have had your own experience of what it is like to go unnoticed and invisible, you are particularly sensitive to the plight of others who are going unheard. The organisation Grandmothers Against Detention of Refugee Children is another example of how older women are putting their skills, time, energy and emotional intelligence to good and important use. Indigenous women, particularly female elders, have long been prominent in the fight for the rights of the original Australians. Faith Bandler led the successful fight for Aboriginal Australians to be accepted as full citizens in 1967. In 2018 the official theme of NAIDOC (National Aborigines and Islanders Day Observance Committee) Week, 'Because of her, we can!', celebrated the contribution of Aboriginal and Torres Strait

Islander women to the survival and progress of black Australians since European settlement. Many of the remarkable women showcased in both mainstream and social media were elders.

Other accomplished women are using their time and money in different ways to effect change. There is a very active philanthropic network called Women Donors. Not all of its members are (as yet) older, but they have had professional success and are getting together to use their wealth to help women who are in less fortunate circumstances. Philanthropy that involves women supporting other women is in its infancy, but as more and more women conquer the previously exclusively male bastions of work and money, this is a form of giving we can expect to become much bigger and more influential. We already know it is the most effective form of philanthropy: according to CARE Australia, if you bring a woman out of poverty she will bring four other people with her.

Because of the different way women see the world thanks to their own life experiences, the power of female giving is likely to bring the circumstances that disproportionately impact on the wellbeing of women and girls into sharper focus. Such things as the impact the lack of reproductive rights, or child marriage, or sex trafficking have on the ability of women and girls to keep themselves and their families out of poverty are situations that women who have birthed children and raised families themselves—albeit in much more fortunate circumstances—are likely to have more understanding about than people who have not had those experiences. Women are much more likely, for example, to empathise with how lack of access to basic feminine hygiene products can keep menstruating girls out of school.

Feminism, although it may as yet be incomplete, is a whole-of-society—indeed, whole-of-world—project. In fact, the threat to feminist gains represented by men's rights activists, conservative religious groups (especially in the US and other soft and hard theocracies) and macho white supremacist movements around the world has energised women who realise that they have not only money and time but also clout. The following are US statistics, but there is no doubt they reveal a trend that is happening all over the developed world. This revolutionary generation of women are vastly more financially formidable than any such generation before them. That is one of the best results of the very different kind of life they have lived compared to the one they were brought up to expect. The fruits of their independence have, for many, been very profitable indeed.

The number of female-owned US businesses turning over US$10 million or above annually increased by 57 per cent in 2013. Forty-five per cent of US millionaires are now women, and 48 per cent of estates worth over US$5 million are female controlled. In 2013, 60 per cent of the wealthiest women had amassed their own assets. There are some estimates that by 2039 two-thirds of the wealth in the US will be controlled by women. No wonder the more bellicose (yet fragile) men in our society are becoming so uneasy. It has never been the hand that rocks the cradle that rules the world—it has always been the hand that signs the cheque. And that hand is increasingly a female one. As more women control more of the world's wealth, power will inevitably be redistributed.

However, while it does this battered old feminist's heart good to see so many women accumulating the money, power and influence that will continue to change society, it is hard to celebrate those gains when so many women continue to miss out. The divide between the women who are doing well and those who are not remains stark. This is not unique to women, of course. Many commentators and economists have become increasingly concerned about growing inequality, particularly in the most prosperous societies. In Australia, the ABS reported in 2017 that the richest 10 per cent of Australians are sixty times wealthier than those in the poorest 10 per cent. That is up from fifty-two times wealthier in 2013–14, a rise of 13.2 per cent. Inequality and the failure of so-called 'trickle-down economics' have also been blamed for the rise of the far right in previously liberal democracies—most spectacularly in Trump's US.

What is also troubling is that as we have watched inequality grow, we have seen a concurrent increase in our tendency to blame those at the bottom for their own misfortune. In the West, at least, there seems to have been a return to the Victorian attitude of the deserving and undeserving poor. In Australia, goaded along by some of the less thoughtful parts of our media, we love to kick the dole bludger. As a result, we spend an inordinate amount of time, energy and confected outrage trying to squeeze every last unearned penny out of those who have very little. The irony of this is that we do so without much awareness about how many unearned pennies we are showering on those who are doing much better. Perhaps we are actually worse than the Victorians, because we have callously and self-servingly divided society into the undeserving poor and the deserving rich.

An interesting example of how blind we are to the amount of middle-class welfare various governments (of all political persuasions) have pork-barrelled away over the decades is the outcry that greeted ALP Opposition leader Bill Shorten's announcement about limiting dividend imputations. Like most of the largesse taxpayers provide to the already comfortable (or downright wealthy), this is a complex, hard-to-wrap-your-head-around scheme that costs the nation's budget an ever-increasing amount, and I do not intend to attempt to give you a full explanation here. Suffice to say, it is a tax device that allows tax paid by a company to be attributed (or imputed) to the shareholders of that company, thereby delivering to them a tax credit. Other countries have similar systems that assess the shareholder's tax liability as zero if the tax has already been paid (or 'franked') by the company. Only in Australia do we actually give money back to people (many of them self-funded retirees) for tax they have not paid. Debate on this question was heavily skewed when opponents claimed that Shorten's proposed change would 'unfairly' affect retirees on what were called low incomes. What the opponents really meant was 'low taxable' incomes, and that is a very different thing, given that many self-funded retirees now pay little or no tax at all thanks to the Howard Government and its superannuation concessions for over-sixties. Such retirees may enjoy quite high actual incomes and accumulated assets but, because of their age, still have low taxable incomes. Whatever you may personally think of the policy suggestion, whether you support the Liberal–National Coalition, the ALP, the Greens, One Nation or the Calithumpians, I give you this example to illustrate how often discussions are confused by small omissions or by providing narrow, technically correct information that only illuminates part of the whole picture. The privileged are particularly good at painting a picture that makes it look as if they are being hard done by. Perhaps that's why they are the privileged. See any men's rights activist website if you doubt me.

Far from it being the poor who are draining Australia dry, new modelling has been released that shows it is the concessions we give to the wealthy that are really costing taxpayers dearly. The Per Capita think tank and Anglicare have shown that the 20 per cent of Australians who are the richest taxpayers cost every worker in the country around $37 per week. That's a higher per-weekly cost to the taxpayer than the age pension ($35), families with dependent children ($20) and people with disabilities ($17). In fact, it turns out that the much-demonised recipients of unemployment benefits, many of whom are older women being humiliated regularly on Newstart, cost workers a measly $6 a week. The $37 a week we rather stupidly give to those who are already doing very nicely, thank you, is made up of the cost to our already tight national budget of all the tax concessions we offer them as a group. These include superannuation tax concessions, negative gearing, capital gains tax concessions, the use of discretionary trusts, the exemption from GST of private health insurance and private education, and the exemption from capital gains tax of a person's principal place of residence.

Many of those who describe themselves as self-funded retirees are fiercely proud of their independence, particularly their financial independence. They are often convinced that their self-funded status means they are the opposite of a drain on the taxpayer. Unfortunately, if they are in the top 20 per cent of Australians in terms of net worth, it turns out they are a bigger drain on the taxpayer than anyone else—a basic inequity that remains largely invisible. Time for some root-and-branch tax reform, perhaps, particularly as the divide between rich and poor grows wider. Moreover, the accumulation of tax concessions like the ones that disproportionately benefit the wealthy, and often the older wealthy, helps drive the growing anti-baby-boomer sentiment and rhetoric that is becoming more noticeable among the young. Who can blame them, particularly given how much we are asking them to give to us? Many women over fifty will benefit from this middle-class welfare alongside their male counterparts. However, given that more women are at the lower end of the socioeconomic scale in our society and more men are at the top, anything that compounds disadvantage disproportionately impacts women. Almost more infuriatingly, anything that compounds advantage disproportionately helps men. Here is a recent example: the LNP's Government's proposed income tax cuts will benefit male taxpayers at about a 2:1 ratio because so many more men than women earn higher salaries.

It is hardly surprising, therefore, that so many of those at the bottom end of our society dread getting older. I recently saw a social media post from a very accomplished female writer and intellectual about her approaching sixtieth birthday. The post was couched in dread. As the full-time carer for her elderly mother, her ability to earn is severely curtailed and she fears that growing older will make it harder for her to find reliable freelance work. Her fears are realistic. As I have said, it is single, older women who disproportionately face poverty as they age. As a whole, older people may generally be richer than younger people. That, however, does not make the prick of poverty any less sharp for those who grow old without enough to support themselves. They are hit by the double whammy. The young who are hard up have years ahead of them where they at least have a chance of turning their fortunes around and gaining more financial security. Far too many of the old find themselves facing a future where their assets can only run down.

Nevertheless, if the major drivers of a changing world are technology and demographics (and I think they are), the mere fact of our ageing population is changing everything. Older people, partly because they live so much longer and there are so many more of them than there used to be, are having an effect on public policy in all sorts of ways. The wealth older people have accumulated in super funds has created investment behemoths that can sway stock markets and economies if said investments change direction. Divestment—the trend for people concerned about global warming to clear their super funds and share portfolios of fossil-fuel stocks—is causing consternation among the big mining companies, particularly when large institutional and national investors, such as some Canadian pension plans and Norway's sovereign wealth fund, lead the way. The retreat of such major investors from fossil-fuel companies has a huge influence. It creates a ripple effect that causes fossil-fuel stocks to dip in value, causing more investors to get out, creating a further dip in value and … you get the picture. This is one important reason why so many energy companies are becoming proactive about diversifying into renewable energy. They fear, quite reasonably, that if their stock prices fall far enough they are in danger of being stuck with stranded assets. They can see the writing on the wall even if governments, particularly conservative governments, can't.

The so-called grey dollar is becoming very powerful in other ways, too. It is the reason that employment growth is greatest in traditionally female occupations such as health and welfare and, particularly, aged care. As manufacturing jobs disappear due to automation, computerisation, technological innovation and—soon—artificial intelligence, so jobs that require human contact, empathy and connection are growing. Yet because they are traditionally female-dominated jobs, they remain very poorly paid. The phenomenon of the working poor is growing in most Western countries, and Australia has not been immune. According to the 2017 census, 1.6 million Australian households have an income of less than $650 per week including all government benefits. That means they earn less than those on the couples pension or the minimum wage. As the consumer price index has risen by almost 10 per cent in the last five years, those low-income households have been slipping further and further behind. Foodbank Australia says that when it opened in 1992 it primarily provided food for the homeless, but the demographic of the people it helps has changed. Increasingly, the organisation says, it feeds the working poor: families who are working but do not earn enough to buy food for an entire week. How on earth are people in that situation—male or female—meant to accumulate enough to keep them in their old age? As women earn less than men right across the spectrum of paid work, and live longer, the prospects for their old age are even worse.

This lifetime of low pay places many older women in a very precarious situation, not helped by the intersection of ageism and sexism that makes it easier for older women to lose their jobs and harder for them to find new ones. A 2015 US study provided concrete evidence of the lack of desirability that older women face in every aspect of life. The researchers put together 40,000 fictional job applications and compared the rate of call-backs for younger women, middle-aged women and older women with older, middle-aged and younger men. They concluded that it was much harder for older women to get jobs than any other group. The call-back rate for younger women (aged 29–31) was much higher than for middle-aged women (49–51), while the call-back rates for middle-aged men was the same as that for younger men. Perhaps this will change as more older women become successful and run their own businesses. Perhaps older women of the future will not find themselves in the perennial catch 22 that has tripped up so many in this generation: that no sooner are women free of their child-rearing responsibilities and ready, willing and able to contribute to the paid workforce than they are judged too old. As I have contended throughout this book, there seems to be no right age to be a woman unless it's a fresh and dewy eighteen.

And if the risk of poverty for older white women is increasing, the risk is even worse for Indigenous women, women of colour, trans women and women with a disability as they get older. As long as women find it harder to keep jobs or get new ones as they age, feminism is incomplete. As long as women's work is taken for granted, unrecognised and undervalued, we still have work to do. (Yes, sorry—more unpaid work for women.) Indeed, even the basic way we value human endeavour is weighted against the work that women do. New Zealand politician and economist Marilyn Waring was one of the first people to do a forensic analysis on how comprehensively we ignore the work of women. Much of women's work is literally invisible, and it is certainly invisible financially. Waring pointed out that we measure a country's wealth according to its gross domestic product (GDP). But GDP only measures marketplace activity. According to Anne Manne, in an article celebrating Waring's contribution to feminism, this means drug dealers are counted as contributors to GDP but hospice volunteers are not. Producing nuclear weapons increases a nation's GDP but women's unpaid work is seen as contributing zero. Waring's most powerful example is breastfeeding. It contributes nothing to GDP because it cannot be bought and sold. On the contrary, GDP unapologetically favours infant formula because it is a commercial product, so the more babies who are not breastfed (against all the recommendations by health experts) the better it is for GDP. Perhaps that is one reason why the Trump administration decided to oppose a UN resolution to protect, promote and support breastfeeding and to try and bully other countries into doing the same. And they tell me men are more rational and logical than women.

If, as the business mantra goes, we only value what we can measure, no wonder so much of the vitally necessary work women do goes unnoticed and is judged as having little or no economic value. But just imagine for a moment what would happen if women stopped doing any and all unpaid work. The entire economy would come to a grinding halt.

In 2015 I wrote a very grumpy essay about why I hate Mother's Day that ran in the online publication *Women's Agenda*. In it, I summarised why I see Mother's Day as a gigantic con, a sop offered to women who labour invisibly every other day of the year. What hadn't struck me when I wrote it is how Mother's Day is also a way to make mothering contribute directly to GDP. The value of the crap we get given every May can be measured—unless, of course, our kids make it themselves. (To be fair, the same goes for Father's Day.) Mothers work away, exhausted, desperate sometimes, unrecognised and unsupported, and then we give them a household appliance, a pair of fluffy slippers or a bottle of overpriced scent as some kind of recompense. Bah humbug! Here's what I said:

> Mothers are among the most discriminated against people on the planet. They work harder, for longer, often in under-valued caring professions where employment is becoming more precarious, but for less pay. They own little land, yet produce most of the world's food. We invest in them less. In the developing world, motherhood can kill yet we restrict women's access to reproductive health. When they are pregnant, even in the West, most religions still regard mothers as little more than a uterus. Her liberty is often lost from the moment the sperm and egg become a zygote.
>
> When mothers get old, we belittle them further. We fire them once they hit 50. We ramp up their insecurity so they'll spend big on futile attempts to look young. We sneer at them when their bellies, thighs, hips and waistlines show the ravages of past pregnancies. Then we encourage them to starve themselves.
>
> Because we routinely pay them less for their work and rarely promote them, they retire with less. Because they often live longer than men, many women, particularly those who spent their

> lifetime caring for others and so compromised their earning potential, must stretch this small sum over a longer time. That's why many women face a very precarious old age. The fastest growing group among the homeless is women over 55.
>
> We claim having children is a 'lifestyle choice' while abortion remains a crime in every state in Australia except Victoria and the ACT. Forget that mothers have given birth to every tax-payer who ever lived, we still begrudge every dollar of tax that goes towards supporting them. Greedy bitches, double dipping for their (miserly) paid parental leave.
>
> And then we add insult to injury by claiming to love them. Frankly, who cares about that kind of love? What good is a feeling to anyone—except to the person who has the smug pleasure of feeling it, perhaps?

What interests me about that article—and I stand by every word I wrote—is that when *Women's Agenda* reposted it in 2018, it seemed to have a much bigger impact than it did the first time around. As we can see with the #MeToo and #TimesUp movements, women are mad as hell and refusing to take it anymore. At the 2018 Sydney Writers' Festival, a scandal erupted when the Dominican-US writer Junot Díaz was confronted publicly by a female writer who accused him of forcibly kissing her. Other women then came forward to tell their own stories of sexist mistreatment by the world-famous author. Díaz immediately cancelled the rest of his scheduled appearances and left Australia. I don't know and do not care to comment on the rights and wrongs of this scenario, but it is important because it illustrates how the tables have turned. Once upon a time women sat silent in audiences and listened to powerful men pontificate and kept their knowledge of that person's hypocrisy a secret or something they whispered quietly to one another in private. The risk if they spoke up was too great for them. Now, the risk is greater for the men who abuse the power that accompanies their fame. US Supreme Court appointee Judge Brett Kavanaugh discovered this in 2018 to his extreme displeasure.

Feminism may be an incomplete project, but it has never been as influential or as powerful as it is today. And things are beginning to change rapidly. Enough women, including older women, now have an independence that few of us have ever had previously, and we are using that independence to make sure that the plight of older women, and all women, remains invisible no longer.

12

REBELS, RESISTANCE FIGHTERS AND ROLE MODELS

Women used to live their lives, die, and then, within a generation or two, just disappear. While there is nothing unusual about this and most people die leaving hardly a trace, it is worth noting that almost every woman who has ever lived has disappeared without there being much of a record—or even a memory—of her existence. Women's invisibility is bad while they are alive, but it is absolute after they die. As Virginia Woolf pointed out, 'For most of history, Anonymous was a woman'.

If women change their names upon marriage, and most of them still do, they become very hard to find and trace, as anyone who has done their family tree will know. If you've ever tried to organise a school reunion for a girls' or co-ed school (I have—three times), you will know how much harder it is to trace old female schoolmates than male ones. On social media, when women try to reconnect with old friends, they often have to explain that they used to have a different last name. We literally erase women's identity as individuals from our memory. The only legacy they are allowed is as the portals through which new generations of people, especially male ones, enter the world. Women in the past—and still, in some parts of the developing world—earned their status entirely as the mothers of sons. Mothers of only daughters, like me, could forget it. My husband was once kindly commiserated with when he told some local women he was working with in Thailand that he had no sons but two daughters. They were astonished when he gently rejected their sympathy and told them he was overjoyed with his daughters and would not trade them for a truckload of sons. 'You are a very good man,' one of the women told him quietly.

The scarcity of women in history, the lack of information about their lives, used to be the only legacy of countless generations of the human female. Their work, their love, their energy, hopes and dreams were regarded as ephemeral and unimportant. No doubt they made an enormous impact on those they lived with—and still do, as countless anonymous women continue to quietly toil away to feed their children and keep them safe, or contribute to their communities in myriad ways—but their indispensable contribution has been taken entirely for granted for millennia. Much of the business of their lives—how they dealt with menstruation, sex, childbirth, all the way to menopause—was rendered literally unspeakable. Trying to find information on such things and how they were dealt with in the past is very difficult. Little exists even though they are the commonly lived experience of half the human race. When we made the functions of women's bodies taboo, we very effectively silenced them about almost everything. If their bodies were invisible, it seems the women became so as well.

Apart from a few major personalities, often only given opportunity by accident of birth (queens such as Elizabeths I and II and Victoria spring to mind), women's lives were lived quietly and invisibly, and their deaths were recorded in the same way. They were the support gender, very rarely the star of the show. And this, I think, is one of the legacies that this revolutionary generation of women has begun to change. Women are demanding they be noticed, reckoned with and remembered in ways they never have before. Quite apart from women having gestated, birthed and (usually) raised every genius who has ever lived, not to mention the research that indicates the DNA inherited from your mother has more influence on your intelligence than that inherited from your father, there are other contributions that many of us, despite the barriers, have managed to make. There are endless memes on social media listing the women who contributed to major scientific, technical and literary steps forward and yet have been written out of history. I was open-mouthed to discover, for example, that the magnificent illustrations in the famous publication *The Birds of Australia* were not created by the credited author, John Gould, as I had always thought, but by his wife, Elizabeth!

There are many other women (past counting, probably) who have been left out of history despite the value and importance of their contribution—not least in science. Rosalind Franklin, whose work using X-rays to take pictures of DNA was critical to its discovery, was entirely ignored when her colleagues James Watson, Francis Crick and Maurice Wilkins were awarded the 1962 Nobel Prize in Physiology or Medicine. How many girls (or boys) were ever taught about Ada Lovelace, daughter of the romantic poet Lord Byron, who is credited with writing the first computer program in 1843? Her contribution to computing was only acknowledged in 2009, when Ada Lovelace Day was created (it's 13 October, if you are interested). Hollywood Golden Age movie star Hedy Lamarr has finally been credited with an invention she made during World War II that led to today's wireless technology. But when my generation of women were at school, did we ever hear about any of them?

I was hungry for female heroes and role models when I was a girl, and it was hard to find any that were not soppy (the Lady with the Lamp), came to a sticky end (Joan of Arc) or were glamorous but reviled (Mata Hari—and she came to a sticky end as well). I clearly remember as a schoolgirl that whenever I stood up for my gender, boys could shut me down easily by asking me to name any woman who had contributed anything to history. I clung to the few I knew about—such as Marie Curie and Elizabeth I—in desperation, but even to me, two seemed like the exception that proved the rule. If only my generation had known about all the women who'd had their contributions ignored, overlooked and dismissed. But we did not. In fact, even when the woman's contribution was so important it could not be entirely disappeared, it was often reduced to an acceptable and sentimentally feminised one. Florence Nightingale (the abovementioned Lady with the Lamp) is the best example of this. She was famous, when I was young, as the archetypal self-sacrificing and nurturing woman who created the modern nursing profession, but I was amazed when I read her biography by Cecil Woodham-Smith (I recommend it) to discover she was a prickly and obstinate rebel who not only transformed nursing but practically ran the British War Office from her invalid's bed, and revolutionised sanitation in both England and India and so saved many millions of lives.

When I was young, and that is not so very long ago, women were still deliberately prevented from making a contribution. When the US began developing its space program in the 1950s, doctors tested both men and women to qualify as the first astronauts. Thirteen out of the nineteen women pilots who applied passed the rigorous tests. Eighteen of the thirty-two male applicants also passed. Yet, in the end, it was decided not to allow the women to fly. Astronaut John Glenn explained their omission as simply being 'a fact of our social order'. Other men were not so subtle: one NASA rocket engineer, when asked why women were not going into space, joked that the male astronauts were very much in favour of the idea and quoted his boss, Bob Gilruth, as saying, 'We're reserving 110 pounds of payload for recreational equipment.' You guys, you're just so damn funny (not). The message my generation of women were constantly being sent was not that men were deliberately holding us back but that we were not good enough. It makes me angry as I write this to think of the hurt and harm such completely false messages did to an entire gender. Our hopes were dashed before we'd even really had a chance to form them.

One of the legacies of this revolutionary generation, accidentally or not, is that they and the women following them are beginning to rediscover and publicise the contributions women have made. People of colour and the LGBTQI community are doing the same. During NAIDOC Week 2018, for example, Indigenous women's contributions were celebrated by people who showcased different women all week on social media. Businesswoman Dr Kirstin Ferguson made 2017 the year of celebrating women by focusing on one woman of achievement a day on Twitter under the hashtag #celebratingwomen. She and Catherine Fox have since co-authored a book, *Women Kind*, about how such a simple idea became a social media phenomenon. As I have already mentioned, comedian Hannah Gadsby became an international sensation in mid-2018 after her confronting one-woman show *Nanette* became a Netflix special. For an hour, alone at a mic on the stage of the Sydney Opera House Concert Hall, Gadsby deconstructs how she has used comedy to disguise the truth of her life, the pain inflicted on her by others for her gender non-conformity, and the pain she has inflicted on herself. It is confronting, uncompromising and also intensely liberating. Gadsby throws off the shame she has carried for so long in front of our eyes.

This rediscovery of the contributions of women has helped us all throw off the sense of innate, inescapable inferiority that so many women of previous generations had to live with, from the disappointment of their birth to their unremembered death. This rediscovery is particularly important for little girls who—just like little boys—need to see achievers they can identify with. After the tradition-shattering royal wedding of Prince Harry, of impeccable royal and aristocratic British pedigree, and mixed-race US descendant of slaves Meghan Markle, I was touched to see an African American mother tweet that her small daughter had turned excitedly to her as she watched the spectacle to exclaim that Meghan's mother, Doria Ragland, had 'hair just like yours'. When human beings see someone who is 'like' them doing something unexpected and admirable, it opens up possibilities that did not previously exist. Lifting the veil covering women of the past and what they have achieved is of vital importance for the future of little girls, and that is a legacy to be proud of.

Shaking off false humility or 'modesty' is enabling many female writers to re-examine the comprehensive erasure of women and their lives from history. Julia Baird has re-examined the life of Queen Victoria through female eyes. Leslie Cannold was inspired to write her novel *The Book of Rachael* when she watched a documentary about Jesus Christ in which his brothers were all mentioned by name but the fact he also had sisters was mentioned only in passing. No-one knows their names. Not one of them was deemed important enough to be thought of as an individual. In response, Cannold has imagined Christ's sisters, giving them names, lives, thoughts and agency. Historian Clare Wright is explicit about the way history has treated the women who participated in the legendary Australian goldminers' rebellion known as the Eureka Stockade. Her book about them is simply called *The Forgotten Rebels of Eureka*. Virginia Woolf's famous feminist essay *A Room of One's Own* is a meditation on what might have happened if Shakespeare had had an equally brilliant sister (spoiler alert: it doesn't end well). Shakespeare may indeed have had a sister, but how would we ever know? Wolfgang Amadeus Mozart certainly had one, and when they were children they toured together as equally brilliant infant prodigies. Mozart's sister was Maria Anna Mozart, nicknamed Nannerl. She disappeared from her brother's story (and from any story at all) when she turned eighteen. She did not die, however, but lived another sixty years in anonymity. One hopes she continued to play the piano, if only in private.

In a small way, I have also contributed to this rediscovery of women and their history by writing a series of young adult novels about Elizabeth I (my long-time hero) telling the story of her life in the first person. I wanted to imagine what it might have been like to *be* her, especially as she is so often seen from the outside and then puzzled over as a lifelong virgin, spinster and female ruler. So odd have these facts appeared to many historians (mostly male) that there has even been speculation that Elizabeth Tudor was not a 'proper' woman at all (whatever that is) and may have suffered from a condition called testicular feminisation. There is little (if any) evidence for this, but if something can be used to imply that such a brilliant and independent woman must really have been a man, it seems that it will be—especially, perhaps, because she was so determined never to marry and never to bear children, and so never hand over any of her power.

This rediscovery, re-interpretation and long-overdue recognition does not happen in a vacuum. It is also the legacy of many generations of women—women such as Mary Wollstonecraft, who dared to suggest during the French Revolution that women might have rights, as men did. (I sometimes wonder if the reason it was an Englishwoman who articulated the limitations placed on women's lives during that turbulent time was, in itself, a legacy of Elizabeth I, whose story must have secretly inspired generations of girls into harbouring seditious thoughts, just as it did me.)

Elizabeth Tudor, along with the other female luminaries of her time (there were so many just after the Reformation that fire-and-brimstone Calvinist preacher John Knox christened them a 'monstrous regiment of women'), such as Mary, Queen of Scots and Catherine de Medici, owned tapestries woven from the illustrations of a book by French late medieval writer Christine de Pizan. *The Book of the City of Ladies*, written in 1405, is a proto-feminist text (yep, women asserting their rights goes back a lot further than we think) advocating for female education and arguing that women are valuable participants in society. The illustrations that were made into the tapestries are even more revolutionary. They show medievally garbed aristocratic women building walls, poring over architectural drawings, even jointing and planing blocks of wood to create their city. It is wonderful to imagine the women leaders of the time gaining strength and solidarity from owning such tapestries. The tapestries, sadly, have long since disappeared, but we still have the book.

The women who followed de Pizan, the queens and Wollstonecraft grasped the baton and continued the fight for equal rights that goes on to this day. Over the following centuries, women fought for their right to keep their own earnings, and to leave an abusive husband and retain some rights to their children. They fought for the vote and to open up higher education for girls. They fought for women's right to information about their own bodies and their right to choose when and whether they would have children. They fought for women to be taken seriously. They are all owed a debt. Then there are the women who got opportunities in the two world wars when they performed their patriotic duty and did men's jobs for the duration and proved—at least to themselves and their daughters—just what women could do. And, as 2018 NAIDOC Week has reminded us, there are the Indigenous women who fought doggedly in the face of endemic racism to keep their families together and hold on to their culture—leaders like Tasmanian Aboriginal elder Truganini; political activist Faith Bandler; activist, writer and intellectual Bobbi Sykes; community worker Mum Shirl; and poet Oodgeroo Noonuccal. There are the women of colour who fought slavery and vicious prejudice in the US, such as abolitionist Harriet Tubman, abolitionist and women's rights activist Sojourner Truth, revolutionary Angela Davis, and writer and poet Maya Angelou. Not to mention courageous trans women who claimed their right to dignity and respect in the face of overwhelming odds, like historian and (sublime) writer Jan Morris and tennis champion Renée Richards. There are lesbian women who bravely emerged from the shadows, such as tennis players Billie Jean King and Martina Navratilova and one of my new heroes, comedian Hannah Gadsby. And there are the women living with disability who have confronted a society that wanted them to live limited lives on the sidelines, such as US writer and celebrity Helen Keller,

Australian comedian and educator Stella Young, and US congresswoman Tammy Duckworth.

Unhappily, despite their grit and determination, for previous generations of women progress remained glacially slow. Entrenched attitudes about female inferiority and the smallness of the feminine 'sphere' hardly shifted. It took technology to create the cataclysmic changes my generation have lived through. It always takes technology. Elizabeth I and the monstrous regiment of women were a direct result of the Protestant Reformation, which, in its turn, was a response to the invention of the printing press. The invention—at last—of reliable contraception made the definitive difference. Women were no longer slaves to their biology, and the rapid escalation of female liberation owes everything to that. Hence, perhaps, the strident opposition to abortion, contraception and women's reproductive rights in general. It's not babies the anti-abortionists want to save: it's male control over women. Protesters agitating for the repeal of the draconian anti-abortion amendment in the Irish Constitution (Amendment 8, which had been added in 1983 and gave a foetus the same rights as the woman who carried it, resulting in many women risking their health) chanted: 'Pro-life, that's a lie. You don't care if women die.' Well, yes, exactly. The sudden escalation of women's demands for their rights that has happened just in the last few years is also because of a technological innovation. Social media and access to the internet have enabled women to connect with one another and support each other like never before. Women marching in the streets protesting against rape in India, Iranian women breaking the law by taking off their hijabs in public or dancing in the streets, Saudi Arabian women finally winning the right to drive cars, are all given oxygen, support and power via their ability to access social media.

The speed of recent change, however, should not belittle the herculean efforts of the women who have gone before. Every generation builds on the work of the last, and pill or no pill, my generation could not have made the strides they have without all the work done by others. The same is true for future generations, although luckily for them the advancement of women is now snowballing. The legacy of the current crop of women over fifty—the accidental feminists—has given a leg up like no other to their daughters and granddaughters, not least through the #MeToo movement.

In the wake of the tsunami of change demonstrated by #MeToo, some prominent older women, including prominent feminists, have reacted with caution. But I would argue that their reservations make little difference. It is to be expected that all of us have a point beyond which we cannot go, and attitudes and beliefs we have been trained to accept since childhood are hard to drop—particularly, perhaps, as we get older. The contribution of women like Germaine Greer, Margaret Atwood and other feminists who have voiced concerns about #MeToo does not negate the fact that it has happened—not in spite of them, but because of them. The battles they fought and largely won have created the climate where the women of today have the tools and the understanding of patriarchy they need to grab the opportunities presented by social media and run with them. Whether or not some older feminists can cope with the monster they have created is beside the point. Their courage and plain-speaking are the reason why feminism is where it's at today. What some older women have perhaps missed about this revolution is that it is not 'sucking it up ['it' being sexual harassment at work] and carrying on regardless' that is courageous. Standing up and objecting to sexist behaviour is what takes real courage. I am not accusing older women of having been cowardly, despite the fact that some of them are rather unhelpfully accusing their younger sisters of 'fragility'. Older women did not speak up because it would have gained them nothing to do so. The world had not changed enough for such behaviour to be taken seriously. But, thanks to them, it has now. The shift in power that #MeToo demonstrates has happened not least because those women found a way to enter the male world of work and survive in it.

The same is true of the less notable members of this extraordinary generation of women. Whether they have espoused feminism or not, they have lived it. Just as sexism is like asbestos in the walls—something we breathe in without even noticing—so is its opposite. It is almost impossible to have lived through the last five or more decades and not have changed your view on what women are capable of, and what they should or should not aspire to do. Even the most conservative person will have changed in ways they once would have thought impossible. On 13 May 2018 (Mother's Day), the passengers on an otherwise perfectly unexceptional Alaska Airlines flight erupted in applause when the captain announced that it was the first-ever such flight for the airline to be captained and co-piloted by two African American women. In 2013 I was a passenger on a Qantas flight from Melbourne to Sydney. As we approached the runway to land, the plane encountered severe turbulence and plummeted through the sky. It was terrifying, and two passengers were injured. The pilot expertly handled the situation, and when we landed in Newcastle after being diverted, the passengers and crew erupted into applause. It wasn't until a couple of days later that I learnt that the pilot who had saved our lives was a woman—the only voice we'd heard from the cockpit was that of the male co-pilot, even after the danger had passed. I could not help wondering if she had been concerned that a female voice would not have been as reassuring to some of the already-traumatised passengers as a man's, and so chose not to speak. Maybe she was just shy, I don't know, but I do not believe a female pilot would have the same reticence today, even after only five years. Things are changing very quickly.

Every generation leaves a legacy they are unaware of, and the consequences of the battles they fought and the attitudes they passed on continue long after they have gone. This generation, most of whom (unless they were born after 1960) are baby boomers, have been particularly powerful and influential through sheer numbers. They began their assault on gender roles right from the get-go, even if they didn't quite realise that is what they were doing. They were the generation of unisex, and loud were the complaints from their elders that from the back you couldn't tell a boy from a girl. One of the clearest and most banal indicators of the blurring of rigid gender lines back in the 1960s and 1970s was the virtual disappearance of barbers and the exponential increase in 'unisex' hairdressers. I dare say Vidal Sassoon thought he was simply changing hair fashion, not that he was at the forefront of a gender revolution—but he was. That's his legacy. (Interesting how the hipster male fashions of today are all about turning young men into elaborately bearded replicas of the Victorian patriarch. Backlash, anyone? Oh, and the barbers are reappearing as well.)

I have never believed that fashion is either trivial or irrelevant (funny how the things women are interested in are so often characterised that way—why isn't sport, I wonder?). I have always thought it was a symbolic and metaphorical representation of the way the times are changing. I had lunch with my 86-year-old mother the other day in a large shopping mall jam-packed with fashion boutiques. As we watched the passing parade she commented: 'The thing about modern fashion is you really can wear absolutely anything.' She is right. Maybe that is one of the legacies of this revolutionary generation too, at least in Western countries: the new belief that diversity is everything, and that you should be, do, wear, love, think, create whatever you want to, including choosing your gender (or lack thereof) and sexuality (or lack thereof).

I cannot help thinking of my infant granddaughter and the legacy that she will inherit. Much of it will be vastly more varied, interesting and exciting than the one my grandmother left to me. Esther will receive at least as good an education as her brother. My grandmother never expected to go to university. That was partly an issue to do to with her class (her husband, my grandfather, didn't expect to go, either), but almost no uni students were female when she was that age. My mother had to fight for her right to take a degree but I was just expected to go to uni, as were my daughters, and so, no doubt, as will my granddaughter. My grandmother did not expect to work for money after she married, and she didn't, apart from a stint running my grandfather's shop when he was drafted during World War II. My mother didn't expect to either, but eventually she desperately wanted to and—in her forties—built an interesting career as a relationships counsellor. Like most of my generation, I have worked professionally, at least part time, all my life.

The worst legacy my generation has left future generations, of course, is our criminal inaction on climate change—but that is a story for another book. What the politicisation of climate change reveals is another legacy of the revolutionary decades this generation of women have both lived through and influenced—and that is the polarisation of political perspectives across the world, including the West, and the possibility of a backlash. Rights that have been hard won can also be lost.

In the US, where the polarisation between the urban, feminist, cosmopolitan and liberal coasts and the rural, masculinist, parochial and conservative inland seems most stark and belligerent, state after state has rolled back access to abortion. After the momentous win of Roe v. Wade in 1973 (when I was sixteen), US women must have felt that the bad old days of dangerous backyard abortions were over. Today, Texas, which has very draconian abortion laws, has the highest maternal mortality rate in the developed world. Backlashes can be fatal, especially for poorer women. Recently, a columnist with the prestigious *Atlantic* magazine called for the death penalty for women who seek abortions. He was fired, but he is not alone in his view. Many regard abortion as murder, and the logical end point of that belief, if you also believe in capital punishment (funny how many so-called 'right-to-lifers' do), is the death penalty for women who end pregnancies. In Australia, where fortunately we no longer have the death penalty, a sitting senator and member of the National Party has nonetheless also voiced extreme views about women who seek to control their own bodies. In July 2017, at a party conference, Senator Barry O'Sullivan spoke in support of Resolution 26 in the Queensland Liberal National Party platform and said this: 'Many in the party and outside would like to lock [pregnant women] up and bind their arms and say "no abortion could occur".'

In the US, things may be about to get even worse. In June 2018, US Supreme Court Judge Anthony Kennedy resigned. His departure and the subsequent successful if contested nomination by the Trump administration of an anti-abortion replacement led to furious demonstrations by those worrying about the safety of the Roe v. Wade decision. American women may soon have to face the possibility of backyard abortions again, particularly if they are young, poor women of colour.

Access to safe, legal abortion and other reproductive health services is not just about autonomy and bodily control for women. The number of children women have and the way they can space their pregnancies (or not) have a direct effect on their ability to earn a living, keep themselves and their children out of poverty, and also prepare for their old age. Women once again find themselves caught between contradictory expectations when it comes to conservative ideas of self-sufficiency and personal responsibility—the judgemental stick most commonly used to beat up on the poor—and those same conservatives' trenchant opposition to safe, legal abortion. How on earth are fertile, sexually active women meant to conform to both?

Given that women in many countries of the world are indeed locked up for the 'sin' of having an abortion, or even for having a miscarriage or stillbirth somebody deems suspicious, we must not think for a second that the legacy of the women who have changed everything will always be benign or forward thinking. Their very success can put women in deadly danger. We have already seen women targeted by mass murderers in the US, which is currently in the grip of an epidemic of mass shootings, of which almost all have been carried out by men. One of the few things that link the men who choose to shoot large numbers of people at random is a history of domestic violence. (Another is that almost all of them are white.) They have often beaten and attacked the women in their lives, and it is common for the first victim of a mass shooter to be a woman who is close to them, as at Port Arthur and Sandy Hook.

In the wake of the mass attack in Toronto in April 2018 by a man who claimed to be inspired by an earlier mass murderer (as described in Chapter 6), a few commentators suggested that there ought to be some kind of 'right to sex' for men who are less successful at attracting women. Writer Ross Douthat argued in the *New York Times* that the idea of a redistribution of the right to sex should not necessarily be dismissed as 'inherently ridiculous'. Well, only if you are not a woman, I guess, who may have to put up with being redistributed (aka raped). The inchoate anger that some men seem to feel towards all women appears to be on the increase, and is finding particularly violent expression in the US. In May 2018, yet another school massacre was perpetrated by a young man who stalked and harassed a young woman because she rejected him romantically. She was one of eight schoolmates and two teachers who he shot and killed at Santa Fe High School in Texas. It is suddenly feeling even more frightening (it's always been a bit risky) for a woman or girl to reject the overtures of a man. Canadian author Margaret Atwood put it brilliantly: 'men are afraid women will laugh at them … women are afraid men will kill them'—an observation gaining increasing resonance. I suppose it is soberingly inevitable that as women gain power, a few men will want to take it away from them again by whatever means possible.

The election of Donald Trump in 2016 is arguably a direct result of the backlash against the progress women, LGBTQI people and people of colour have made. White, conservative voters simply could not contemplate a female president following a black one. Trump's campaign slogan directly plugged into that sentiment. 'Make America Great Again' was backward looking. It was about returning to a world that was run by white men, where all women knew their place (not just the 52 per cent of white women—who voted at all—who voted for Trump), LGBTQI people were closeted, and people of colour were restricted to menial and domestic labour. The slogan and the president it helped elect are a direct rejection of the legacy of the accidental feminists. No wonder women all over the world were gripped by the TV adaptation of Atwood's dystopian 1985 novel *The Handmaid's Tale*. I remember reading the book when it was first published and enjoying it. Even then, the fate of the women in the story didn't seem that impossible to me. However, the reason it resonates so powerfully now is because the ghastly misogynistic regression it dramatises seems more possible than ever. As Atwood herself has said, everything in the book has happened to some women, somewhere, at some time.

The vitriolic, sexualised abuse that outspoken women experience on social media is another example of the anxiety that has been generated by the rise of the female gender. The statement 'The more they hate you, the more effective you are being', while true, can be cold comfort if you are facing a barrage of hate and abuse for simply expressing an opinion. In Australia, outspoken feminists such as Van Badham, Tracey Spicer and Clementine Ford face appalling abuse simply for being articulate and forthright. Morning TV host Yumi Stynes lost her job at *The Circle* in response to out-of-proportion vitriol about a careless remark, while the behaviour of her male colleague, George Negus, who laughed along with her, raised barely an eyebrow. The 2015 Young Queenslander of the Year and engineer Yassmin Abdel-Magied was forced to leave the country, such was the level of insulting commentary aimed at her in response to a pretty unexceptional tweet about Anzac Day. Data analyst and writer Ketan Joshi estimated that after posting her seven-word tweet, Abdel-Magied had 207,979 words written about her, most of them negative. These pile-ons can have serious, real-world effects beyond even the loss of job or country: Abdel-Magied was recently refused entry to the US. Stynes and Abdel-Magied, perhaps not coincidentally, are both non-Anglo Australians—Stynes is of Japanese descent and Abdel-Magied Sudanese—but being white and Aussie offers thin protection if you are female. Female journalists and politicians routinely experience more intense and more gendered abuse than their male colleagues do. Former human rights commissioner Gillian Triggs, former prime minister Julia Gillard, ABC TV journalist and columnist Emma Alberici and Greens senator Sarah Hanson-Young are all white women who have been subject to intense media campaigns against them.

In a way, the intensity of the backlash is merely a reflection of feminism's overwhelming progress. The rise of women has generated real fear in some men and, it must be said, some women. Why else would they react so viciously to the—perfectly reasonable—attempts by female gamers to make gaming less misogynistic? Prominent US gamer and feminist campaigner Anita Sarkeesian has had to have police protection as a result of her campaign, and gave up speaking in public for a time. The so-called men's rights activists routinely use organised onslaughts of abuse and intimidation on social media to attempt to silence women who speak up for their gender. Mary Beard, the venerable and authoritative British academic and expert on ancient Rome (and co-host of *Civilisations*, at least in Britain) whom I wrote about in Chapter 2, faced unbelievable abuse when she began her later-in-life TV career about her appearance, her 'arrogance' at assuming she knew her subject (she is an acknowledged world expert), and her cheeky insouciance. A British woman who merely lobbied to have a woman other than the Queen appear on one denomination of British currency (eventually Jane Austen was chosen) brought a storm of absurd protest down upon her head, most of it personal, abusive and sexualised. Tragically, this is also a legacy of the women who have changed everything. They have helped advance the feminist project considerably, and the feminist project is, of course, nothing less than a redistribution of political, social and financial power more equally between men and women.

For women to gain some power, men may have to lose a little—and some of them don't like that at all.

Nonetheless, I remain cautiously optimistic. I don't believe half of the human race will ever be as easy to intimidate and control as they once were. Thanks to every generation of women from every culture on earth who ever lived, thanks to every woman who ever voiced a seditious thought or pursued her talents regardless of invisibility, my generation of women have been able to live a life different from the women who came before us. That doesn't mean every one of us has had a good life, or realised our dreams—of course it doesn't. Feminism is not a cure-all or a magic wand able to deliver perfect happiness. All it claims to do is give women the same rights as men to decide the shape of their own lives. And, for better or worse, the legacy this generation of women is leaving to the future is about our right to make our own decisions about our own lives.

13

STRATEGISTS, POLICY MAKERS AND PROBLEM SOLVERS

A powerful legacy of the accidental feminists is the new and growing recognition of the plight of so many women as they grow old. There is nothing new about women struggling financially as they age. It is a story as old as history, we just haven't paid much attention to it before. In eras when women could not inherit and had to rely on the kindness of male relatives for any kind of decent life if they were unmarried or after their husband died, they were fundamentally reduced to dependents at best and beggars at worst. The dreaded workhouses made famous by Charles Dickens were well supplied with elderly women as residents, particularly after the passing of the infamous Poor Laws in 1834. These laws resulted in many elderly people having to leave their parish—which had previously taken responsibility for its ageing citizens—and be housed collectively with others unable to provide for themselves. There, driven by the sort of pitiless judgements reminiscent of the sanctimony behind today's work-for-the-dole schemes, the old, the very young, the poor, the fallen and the sick were put to work in return for room (well, a bed in a dormitory) and board (well, gruel, bread and cheese and the occasional watery stew). Hence the name 'workhouses'.

Without any kind of safety net, women dependent on the men they married for economic security easily found themselves facing unpalatable fates. Dickens' own mother had no recourse but to move herself and her children into a debtors' prison when her husband, John Dickens, could not pay his creditors. Charles never forgave her for not protecting him, and for forcing her eldest son (him) to live in digs and work for a pittance in a blacking factory rather than continue his schooling. It always struck me as profoundly unfair that it was his mother who copped the blame, but perhaps she was the only parent he could ever rely on, and when she failed, when he was still only a boy, he had no-one else. Women suffered fates such as these more or less silently. Austen wrote about it, albeit gently; Dickens also, but with less compassion for female victims—many of his older female characters are caricatures. Of the Victorian social novelists, Elizabeth Gaskell is probably the most generous-spirited about the plight of the elderly single woman, especially in her wonderful book *Cranford*. Read it, if you haven't already.

Unlike the women of the past, women today are the beneficiaries of not just a welfare safety net (although it is looking a bit threadbare) but also the shift in power between the genders that has taken place. Men are not as dominant as they once were. Thanks to all the work of generations of women building the strength and legitimacy of feminism, the plight of older women is no longer so easy to ignore. At last there is real concern, rather than faux pity, about the fact that the fastest-growing group among the homeless is women over fifty-five. There is real discomfort about the statistics that reveal women retire with so much less than men. It is no longer possible to consider it a 'private' matter or due to a woman's personal choices. After all, if most women now work for wages for most of their life, then it is quite outrageous that they should be left high and dry in their old age. (It was always outrageous, in my view, whether they worked for wages or not. Women have always worked, both paid and unpaid. They don't call childbirth 'labour' for nothing.) It is particularly galling if the major reason why they lack the wherewithal to support themselves is precisely because they spent so much time looking after the rest of us. Natural justice would dictate, whatever your politics, that it is now our turn to look after them. Yes, I can hear some libertarians (ever noticed how many of them are white, privileged men?) squawking about 'personal responsibility', but, of course, that is just part of the problem. Women are expected to take responsibility for the care and nurture of others and put their own needs last—even their own needs to earn a living or have a decent income when they age. They are told they will be cared for in return for doing so, but far too often that promise is not kept.

The harsh expectations that women will put the needs of others ahead of their own, no matter what, are driven by ancient patriarchal religious ideas. I caused a bit of a kerfuffle when I said on ABC TV during a debate about the Irish referendum to repeal the anti-abortion eighth amendment, that women don't give up their human rights when they become pregnant. Apparently that was quite a new thought for many people, revealing that perhaps women are unconsciously seen as becoming slightly lesser when they conceive. We become a vessel for someone else rather than simply a person in our own right. One of the more ghastly forms of domestic violence is reproductive coercion, where a woman is forced by an abusive partner either to have a child against her will because her partner sabotages contraception, or to end a wanted pregnancy. Making a woman pregnant is, of course, a very good way of keeping her dependent and making it even harder for her to leave an abusive relationship. Bad as that is, pregnant women and new mothers in their first postpartum year are at risk of even worse treatment. According to US research, the leading cause of maternal death in pregnancy in the US is murder. One in five of the pregnant women who die is killed by the father of her unborn child.

Julia Baird, a devout Christian, has been relentless in her investigative journalism exposing attitudes towards domestic abuse among those of different religious faiths, including her own Anglican denomination. She has revealed a terrifying tendency by religious leaders, most of whom remain male, to send women back into violent and abusive homes using 'headship' doctrine as a rationalisation. She has also shown that some male religious leaders are themselves perpetrators of domestic violence. Her contention is that the idea of the hierarchy of God over man, and man over woman, is dangerous—not just to women, but, as revealed by the Royal Commission into Institutional Responses to Child Sexual Abuse, to children too. The idea of blind obedience by the subordinate members of the family to the dominant husband and father can be a deadly one. We tell women their place is in the home, and then we make it one of the most unsafe places for them to be. As I have pointed out, the major precipitating event that causes a woman to become homeless is fleeing domestic violence. We tell women in abusive relationships to leave, but then give them nowhere to go.

As I have been researching and writing this book, I have found it hard to escape the feeling that I am writing in circles. It does not matter which particular sector or life stage I am writing about, it seems we make it harder for women to successfully navigate their way through it. Whether it is the way we're raised, the world of work, the way we're marketed to, how much we're paid, our caring responsibilities, how likely we are to get hired or promoted or to keep our jobs, whether it's our health, our wealth or how safe we are in our own homes, it is harder to be female. If you are female and you try to get ahead, there will be bigger, wider and deeper obstacles in your way. That is bad enough, but what is infuriating is how the very existence of such obstacles is still denied. Not only must we jump higher and further than our male competitors to get over them, we must do so smiling and in high heels. What we must not do is point out their existence or demand they be reduced. To do so is to whine or play the gender card or act like a victim.

Such attitudes are particularly prevalent on the conservative side of politics. It is common to hear conservative politicians—even female ones—argue that they believe in promotion on merit, and that for women to get ahead they must simply 'work harder'. Tell that to the women who have worked hard all their lives as mothers, wives and dutiful daughters, who have been reduced to part-time, casual, poorly paid work because of the demands of their caring responsibilities, and who, in their old age, have ended up living out of their car. Tell them they failed to find security in old age because they 'lacked merit' and did not work hard enough. Go on, I dare you. We as a society set these women up to fail. We took advantage of them. We lied to them. We changed the rules to benefit the already privileged and to further handicap these women. We told them to stay home and look after their kids, then we told them they were too old and unskilled to be worth employing. Finally we administered the coup de grâce and told them it was all their own fault. We have to change, and now.

There have been some important improvements in policy settings taking into account the revolution in women's lives in the last half-century or so. In 2002 the Family Law Act was amended to include 'superannuation splitting' laws because it was recognised that the previous way superannuation was divided—or, more frequently, not divided—was very detrimental to women, who almost always had less super than their husbands (or none) due to the fact that the women were (and are) usually the partner who gave up paid work to care for children. Mind you, the 2002 amendments only applied to married couples: it was not until 2009 that superannuation splitting was also applied to those in de facto relationships. Women who were divorced prior to 2002 often received little or none of their partner's super. And this had profound implications for their future. Yet the work women do in the home is vital to their partner's ability to progress in his career, earn a decent income and accumulate that all-important super. It is this basic structural disparity that has led to women retiring with an average of half the super of men, or even none at all. Imagine if you had to pay someone to do what women routinely do? In 2013 salary.com estimated that you'd have to pay a woman engaged in 'home duties' over US$113,000 per annum in wages. If a father were forced to hire someone to do the work a wife and mother provides more or less for free, you can imagine what the effect on his economic wellbeing might be. Perhaps you can see why she deserves some of his super if the relationship breaks down—yes, even if she leaves him. Many of the older women currently struggling to keep a roof over their heads may well have been divorced prior to 2002, or 2009 if their relationship was de facto.

Superannuation splitting laws are better than nothing, but they do not go far enough. One of the issues we have to look at as a society is why it is acceptable for women to go into retirement (whether voluntarily or because they have no choice—I am looking at you, nexus between ageism and sexism) with so much less behind them than their male peers. A society and an economy structured to make that a real and substantial risk for large numbers of women are patently not operating properly. Yet it seems to require women being in positions of power before anyone bothers to do something about it. The increasing numbers of women at the top are already starting to have an effect on bringing women and their economic future into focus. It seems women leaders, when they are not the remarkable exception but have a few female peers, do pay more attention to female workers and their lives. I was the master of ceremonies (a frequent part of my work) at the 2018 International Women's Day (IWD) event for private health insurer HCF. In August 2017, HCF appointed its first female CEO, Sheena Jack. At the event, Jack gave a short welcome and while doing so made a major announcement: she revealed that HCF had decided to continue paying its employees superannuation while they were on the unpaid portion of their parental leave, up to fifty-two weeks. Given that the vast majority of workers who take parental leave are women, this was an initiative mainly aimed at them and at closing the super gap between the genders. Most Australian workers are entitled to eighteen weeks' parental leave at the minimum wage of $719 per week, and they then take unpaid leave depending on what their employer will allow. Unfortunately, there is no obligation for employers to continue to pay superannuation entitlements while someone (usually a woman) is on paid or unpaid parental leave. You can see how this deficit would accumulate over a lifetime, even if a woman only has one or two children. If she has more children, or a child with special needs, her long-term disadvantage keeps compounding. HCF and Jack are to be congratulated for their initiative, and we can only hope that their example leads more employers to follow suit. However, leaving such important decisions to the vagaries of individual companies, executives and boards remains a shaky situation for women. I cannot help thinking that, like the superannuation splitting laws, what we really need is for this to be enshrined in legislation or, even better, to be paid by government to all women and the as yet small number of men who take parental or carer's leave. After all, when you take parental leave you are gestating, birthing and raising the next generation of taxpayers.

The above may seem obvious, but such ideas are relatively new. Paid parental leave only came into existence in Australia in 2010—much later than in most of the rest of the world—and it was designed as a welfare payment. Hence the limitation of it being paid at the minimum wage regardless of how much the recipient (usually a woman) actually earns. It is also only paid to people (mostly women) who earn less than $150,000 a year. This may seem sensible at first glance, but I believe that until parental leave is seen as a workplace entitlement that is paid as a percentage of your salary in the same way as holiday pay, sick pay and, indeed, superannuation, it will do little to close the yawning gender pay and superannuation gaps. It also encourages the lower earner in a couple to take the time off, and that is generally the female partner, thereby perpetuating the very problem it is meant to be doing something to alleviate. And it leads to a situation where many new mothers feel compelled financially to return to work after eighteen weeks regardless of how they or their very young babies may feel about it. It forces far too many women to return to work part time, which also, of course, limits their ability to earn and accumulate super. Paying parental leave at the minimum wage also, subtly but powerfully, perpetuates the idea that work is for men and that society is doing women a favour by letting them participate. Women are meant to feel grateful and (mutually) obligated for the 'welfare' they receive. It's funny, isn't it, how even though women have given birth to every taxpayer who ever lived—not to mention being taxpayers themselves—we begrudge every penny of tax we spend on them.

Other women are noticing this too, and again, as with HCF, when a woman occupies the corner office, it seems these problems get taken much more seriously. On the eve of IWD 2018, EnergyAustralia CEO Catherine Tanna announced that her company would be spending $1.2 million immediately to increase the pay of the 350 female employees in the organisation who were not being paid the same as their male colleagues (it was a big twenty-four hours for women and their pay). She also apologised that it had taken the company so long to rectify the situation. The times, they are a-changing.

For too long male leaders, both in private industry and in our parliaments, have basically trivialised the need for women to receive equal pay for equal work. Old-style patriarchal leaders like John Howard are on record saying that women will never achieve fifty-fifty representation in parliament (or anywhere else) because of their caring responsibilities. This is what I said in response to Howard's remarks in an article in the online publication *The Big Smoke* in 2016:

> Not only must we have 50 per cent of women in our parliaments and in every other corridor of power, Mr Howard, we must also

> have 50 per cent of the caring responsibilities shouldered by men. Only then will we have a society that fairly distributes the responsibilities and the rewards.
>
> Women are disproportionately finding themselves facing poverty and desperation in their old age precisely because they have relied on men to take care of their interests, while they were busy caring for others. They weren't just relying on their husbands, either, they were—and still, sadly, are—relying on men in positions of power in government, business and every other sector of society to make decisions that took, and take, women's lives into account.
>
> And, frankly, Mr Howard, you blokes have let them down. Every older woman facing the possibility of living in her car is proof of that. Women must take their seat at the decision-making table in equal numbers to men. Only then will they have any chance of improving their own lives.

The trouble is that men like Howard fail to understand why equality matters so much. They assume that women will be adequately looked after by a male breadwinner while they undertake their caring, and that they will continue to be provided for into old age. I doubt that such a situation has ever satisfactorily existed, but we can see just how rare it is in front of our faces with the statistics on women and poverty. In every country of the world there are more men than women in positions of power and influence, and, I would argue, not coincidentally, in almost every country of the world women make up the majority of the poor. In Australia, 44 per cent of the homeless are women and 59 per cent of those being supported by specialist housing services are women. The overall poverty rate in Australia is slightly higher for men than women, but it is single men aged between eighteen and sixty-four who are the most likely of their gender to be poor in this country. For women it is older women and single mothers, indicating that it is our greater vulnerability as we age and our much greater caring responsibilities that predispose women to poverty.

It really does seem, sadly, that it is not until we have more women in positions of power that women's plight will become the focus of public policy makers. And there is nothing new about the need for representation by people like you before you get a fair hearing. I think an entire nation was formed on the principle of no taxation without representation: they call it the USA. My favourite example of how women at the top make a real difference is from two centuries ago, when chloroform was first invented. Doctors heralded it as a boon for birthing mothers in that it could help reduce their pain and so help save their children and themselves from the very real risk of death that could result from exhaustion during a long and painful labour. Unfortunately, religious leaders did not greet this lifesaving invention with the same enthusiasm. Instead, they decreed that it was ordained by God that women must suffer the pangs of childbirth as punishment for the temptation of Adam back in the Garden of Eden. (Eve suggested Adam eat an apple; he agreed. Get over yourselves, men.) Thankfully for women everywhere, the head of the Church of England at the time was herself a birthing mother. Queen Victoria, who had already had seven children and would go on to have another, grabbed the chloroform with both hands and told her sanctimonious, exclusively male church hierarchy to sod off. I doubt she used those words, sadly, but the effect was the same. Thanks to a woman and a mother being in a position of power, chloroform and all further forms of pain relief in childbirth became acceptable, and no doubt saved many millions from trauma, injury and death.

Although I am by nature cautious about advances for women (see my fear of a coming backlash in the previous chapter), I cannot help being excited by the extraordinary breadth and depth of the responses to the fundamental shift of power that are the result of the #MeToo movement. Power is a word that many women are uncomfortable with. They see it as something that is nasty, ruthless, self-serving and, I am afraid, quintessentially unfeminine. I believe that this is at the root of many women's discomfort with unequivocally identifying as feminists, even though they may share all of feminism's beliefs. Feminism, after all, is a revolutionary movement. It aims to redistribute power, which is what all revolutions set out to do. The wonderful and singular characteristic of feminism, unlike most other revolutionary movements, is that it aims to do so without arming itself or its followers, and without shedding a drop of blood. There have been feminist martyrs, sure enough, but there are no sentient feminist victims. Feminists, after all, love their enemy. The power structure they fight is made up of their fathers, husbands, brothers and sons. That is why we have used persuasion, logic and pressure rather than violence to further our progress. Even the suffragettes, who shocked society with their 'unladylike' tactics, only attacked property. Their targets were empty houses, postboxes and plate-glass windows. We have come a long way using such methods, but it has been slow—too slow. Too much potential and talent have been wasted. Too many women have languished in poverty and miserable marriages. Too many women have lived limited lives, helping others to achieve glory without ever being given a chance themselves. Too many women have been brutalised and humiliated and yet been forced to absorb the shame of others' bad behaviour. Too many have been locked up, reviled, even killed for speaking up and saying what those in power did not want to hear. Too many women have simply been forgotten and written out of history.

It is only in the last few months, as I write these words, that something momentous may at last have changed. Women have finally learnt how to exercise their power. The toppling of Harvey Weinstein and other famous and influential men who until very, very recently believed their fame and success insulated them from any unpleasant consequences no matter how appallingly they behaved, has sent a clear message to many across the world. Women will not be silent anymore and—even worse for those who fear exposure—when they speak up, people will listen to them and will act. There are now serious consequences for exploiting and abusing women (and some men) in a way there literally never have been before. And that's all power is. Power is the ability to make change, and change only happens in human society when it gets too uncomfortable for things to stay the same. #MeToo and all the brave women who have spoken up about their abuse, be it major or comparatively mild, criminal or merely humiliating, have made it too uncomfortable for powerful men to behave the way they used to. Whether or not Australia's strict defamation laws obstruct men from being brought properly to account for their behaviour, those men are now on notice that the women they attempt to exploit are more likely to resist, more likely to tell someone, and more likely to be believed. On 25 May 2018, theocratic Ireland voted in a landslide (66.4 per cent voted yes) to repeal the eighth amendment to its Constitution. After its equal-marriage victory and now this resounding endorsement of women's full rights as sentient human beings, even conservative Ireland has put the patriarchy on notice that its grip is slipping.

And all but a few diehards can see the writing on the wall. According to figures released by the Australian Institute of Company Directors, 52 per cent of new board appointments in the top 200 companies in the first quarter of 2018 were women. This is the first time that has happened. You may see this as a long bow, but I think it is a direct consequence of the ripple effect (more like a tidal wave) of #MeToo. I can hear the board discussions ringing in my ears as directors start to worry about what might be going on in their own organisations behind closed doors, and how vulnerable (and liable) they and their shareholders might be if accusations are made. I can see how they might start to realise they need more women at the table to talk about what they can do and how they can begin to reform their organisations to be more respectful of women and their contribution. After all, can you really blame some immature men for feeling they are entitled to treat female colleagues badly when they know perfectly well that their own organisation refuses to pay those women what they are worth? Why would male employees not feel free to abuse female workmates when their employers already do so through the women's pay packet and super payments? Every time we disrespect a woman's contribution by valuing it at less than a man's, however we do it, we encourage men and boys to think less of women, and women and girls to think less of themselves. That may, of course, be the purpose of such behaviour.

There has been a backlash recently, in response to the wrongdoing exposed by the Royal Commission into Misconduct in the Banking, Superannuation and Financial Services Industry, to the increasing numbers of women on boards. Almost predictably, it has been largely women directors who have been thrown under the bus by being expected or forced to resign when wrongdoing has been exposed. No doubt some of them richly deserved their fate, women being no more or less likely than men to do the wrong thing if they think they can get away with it. However, it is impossible to credit that women are more responsible for the systemic poor behaviour and rorts in our banking system, given how recently banks have opened up senior positions to women and how relatively few senior women there still are. Nevertheless, the fall of a handful of them has been pounced on gleefully by those who oppose the advancement of women, and has been used as an example of why women cannot be trusted with power. The more things change, it seems, the more they stay the same.

One reason that this handful of female directors has been held up as an 'awful warning' about what happens when you don't promote on what such critics claim as 'merit', is the fear of the push for quotas for women on boards and in senior positions. I am an unequivocal supporter of such quotas, and I have four reasons for supporting them. The first and most important is that I do not think things will change without them. You can change attitudes (and we have done so) without changing behaviour. In the 1970s and 1980s, research showed that advertising campaigns had convinced Australians that they should not drink and drive, but despite people's change in attitude, they continued to do exactly that. It wasn't until random breath testing that most of us changed our behaviour and the death toll on the road fell. Quotas are like random breath testing. They create real consequences, and that is how you get behavioural change.

The second is that we already have all sorts of quotas for people in positions of power. Barnaby Joyce, for example, until his recent fall from grace, was only deputy prime minister because he was leader of the National Party. That is a quota. Now our deputy PM is Mike McCormack, a man few Australians had heard of before he was elevated to the position. He has gained the second job in the land by being the new leader of the National Party and so gaining access to the quota. Indeed, the entire cabinet is made up of quotas of various kinds—there must be x number of representatives from WA, Queensland and Tassie, for example, which are geographic quotas. There are factional quotas as well: deals are done to ensure there are representatives from the right, left and moderate wings of the parties in power. Many boards also insist on interstate directors and some have staff representatives—quotas, quotas and more quotas. Why is it that the only quotas we object to are those that would apply to women?

The third and most compelling reason is how fundamentally unfair, ignorant and self-serving it is for men to oppose quotas given how much they have benefited from them. Do they forget the 100 per cent quota that operated in their favour for virtually all of recorded (and probably unrecorded) history? Every incursion women have made into schools, higher education, the professions, paid work, political representation, inheritance and any public position at all has had to be fought for against the 100 per cent male quota that still appears to exist in some parts of our world. And if there are any men or their apologists who think that such a quota didn't give their gender one hell of a leg up, they are kidding themselves. By comparison, women like me who are in favour of quotas for our own gender are positively meek. We're only asking for 30–40 per cent of the positions. If we were really going for even-stevens we'd be demanding 100 per cent for the next 2000 years.

The final reason is that I think there is plenty of evidence (much of it gathered in these pages) that we need women in positions of power before women's secondary status will change. Women look at women's lives through a different lens. If we want to improve our lot—for everyone who identifies as a woman—we must have women at the decision-making tables. Not all women defend women (just as not all men ignore women's plight), but it is inevitable that more of us will more thoroughly understand what women need and will agitate to provide it. The men who resist our progress (and most men have throughout history) must on some level understand this; otherwise, why would they bother to object?

The desperation of the attempts to demonise the few women in power is further proof that the patriarchal construction of our society is on notice—that its days are numbered. To their very great credit, there are many men who could not be more delighted to see it crumbling. In the recent Irish referendum 65.9 per cent of men voted in favour of repealing the anti-abortion, anti-women eighth amendment. They were just as clear as the 72.1 per cent of Irishwomen who voted the same way that a clump of a few hundred cells cannot have equal rights with a sentient human female.

The women of my generation have many ideas about what could and should be done to avoid another generation of women growing up to face a precarious financial future. Here are just some thoughts on what we could do, from the women I interviewed.

> 'Don't listen to your elders—watch them.'

> 'Pay adequate levels of social security and introduce a universal basic income to stabilise families (and) communities and reduce our vulnerability to global financial fluctuations.'

> 'Provide affordable and public housing that takes advantage of every possible sustainable technology. Charge very high taxes on any investment property that is not occupied.'
>
> 'Teach kids at school about superannuation and finances.'
>
> 'Superannuation rules need to be (such) that super companies can't make life insurance premiums a default setting. There should be some cap on admin fees.'
>
> 'Introduce early intervention programs to help reduce intergenerational poverty, violence and religious abuse.'

There are many more things we need to do urgently. We must do something now for the generation of older women who are facing a poverty-stricken old age and the real risk of homelessness. This will involve building low-cost housing fast. Former ALP senator and inaugural age discrimination commissioner Susan Ryan (now retired) has suggested that we reduce tax concessions, such as negative gearing, for investors in the housing sector. She has suggested that developers should be required to include 25 per cent of units as affordable housing in their plans or pay an equivalent levy to local councils to provide such housing. She also argues that we should urgently increase direct public funding to community housing providers. We must remove the structural problems that make housing too expensive for too many people, because in the face of rising house prices and rocketing rents combined with stagnant wage growth and absurdly low fixed incomes, homelessness is exploding. (According to 2016 ABS census data, the number of homeless women over fifty-five increased by 31 per cent between 2011 and 2016, and the number of homeless men in the same age group by 26 per cent.) We must do something about all the elderly women and men living on Newstart. We must up its rate. We must also put policy settings in place that encourage employers to employ older workers and keep them employed. We must change the way we contribute to women's super. Perhaps we could abolish Family Tax Benefits A and B because they create an impediment to women returning to work after having children. (Combined with the loss of other concessions, mothers returning to work can face a marginal tax rate of between 85 and 95 per cent.) Instead, we should use the savings to pay superannuation while parents take time out of the workforce. All carers should have their super contributions continued whether or not they are in paid work. By looking after the vulnerable—the very old, the very young, the disabled and the sick—carers save the economy billions. We must urgently close the earning gap between men and women. We must offer fathers incentives to spend at least some part of their children's infancy at home as the primary carer. We must stop undervaluing women's work, whether it be at home or in feminised industries or anywhere else. We must value caring work properly. Without it, society would cease to function. We must also urgently do something about the out-of-control cost of child care. If we make these changes, we may avoid seeing another generation of women face poverty in their old age as a reward for caring.

The women who were accidental feminists at first, but who now in the main identify with the only force that has ever consistently improved their lot, are starting to see the fruits of their long decades of labour, and for many of us they are very sweet and juicy indeed. For too many, as I have pointed out, such rewards are out of reach, usually through no fault of their own. What is so heartening now is that the scales have finally fallen from the eyes of most women (and many men) thanks to the free-for-all (for good and bad) that is the internet, and they are finally seeing sexism for what it is. Yet even before this latest tectonic shift in power, the women of my generation were fighting for their rights.

Do you remember my old schoolfriend Kerrie? The girl whose grief at being forced to curtail her education by her no doubt loving but nevertheless sexist father began this book? After she left school, she disappeared into the anonymity and menial jobs that swallowed up so many of my bright female friends. Yet I have reconnected with her in recent years thanks to Facebook (I know it's much reviled at the moment, but it certainly has its uses). I do not know if she did manage eventually to get the education she so much wanted, and I feel it would be impertinent to ask. But I do know she now lives in Europe and has remained as sharp, opinionated and quick-witted as she was as a girl.

And perhaps that was always patriarchy's fatal flaw. No matter how much they held us back, no matter how many obstacles they put in our way, no matter how low our self-esteem or bitter our disappointments, they could not drain our brains out of our ears, or (totally) smash our spirit and our desire to participate in and contribute to the world. Many of us, throughout history, found a way. Now, thanks to the efforts and determination and courage of countless generations of sometimes noisy, sometimes quiet, revolutionaries, most of us have found ways to put our brain, character and heart to good use. All that remains is for us to be paid fairly for it, all our lives, into our old age.

ACKNOWLEDGEMENTS

Accidental Feminists is the result of an unexpected phone call. I was watching TV one evening and my mobile rang. It was from an unknown number but—hey—curiosity always gets the better of me, so I answered. The call was from Louise Adler from MUP.

As soon as she identified herself I sat up a little straighter. I knew who she was and had long admired her from afar.

Louise launched straight into the reason for her call. She had read a piece I'd just had published on ABC Online, *Women over 50: A Tale of Two Fates*. In her warm but brook-no-opposition fashion she told me it was a book and she wanted me to write it for her.

As you can see, I did. I am eternally grateful to her for making that call.

Everyone at MUP deserves my acknowledgement and they have all been a dream to work with, but special mention must go to Sally Heath, who nursed me through the research and writing. I always felt supported and encouraged by Sally, even when she challenged me. That is a gift in a publisher and a boon to a writer. She gently nudged me to do better.

Kate Purvis, my editor, kept me honest and rigorously insisted on solid references, correct grammar and precise explanations. MUP Senior Editor Louise Stirling backed her up with further fine-tooth corrections and clear-eyed queries. If this book reads well, it is down to them.

The book's cover, designed by Josh Durham, is a triumph. It encapsulates perfectly what I wanted this book to say. I loved it the moment I saw it.

I want to also thank publicist Tessa Connelly and MUP marketing manager Emma Rusher. Their enthusiasm, energy and expertise were infectious.

Accidental Feminists may have my name on the cover but there are many who are responsible for its final shape and I owe each of them a debt.

Not least are the women I sent questionnaires to for this book. Their responses were generous, honest and raw. I hope that in some slight way this book helps build the momentum that sees women rewarded appropriately for their work—at home and in more conventional workplaces—throughout their lives so that none of them are ever again forced to enter old age filled with fear, shame and dread. If this book does help increase awareness of the plight of far too many women, it will in no small measure be due to their peers quoted in these pages who were willing to lay open their own lives in the hope their experiences would help others.

I owe them a great deal. So do we all.

NOTES

1: DAUGHTERS OF FEMINISM

US Civil Rights Act: Gillian Thomas, 'Women were included in the Civil Rights Act as a joke', *Longreads*, 7 July 2016.

Savile: Chris Greenwood and Richard Spillett, 'Girls' school head won't be charged over Savile', *Daily Mail Australia*, 29 April 2015.

2: HAGS, CRONES, WITCHES AND MOTHERS-IN-LAW

Clarks shoes sexism: Maev Kennedy, 'Clarks withdraws girls' school shoe after accusations of sexism', *Guardian Australia*, 14 August 2017.

Billabong sexism: Karen Knowlton, 'F★ck you Billabong. Seriously, f★ck you', *Women 2.0*, 9 August 2017.

Taking up space: Madonna King, 'What our kids' pocket money says about the pay gap', *Sydney Morning Herald*, 4 July 2018.

Beard: Hannah Furness, 'Mary Beard "cut" from US version of *Civilisations*, fearing "slightly creaky old lady isn't ideal for US TV"', *The Telegraph*, 17 April 2018.

Film extras: Megan Carpentier, 'Why are women still (mostly) silent film stars?', *The Guardian*, 13 April 2016.

Women protagonists in film: Rachel Montpelier, 'Study: Number of women protagonists in top 100 films climbed to 29% in 2016', *Women and Hollywood*, 21 February 2017.

Gender in children's books: Alison Flood, 'Study finds huge gender imbalance in children's literature', *The Guardian*, 6 May 2011.

Hunter-gatherers: Lindsay Abrams, 'The evolutionary importance of grandmothers', *The Atlantic*, 24 October 2012.

Anti-ageing market: 'Global anti-aging market to reach US$191.7Bn by 2019', Transparency Market Research, May 2018.

Witch-hunting in Papua New Guinea: Ian Lloyd Neubauer 'Why is Papua New Guinea still hunting witches?', *The Diplomat*, 17 January 2018.

Wealth transfer: Juliette Fairley, 'Women to benefit from $22 trillion in wealth transfer by 2020', *The Street*, 17 November 2014.

3: DUTIFUL DAUGHTERS, WIVES, MOTHERS AND GRANDMOTHERS

Howard: Tom McIlroy, 'John Howard says 50/50 gender split in politics is unrealistic due to caring responsibilities', *Sydney Morning Herald*, 7 September 2016.

'Spit-roasting': Conor Gallagher, 'Inside Court 12: The complete story of the Belfast rape trial', *Irish Times*, 28 March 2018.

Australian sporting team sex scandal: Rebecca Barrett, 'Matthew Johns in group sex scandal', ABC News, 6 May 2009.

Rape case figures: Jane Gilmore, 'Terrifying truth about rape convictions: it shatters your belief the world is a safe place', news.com.au, 23 February 2017.

Shotgun weddings: Sharon Jayson, 'Shotgun weddings becoming relics of another time', *USA Today*, 26 April 2014.

Mothers in the workforce: Jennifer Baxter, 'Parents working out work', Australian Institute of Family Studies, April 2013.

Cost of caring: Katy Abel, 'The price of motherhood: An interview with Ann Crittenden', *Family Education*, c.2010.

Pocket money: Madonna King, 'What our kids' pocket money says about the pay gap', *Sydney Morning Herald*, 4 July 2018.

Child care v. returning to work: Polly Dunning, 'If childcare costs more than my salary, don't expect me to return to work', *Sydney Morning Herald*, 21 August 2017.

Expensive child care: Natasha Bita, 'Australian childcare system among the world's most expensive: OECD', *The Australian*, 24 November 2015.

Wage stagnation: Matt Wade, '"A new era" of stagnant incomes: How wages aren't matching the growth of national income', *Sydney Morning Herald*, 15 March 2017.

Grandparents doing child care: Bridget Jenkins, 'Grandparent childcare in Australia: A literature review', *Elder Law Review*, vol. 6, 2010.

Alzheimer's numbers: 'Alzheimer's disease to quadruple worldwide by 2050: Video interview with Ron Brookmeyer', Johns Hopkins Bloomberg School of Public Health, 10 June 2007.

Elder abuse: Rae Kaspiew, Rachel Carson and Helen Rhoades, 'Elder abuse: Understanding issues, frameworks and responses', Australian Institute of Family Studies, February 2016.

Seniors Rights Victoria helpline data and Ryan: Christine Long, 'How to stop elder financial abuse at the hands of loved ones', *Sydney Morning Herald*, 18 February 2016.

4: GOLD-DIGGERS, BEGGARS AND THIEVES

Professional pay levels: RMIT/ABC Fact Check, 'Fact check: Have women become better educated whilst the gender pay gap hasn't budged?', ABC News, 16 July 2018.

GP gender pay gap: Grace FitzGerald, 'The gender pay gap in medicine', Level Medicine, n.d. <http://levelmedicine.org.au/resources/completed-fellowship-papers/gender-pay-gap/>, accessed 9 August 2018.

Products aimed at women cost more: Catey Hill, '6 times it's more expensive to be a woman', *MarketWatch*, 12 April 2016.

Clinton approval rating: Patrick O'Connor, 'Hillary Clinton exits with 69% approval rating', *Wall Street Journal*, 17 January 2013.

Wilkinson and Channel 9: Andrew Hornery, 'How the deal went down: Inside Nine's Wilkinson star chamber', *Sydney Morning Herald*, 17 October 2017.

Girls outperforming boys at school: Alice Park, 'Girls beat boys in every subject, and they have for a century', *TIME*, 29 April 2014.

Australian divorce numbers: 'Divorce in Australia', Australian Institute of Family Studies, 2018.

BBC equal-pay fight: '"The BBC doesn't do equal pay": Why female staff are fighting back', *The Guardian*, 30 January 2018.

Asking for pay rises: Jamiles Lartey, 'Women ask for pay increases as often as men but receive them less, study says', *The Guardian*, 6 September 2016.

Gender pay gap at the top: Leah Hunter, 'The gender pay gap is even worse at the top', *Fast Company*, 28 June 2016.

Industries dominated by one gender: Joanne Gray, 'WGEA boss wants to challenge Australia's highly gender-segregated workforce', *Financial Review*, 12 December 2016.

Part-time employment rates: '12 countries with the highest rates of part-time employment', *World Atlas*, 25 April 2017.

Part-time and casual working women: 'Gender workplace statistics at a glance', Workplace Gender Equality Agency, Australian Government, February 2018.

Women's low workplace participation: Clay Lucas, 'Australia's women most empowered in world', *Sydney Morning Herald*, 17 October 2012.

5: WOMEN'S WORK

Ratio of male and female university students: Nick Parr, 'Who goes to university? The changing profile of our students', *The Conversation*, 25 May 2015.

Workforce participation rates: 'Gender workplace statistics at a glance', Workplace Gender Equality Agency, Australian Government, February 2018.

Percentages of working women: 'Paid work: Trends in women's employment', Australian Bureau of Statistics, 3 June 1998.

Housework hours: Karl Quinn, 'Back in Time for Dinner is the convenience food of history shows', *Sydney Morning Herald*, 30 May 2018.

Housework in 2018: Carolyn Tate, 'Women are doing less housework—but it's not men we have to thank', *Essential Kids*, 17 April 2018.

Men doing housework: Daniel Carlson, 'Not all housework is created equal: Particular housework tasks and couples' relationship quality', Council on Contemporary Families, 3 April 2018.

Child care not tax deductible: Nassim Khadem, 'Why we need to get high-income women back to work: The case for tax deductible childcare', *Sydney Morning Herald*, 23 October 2017.

Howard and family tax benefits: Brian Lawrence, 'Who fathered the Family Tax Benefit?', *Eureka Street*, 29 May 2014.

Women's loss of potential earnings: 'The gender pay gap over the life cycle', Australian Council of Trade Unions, March 2016.

Women retiring with no super: Laura Hartnell, 'Superannuation: 1 in 3 women retire with nothing, Senate report finds', ABC News, 28 February 2017.

Emotional labour: Gemma Hartley, 'Women aren't nags—we're just fed up', *Harper's Bazaar*, 28 September 2017.

Sexual harassment in the medical profession: 'Just give in to sleazy bosses, top surgeon Dr Gabrielle McMullin says', *Sunday Telegraph*, 7 March 2015.

Violence against nurses: David Terry et al., 'Workplace health and safety issues among community nurses: A study regarding the impact on providing care to rural consumers', *BMJ Open*, 12 August 2015.

Lipsyte on workplace sexual harassment: Robert Lipsyte, 'How we men can—and must—bring down sexual predators', *The Guardian*, 19 November 2017.

6: SLAGS, SLUTS, GOSSIPS AND STACEYS

Fear of female brainpower: Robert Burriss, 'Are men just not interested in clever women?', *Psychology Today*, 22 September 2016.

Smart women applying for jobs: Kasey Edwards, 'Why employers don't hire smart women', *Sydney Morning Herald*, 22 April 2018.

Husband denies inflicting injuries: Jane Caro, 'Why do women stay with violent men? Because they're addicted to hope', *Daily Telegraph*, 23 November 2015.

Victoria Police victim-blaming language: Melissa Cunningham and Erin Pearson, 'Ashton says police could have used better language on Eurydice death', *The Age*, 18 June 2018.

Winton on masculinity: Tim Winton, 'About the boys: Tim Winton on how toxic masculinity is shackling men to misogyny', *Guardian Australia*, 9 April 2018.

Divorces instigated by women: Douglas LaBier, 'Women initiate divorce much more than men, here's why', *Psychology Today*, 28 August 2016.

Levels of marital satisfaction: Bella DePaulo, 'Is it true that single women and married men do best?', *Psychology Today*, 11 January 2017.

Increased workload when married: Claire Kamp Dush, 'Dual-earner couples share the housework equally—until the first baby comes', *The Conversation*, 8 May 2015.

Effect of marriage on women's health: Sarah Knapton, 'Marriage is more beneficial for men than women, study shows', *The Telegraph*, 11 June 2015.

Knowledge about the clitoris: Edward Clint, 'The clitoris revealed, and how io9 got it wrong', *Incredulous*, 12 August 2013.

Men shaming their sex partner: Jen Gunter, 'My vagina is terrific. Your opinion about it is not', *New York Times*, 16 November 2017.

Draconian abortion laws: Nathalie Baptiste, 'This is what happens when abortion is outlawed', *American Prospect*, 17 June 2015.

Queen Victoria: Robert C. Abrams, 'Sir James Reid and the death of Queen Victoria: An early model for end-of-life care', *The Gerontologist*, 55(6), 2015, pp. 943–50.

Older women and alcohol: Siw Ellen Jakobsen, 'Older women want their wine', *ScienceNordic*, 19 March 2014.

7: INVALIDS, LIARS, HYSTERICS AND MADWOMEN

Male v. female teacher behaviour: Seth Nichols, 'Why teachers are walking out', *Known Blog*, 17 May 2018.

Mesh implants and slings: Hannah Devlin, 'Women harmed because vaginal mesh regulation "not fit for purpose"', *The Guardian*, 7 December 2017.

Endometriosis: 'Endometriosis: The silent condition that can be ignored for years', Premium News Network, 1 August 2017.

Medical research extrapolated: Cathy Johnson and Natasha Mitchell, 'Man flu, headaches and heart attacks: Health issues affect men and women differently', ABC News, 2 September 2017.

Misdiagnosed heart disease: André Picard, 'Heart disease isn't just for men, after all', *Globe and Mail*, 12 May 2018.

Women's pain: Diane E. Hoffmann and Anita J. Tarzian, 'The girl who cried pain: A bias against women in the treatment of pain', *Journal of Law, Medicine & Ethics*, 29(1), 2001, pp. 13–27.

Yentl syndrome: Joe Fassler, 'How doctors take women's pain less seriously', *The Atlantic*, 15 October 2015.

First diagnosis of hysteria: Cecilia Tasca et al., 'Women and hysteria in the history of mental health', *Clinical Practice & Epidemiology* in *Mental Health*, vol. 8, 2012, pp. 110–19.

Hysteria 'cures': Hugo Schwyzer, 'Vibrators and clitoridectomies: How Victorian doctors took control of women's orgasms', *Jezebel*, 31 May 2012.

Pelvic massages: Catherine Pearson, 'Female hysteria: 7 crazy things people used to believe about the ladies' disease', *Huffington Post*, 7 December 2017.

Desecration of Dixon memorial: Tammy Mills and Erin Pearson, 'Comedian charged over offensive graffiti at Eurydice Dixon's memorial', *The Age*, 4 July 2018.

Cosby: 'Bill Cosby convicted of sexual assault of Andrea Constand in retrial', ABC News, 27 April 2018.

Sixty Cosby accusers: Carly Mallenbaum, Patrick Ryan and Maria Puente, 'A complete list of the 60 Bill Cosby accusers and their reactions to the guilty verdict', *USA Today*, 27 April 2018.

Hanson-Young and Leyonhjelm: Leah MacLennan and staff, 'Sarah Hanson-Young confirms she will sue David Leyonhjelm for defamation, crowdfunding legal costs', ABC News, 10 July 2018.

Male violence statistics: 'Facts and figures', Our Watch, n.d. <https://www.ourwatch.org.au/understanding-violence/facts-and-figures>, accessed 12 August 2018.

Victoria Police 2013–14 figures: Jane Gilmore, 'No, women aren't as likely to commit violence as men', *Sydney Morning Herald*, 19 November 2014.

Thurman's anger: Maureen Dowd, 'This is why Uma Thurman is angry', *New York Times*, 3 February 2018.

Internalised anger: Audrey Nelson, 'Nice girls don't do conflict', *Psychology Today*, 23 November 2010.

Gaslighting: Stephanie A. Sarkis, '11 warning signs of gaslighting', *Psychology Today*, 22 January 2017.

8: VESSELS OF REPULSION

Women who will never have a baby: 'Family formation: Trends in childlessness', Australian Bureau of Statistics, 9 May 2002.

Enright on eighth amendment: Anne Enright, 'Time for change: Anne Enright on Ireland's abortion referendum', *The Guardian*, 24 March 2018.

Massacre of older Yazidi women: Sophy Ridge, 'Mass graves of women "too old to be Isil sex slaves"—this is what we're up against', *The Telegraph*, 17 November 2015.

Trump on Brigitte Macron: Clark Mindock, 'Donald Trump to Emmanuel Macron's wife Brigitte: "You know, you're in such great shape ... beautiful"', *The Independent*, 13 July 2017.

Movie age gaps: Laura Whitmore, 'Hollywood sexism: Graph exposes huge age gap between male actors and their female love interests', *Stylist*, 2015.

Older people having sex: Marilynn Marchione, 'Sex and the seniors: Survey shows many elderly people remain frisky', *New York Times*, 22 August 2007.

Widowhood statistics: 'The demography of widowhood', medicine.jrank.org, n.d. <http://medicine.jrank.org/pages/1840/Widowhood-demography-widowhood.html>, accessed 13 August 2018.

Remarriage after widowhood: Christiane Delbès and Joëlle Gaymu, 'The shock of widowhood on the eve of old age: Male and female experiences', *Population*, 57(6), 2002, pp. 885–914.

Remarriage after divorce: 'Family formation: Remarriage trends of divorced people', Australian Bureau of Statistics, 24 June 1999.

Widow Allowance: 'Payment rates for Widow Allowance', Department of Human Services, Australian Government, July 2018.

Restart incentive scheme: 'Restart: Help to employ mature workers', Department of Jobs and Small Business, Australian Government, July 2018.

Anglicare rental snapshot: '2018 rental affordability snapshot', Anglicare Australia, 2018.

Heart Foundation statistics: 'Overweight and obesity statistics', Heart Foundation, n.d. <https://www.heartfoundation.org.au/about-us/what-we-do/heart-disease-in-australia/overweight-and-obesity-statistics>, accessed 13 August 2018.

Physical activity statistics: 'Sport and physical recreation', Australian Bureau of Statistics, 29 June 2011.

9: LOSS AND LAMENTATION

Women over eighty-five living with partner: Gareth Hutchens, 'Census 2016 finds Australia getting older and more female', *Guardian Australia*, 27 June 2017.

Elder financial abuse: Melanie Joosten, 'National Ageing Research Institute and Australian Association of Gerontology', National Ageing Research Institute, 17 August 2016.

ABA protections for bank staff: James Eyers, 'Banks should broaden whistleblower protections, says report to ABA', *Financial Review*, 12 October 2016.

Manslaughter of mother: 'Brothers charged over death of 73-year-old mother left in "abhorrent" conditions', 9 News, 3 May 2018.

Domestic violence risk factor: Kim Webster, 'Family violence a bigger health risk for women than smoking, drinking, obesity: Study', ABC News, 1 November 2016.

Domestic violence and homelessness: Nicola Heath, 'A tragic reality: Domestic violence is the main cause of homelessness in Australia', SBS Life, 30 June 2017.

Chances of staying married: Renée Peltz Dennison, 'Do half of all marriages really end in divorce?', *Psychology Today*, 24 April 2017.

Suicide rate of elderly men: Ky Chow, 'Australian men aged over 85 have the highest rate of suicide, ABS data shows', ABC News, 31 May 2017.

Women more likely to instigate divorce: Douglas LaBier, 'Women initiate divorce much more than men, here's why', *Psychology Today*, 28 August 2016.

Suicide rates and marital status: 'Suicide: Marital status and the family', family.jrank.org, n.d. <http://family.jrank.org/pages/1659/Suicide-Marital-Status-Family.html>, accessed 13 August 2018.

Alzheimer's more common in women: J. Viña and A. Lloret, 'Why women have more Alzheimer's disease than men: Gender and mitochondrial toxicity of amyloid-beta peptide', *Journal of Alzheimer's Disease*, vol. 20, supplement 2, 2010, pp. 527–33.

Men more likely to suicide: Daniel Freeman and Jason Freeman, 'Why are men more likely than women to take their own lives?', *The Guardian*, 21 January 2015.

Nursing-home scandals: Andy Kollmorgen, 'The hidden costs of retirement village contracts', *Choice*, 26 June 2017.

Sontag on loss of sex appeal: Susan Sontag, 'The double standard of aging', *Saturday Review*, 23 September 1972.

Desire to be taken seriously: Hugh Mackay, *What Makes Us Tick? The Ten Desires that Drive Us*, Chapter 1, Hachette, 2010.

Dying in hospital: James Bullen, 'Can you die from old age?', ABC News, 14 June 2017.

CPR on the elderly: Darrell Brewer, 'CPR risks for the elderly', HopeTree Care, 28 September 2015.

10: PAST OUR USE-BY DATE

Women's life expectancy: 'Deaths in Australia', Australian Institute of Health and Welfare, Australian Government, 18 July 2018.

Life expectancy 100 years ago: 'Life expectancy at birth (years) by sex, Queensland and Australia, 1881–1890 to 2014–2016', Queensland Government Statistician's Office, December 2017.

Average retirement age: 'What is the retirement age in Australia?', AMP, 24 January 2018.

Increase in women's homelessness: Miki Perkins and Matilda Boseley, 'Older women, migrants swell the ranks of Australia's homeless', *Sydney Morning Herald*, 14 March 2018.

Homeless women seeking assistance: 'Specialist homelessness services annual report 2016–17', Australian Institute of Health and Welfare, Australian Government, 12 February 2018.

Workplace-related injuries: 'RSI statistics', RSI-Therapy.com, n.d. <http://www.rsi-therapy.com/statistics.htm>, accessed 13 August 2018.

Centrelink robo-debt: Jonno Revanche, 'After the "robo-debt" debacle, traumatised users find support in online communities', *Guardian Australia*, 4 January 2018.

Putting off going to the doctor: 'Thousands delay GP visit because of cost', SBS News, 1 February 2017.

Effects of neighbourhood on mortality: Hans Bosma et al., 'Neighborhood socioeconomic status and all-cause mortality', *American Journal of Epidemiology*, 153(4), 2001, pp. 363–71.

Life expectancy of homeless people: Wilma J. Nusselder et al., 'Mortality and life expectancy in homeless men and women in Rotterdam: 2001–2010', *PLOS One*, 8(10), 2013.

Tasmanian homeless study: Danny Tran, 'Homeless Australians have shorter lifespan than Africans: Study', ABC News, 12 September 2014.

Effect of income on life expectancy: Max Ehrenfreund, 'How income affects life expectancy', World Economic Forum, 25 September 2015.

Indigenous people's life expectancy: 'Deaths in Australia', Australian Institute of Health and Welfare, Australian Government, 18 July 2018.

Disadvantages for Indigenous people: 'Adult health: Risk factors and socioeconomic status', Australian Bureau of Statistics, 17 February 2011.

Socioeconomic status and lifespan: Cayla Dengate, 'Low socioeconomic status affects life expectancy more than obesity', *Huffington Post Australia*, 27 March 2017.

Smoking rates: Tobacco Control Unit, Cancer Council NSW, 'The reciprocal relationship between social disadvantage, financial stress and smoking: What does the research tell us? What can community service organisations do?', NCOSS and Cancer Council NSW, July 2008.

Single older women and homelessness: Lina Caneva, 'Homelessness for older Australian women a "sleeping giant"', Pro Bono Australia, 10 November 2016.

Hartman and Darab report: Sandy Darab and Yvonne Hartman, 'Understanding single older women's invisibility in housing issues in Australia', *Housing, Theory and Society,* 30(4), 2013, pp. 348–67.

11: INVISIBILITY V. INDEPENDENCE

Mental illness and age: 'Facts and stats about mental illness in Australia', Mindframe, n.d. <http://www.mindframe-media.info/for-mental-health-and-suicide-prevention/talking-to-media-about-mental-illness/facts-and-stats>, accessed 14 August 2018.

Knitting Nannas Against Gas: Maxine Newlands, 'Nannalution gathers pace: Australia's Knitting Nannas activists and the anti-fracking movement', *The Ecologist*, 9 September 2016.

Bringing women out of poverty: 'Ethiopia: Help one woman out of poverty and she will bring four others with her', CARE Australia, 21 February 2012.

Women having more money and clout: Marianne Schnall, 'The rising activism in women's philanthropy', *Forbes*, 2 February 2018.

US wealth controlled by women: Kiersten Marek, 'Empowered women are changing philanthropy. These experts explain how', *Inside Philanthropy*, 15 August 2017.

Increasing inequality in Australia: Christopher Sheil and Frank Stilwell, 'The ABS is wrong: Inequality is getting worse in Australia', ABC News, 15 September 2017.

Richest taxpayers' $37 per week: Emma Dawson and Warwick Smith, 'The cost of privilege', Per Capita for Anglicare Australia, March 2018.

Proposed income tax cuts benefiting men: Katharine Murphy and Gareth Hutchens, 'Men to receive almost two-thirds of Coalition tax cuts after 10 years', *Guardian Australia*, 6 June 2018.

Drivers of a changing world: 'Drivers of change', World Economic Forum, n.d. <http://reports.weforum.org/future-of-jobs-2016/drivers-of-change/>, accessed 14 August 2018.

Divestment of fossil-fuel stocks: Olaf Weber, Truzaar Dordi and Vasundhara Saravade, 'How divesting of fossil fuels could help save the planet, *The Conversation*, 11 December 2017.

Low-income households slipping behind: Rob Burgess, 'The working poor: One-in-five households being left behind', *New Daily*, 29 June 2017.

Foodbank and the working poor: Emma Sykes, 'The "working poor" are Australia's hungriest', ABC News, 17 October 2011.

Job call-back rates: Lauren Stiller Rikleen, 'Older women are being forced out of the workforce', *Harvard Business Review*, 10 March 2016.

Manne on Waring: Anne Manne, 'Making women's unpaid work count', *The Monthly*, May 2018.

US opposes UN breastfeeding resolution: Polly Dunning, 'Shocking double standard on display as US bullies on breastfeeding', *Sydney Morning Herald*, 10 July 2018.

Mother's Day: Jane Caro, 'The hypocrisy is blatant & barefaced: Why Jane Caro can't stand Mother's Day', *Women's Agenda*, 14 May 2015.

Díaz sexual misconduct scandal: Jennine Khalik, 'Junot Diaz withdraws from Sydney Writers' Festival after sexual harassment allegations', ABC News, 6 May 2018.

12: REBELS, RESISTANCE FIGHTERS AND ROLE MODELS

Influence of mother's DNA on intelligence: 'Is intelligence inherited from the mother or the father?', *TRT World*, 20 April 2017.

The Birds of Australia illustrations: Kate Evans, 'Elizabeth Gould, illustrator of Birds of Australia, brought out of her husband's shadow', ABC News, 25 November 2016.

Franklin ignored for Nobel Prize: Jane J. Lee, '6 women scientists who were snubbed due to sexism', *National Geographic*, 19 May 2013.

Ada Lovelace Day: Miss Cellania, 'Ada Lovelace: The first computer programmer', *Mental Floss*, 13 October 2015.

Lamarr's invention: 'Hedy Lamarr: Invention of spread spectrum technology', Famous Women Inventors, n.d. <http://www.women-inventors.com/Hedy-Lammar.asp>, accessed 14 August 2018.

Women not going to space: Marina Koren, 'Why women weren't allowed to be astronauts', *The Atlantic*, 10 March 2017.

Maria Anna Mozart: Sylvia Milo, 'The lost genius of Mozart's sister', *The Guardian*, 8 September 2015.

Elizabeth I 'not a woman': Claire Ridgway, 'Elizabeth I: A virago, genetically male or simply a strong woman?', The Elizabeth Files, 12 November 2009.

Lost tapestries: Susan Groag Bell, *The Lost Tapestries of the City of Ladies: Christine de Pizan's Renaissance Legacy*, University of California Press, 2004.

Influence of technology: Jane Caro, 'The virtual Reformation', *Kill Your Darlings*, 16 January 2017.

Alaska Airlines flight: 'Video: Alaska Airlines flight piloted by two female African Americans for the first time', One Mile at a Time, 16 May 2018.

Maternal mortality rate in Texas: Molly Redden, 'Texas has highest maternal mortality rate in developed world, study finds', *The Guardian*, 20 August 2016.

Atlantic columnist: Cristina Cabrera, 'Atlantic writer fired over calling for execution of women who get abortions', *Talking Points Memo*, 5 April 2018.

View that abortion is murder: Anna North, 'Plenty of conservatives really do believe women should be executed for having abortions', *Vox*, 5 April 2018.

O'Sullivan on abortion: Gina Rushton, 'The Liberal National Party has committed to new abortion controls', Buzzfeed News, 18 July 2017.

Abortion illegal in many countries: Anastasia Moloney, 'Salvadoran woman jailed for abortion crimes hopes for early release: Rights groups', Reuters, 9 December 2017.

US mass shootings: Roxanne Dunbar-Ortiz, 'Inside the minds of American mass shooters', *The Guardian*, 10 November 2017.

The right to sex: Ross Douthat, 'The redistribution of sex', *New York Times*, 2 May 2018.

Trump elected due to backlash: 'Will America ever have a woman president?', *Politico*, 4 November 2017.

Social media abuse: Georgina Dent, 'The perils of being a woman with a platform: Emma Alberici the latest target', *Women's Agenda*, 21 May 2018.

13: STRATEGISTS, POLICY MAKERS AND PROBLEM SOLVERS

Workhouses: Jennie Walters, 'The workhouse', jenniewalters.com, n.d. <http://www.jenniewalters.com/history/workhouse.php>, accessed 14 August 2018.

Murder of pregnant women: Andrea Todd, 'Death by pregnancy: Why are so many moms-to-be dying?', *Women's Health*, 20 October 2017.

Baird on domestic abuse in religion: Julia Baird with Hayley Gleeson, '"Submit to your husbands": Women told to endure domestic violence in the name of God', ABC News, 23 January 2018.

Home the most dangerous place for women: Patrick Wood, 'Landmark report reveals a woman dies every week due to Australia's domestic violence crisis', ABC News, 28 February 2018.

Superannuation splitting: 'Superannuation splitting laws: Frequently asked questions', Attorney-General's Department, Australian Government, n.d.

Estimated salary of wives/mothers: Mandi Woodruff, 'Here's how much it would cost to replace your mom', *Business Insider*, 10 May 2013.

Paid parental leave: 'Who can receive Parental Leave Pay', Department of Human Services, Australian Government, July 2018.

EnergyAustralia pay rises for women: Elysse Morgan, 'Energy Australia closes gender pay gap overnight, literally', ABC News, 7 March 2018.

Caro response to Howard comments: Jane Caro, 'John Howard's comments: Lack of foresight, lack of understanding', *The Big Smoke*, 9 September 2016.

Women make up majority of the poor: 'Why the majority of the world's poor are women', Oxfam International, n.d. <https://www.oxfam.org/en/even-it/why-majority-worlds-poor-are-women>, accessed 14 August 2018.

Homeless women in Australia: 'Homelessness and women', Homelessness Australia, [2017].

Poverty in Australia: *A Hand Up Not a Hand Out: Renewing the Fight Against Poverty (Report on Poverty and Financial Hardship)*, Chapter 3, Commonwealth of Australia, 2004.

Irish eighth amendment referendum: Harriet Sherwood, 'Irish archbishops say abortion vote shows church's waning influence', *The Guardian*, 27 May 2018.

Female board appointments: Chris Pash, 'ASX200 boards are for the first time appointing more women directors than men', *Business Insider Australia*, 13 April 2018.

Tax rate for mothers returning to work: Miranda Stewart, 'Mothers have little to show for extra days of work under new tax changes', *The Conversation*, 20 June 2018.